THE

EVERYTHING

MAGIC BOOK

Everything you need to amaze,
baffle, and entertain your friends

Greg Davidson

Adams Media Corporation
Avon, Massachusetts

To Phoebe Irene Pegg, October 6, 1904–May 25, 1999

I would like to dedicate this book to the life, love and sense of humor of Irene Pegg, my Grandmother who everyone called "Granny." At one time or another, Granny served as my rehearsal audience, seamstress, prop builder, chauffeur, public relations manager, song partner, and dedicated fan. We also shared the same birthdate. I know if I could tell her I had written a new book, Granny would say something like, "_Written_ one? Don't you think that you had better _read_ one before you write one?"

An Everything® Series Book.
Everything® is a registered trademark of Adams Media Corporation.

Published by Adams Media Corporation
57 Littlefield Street, Avon, MA 02322. U.S.A.
www.adamsmedia.com

ISBN: 1-58062-418-9

Printed in the United States of America.

J I H G F E D C B

Library of Congress Cataloging-in-Publication data
available upon request from the publisher.

This publication is designed to provide accurate and authoritative information with regard to the subject matter covered. It is sold with the understanding that the publisher is not engaged in rendering legal, accounting, or other professional advice. If legal advice or other expert assistance is required, the services of a competent professional person should be sought.
— From a _Declaration of Principles_ jointly adopted by a Committee of the American Bar Association and a Committee of Publishers and Associations

Illustrations by Barry Littmann.
Interior instructional photographs and line drawings by Greg Davidson.

This book is available at quantity discounts for bulk purchases.
For information, call 1-800-872-5627.

Visit the entire Everything® series at everything.com

Contents

CONTENTS

Introduction

Are you going to learn secrets in this book? Yes, you are! But I'm not simply going to reveal secrets for no reason. Successful magic, after all, relies partly on the secrets held by the magician. This book will give you a solid background in the rules of magic; it will reveal the *real* secrets of success behind magic, the ones that elude you as you watch magic on television or on stage in Las Vegas. The secrets are not within the gimmicks, boxes, and pockets used by the magician but rather in the preparation work and knowing magic inside and out.

To help you understand the components of magic and how to launch your career in magic, I've divided the book into three Parts:

Part I: Hocus Pocus—Learning the Basics will take you through some of the basic elements of magic and explain how learning magic can help you personally, socially, and professionally.

Part II: Learning the Magic—the Tricks of the Trade represents the bulk of the book and devotes a chapter or more to each of the basic forms of magic: Close-Up Magic (with all its variations), Parlor Magic, Stage Magic, Illusions, Comedy Magic, Mental Magic, and Escape Magic. Within these chapters, you'll also get detailed step-by-step instructions on how to perform tricks or effects, in many cases accompanied by helpful photographs that illustrate each step for you. In addition, this part includes chapters on specialty magic—that is, magic for both kids and adults, street magic, head scratchers (or puzzles), and magic with science. It's got a little bit for everyone.

Part III: Introducing "You"!—Putting on the Show tells you how to prepare yourself for performing magic, from deciding which type of magic to do to rehearsing to the actual performance. You'll learn about props, costumes, makeup, lighting, sound, and a whole host of components that will make your act a success.

In addition, you'll find the following special features:

- **Definitions Please.** These sidebars present the meanings of many of the terms you'll encounter throughout your study of magic. Although every magic book differs slightly in how it teaches the material, and quite often these differences can be seen in the lack of standard terminology for the various elements of magic, I have attempted to provide the basic language that the rest of the magic world speaks.

The Magician's Code—the "Don'ts"

- Never tell anyone how a trick is done
- Never perform a trick without sufficient practice
- Never do the same trick for the same audience

- **Master Magicians.** Throughout the book, you will find brief biographies of some of the most well-known magicians of our time. Many of these will inspire you to set your goals and pursue putting together the magic act that has "you" written all over it.
- **Did You Know?** A smattering of magic trivia is included throughout the book, just because! It's fun!
- **Dollars and Cents.** Let's face it, performing magic costs some money and I've tried to give you an outline for what your cash *outlay* may be.

I've ended the book with a helpful Appendix that provides you with lists of all things magic: suppliers of magic products, magic magazines and periodicals, Web sites featuring information on magic, organizations for magicians, and much more.

Throughout this book, I refer to the magician as "he" merely for the sake of simplicity. Men and women alike have proven successful in the world of magic. I have, however, referred to the spectators, assistants, and helpers as both "he" and "she" for inclusiveness.

I also tried to keep from mentioning left or right hands whenever possible to take into consideration the issue of handedness. You will automatically use your dominant hand, and rather than write the book for the majority of right-handed people, I chose to omit this detail for simplicity's sake. In certain instances, of course, it was necessary to include such details.

A Wonderful Art . . . and Gift

My hope for you as you read *The Everything® Magic Book* is that you will take this information and both guard and share it. Magic is not only a wonderful art to be perfected but also a gift to others. I have seen it offer enchantment for people in hundreds of different shapes and packages. I appreciate the opportunity to pass on the secrets of magic. Isn't it ironic that the real secret is only kept if it's shared?

Welcome to the world of magic with all of its challenges, mystery, and enchantment.

Greg Davidson
Roswell, Georgia

PART I

Hocus Pocus—Learning the Basics

CHAPTER 1

Now You See It . . . but Where?

First of all, how many different kinds of magic are there? A "kajillion," that's how many. Every day it seems that a new or different type of magic is emerging somewhere in the world, especially if you are in tune to it. Based upon new creativity, technology, skill levels, and study techniques—and, of course, more people than ever before who are interested in magic—it has taken on a whole new full head of steam. Although these factors seem to push the envelope for more and more possibilities, the tried-and-true styles, divisions, and categories of *prestidigitation* (that's magic) still seem to stay intact. In Chapter 2, you'll learn the various categories of magic that may interest you.

The reason that there are so many kinds of magic is because there are so many kinds of people. Magic has not only grown and evolved to suit the needs of the magician but also because audiences have matured as well. People are more technically minded these days than ever before and the methods of magic therefore have to be more sophisticated. Public interest in magic is at an all-time high, with more venues for the performance of magic than ever. And, as each performer looks to capture his segment of spectators, new acts and types of magic are developed. The classics are still the same, though, and we'll focus mostly on these in this book.

So, Where Should I Begin?

You can get started by reading this book. Within these pages, you'll get a good primer on magic. From there, you should have a solid foundation upon which to grow. To learn more refer to the resources listed in the Appendix. And, above all, start practicing!

How Long Will It Take?

Not long, and forever. Magic can be learned on an entry level very quickly, but learning magic, as in *all* of magic, would take forever. Magic is ever changing and ever developing, so it's perfect for a hobby or a job. It never gets boring, and it's always full of new surprises, pay-offs, and new friends.

Becoming proficient in any area of magic, whether it be Close-Up Magic or Escape Magic, depends on how amazing you want your magic to be. The bottom line is that you have to practice until the magic works . . . or until you fool someone with the trick. There is no connection between the size of the magic and the amount of practice you'll need. In other words, some coin moves take years to perfect while some giant box tricks almost work all by themselves. It's possible to learn a basic coin vanish, such as the French Drop, in under an hour. That would be enough time to follow the instructions, learn the "how" part, and begin to experiment, making it natural and smooth. However, to understand the "where and when" part of any trick will probably take longer. In any case, I agree with Eugene Burger's advice: "When you think you are ready to perform a magic trick, don't. Wait 30 more days. If you can't wait, try out your magic on a family member or a friend who knows you are still in the learning stage."

Can Anyone Learn Magic?

Yes, everyone can learn at least some form of magic. Depending on your individual interest and the level of your dedication, you can quickly become an amateur and eventually become a pro. I have met very few people who couldn't learn some kind of magic, and I have never met anyone who didn't love it when they did. No matter what your age, magic can add a new dimension to your life.

Learning magic is not difficult, but it takes time. Was learning to ride a bike difficult? Well, back then it may have been but now it's hard to imagine not being able to do it. This book has a systematic approach for learning great magic, with advice and tricks from some of the world's greatest magicians.

How Much Will It Cost?

Learning magic won't cost you much at all. Of course, you can spend as much money as you want to continue on. Just like with all other arts, you can spend money but you don't have to. The

Mark Wilson

In 1958, Mark Wilson and his wife Nani Darnell were already producing a local TV show called *Time for Magic* when they decided to go to Los Angeles to try to sell a magic show for national television. TV executives there told them to go back to Texas, claiming that magic wouldn't work on television. Mark wouldn't give up and eventually he struck a deal with Kellogg's as a sponsor. This time, CBS opened the door when he came knocking.

Mark Wilson's *The Magic Land of Allakazam* premiered on October 1, 1960, and became the first commercially sponsored magic series on any American television network. He was the first to stress the use of a live studio audience and continuous taping so that viewers could be sure no trick photography was being used. Magician Bev Bergeron also appeared on the show as "Rebo" the clown.

Melinda

Melinda is known as the "First Lady of Magic" and has been described as the leading female magician in history. USA Today has ranked her as one of the top three magic acts in the world, along with David Copperfield and Siegfried and Roy. Melinda became the first and only woman to star in her own primetime magic television special, "Disney's Melinda, First Lady of Magic," and in 1998 she was named "Magician of the Year" by the International Society of Magicians.

Nancy Glass of American Journal described Melinda as "part David Copperfield and part Cher." Some of Melinda's greatest illusions include making a jet appear, a sports car vanish, and being impaled by a giant industrial "Death Drill."

basic skills are all you need to start with, which you will learn from this book. From there, it's up to you. If you feel you need a gold wand with pearl handles, who am I to talk you out of it? I would suggest not worrying about it for a while.

The amount of money you will spend will depend largely on what type of magic you are interested in. For instance, this book shows you how to do Close-Up Magic with many items you might find around the house. Or, you can perform a whole range of card tricks with a deck that costs less than $5. On the other hand, if you are interested in larger magic, the prices for these props start around $20 to $30 for small props and climb to $1,000 or more for most stage illusions. In fact, you'll find that learning the magic is the least expensive part. By purchasing a few books and videos and attending some lectures, your initial investment should be less than $100. That's the best place to start.

How Will I Know When I'm Good Enough?

This book gives you the tools you need to not only *learn* but also *study* your own magic and the steps to take to track your progress. Combine these tools with actually performing magic, get some feedback, and you'll have a sense if you're ready.

You'll be able to perform some magic as soon as you learn it. Certain tricks and stunts are easy to pick up immediately, as soon as you know the secret to doing them. Some examples of these effects are bar bets, brainteasers, and self-working tricks. In short, you should be able to pull together a small repertoire of trickery within a month or two, depending on how dedicated you are. After that, with practice and helpful feedback, your skills should grow noticeably within no time.

The Elements of Magic

The following elements of magic will appear throughout this book. When a new trick, or effect, is introduced, it will often be followed up with these four sections: *effect* (which describes the trick in general terms), *preparation* (which tells you how to prepare), *setup* (which explains the physical setup that's required), and *routine* (which tells you how to do the effect step by step).

Trick or Effect

The words "trick" or "effect" describe the desired scene, that is, what happens and what the audience experiences when a piece of magic is executed correctly. The effect is what the magic "looks like." I prefer the word "effect" over the word "trick," with the optimism that no serious magician would ever choose to just trick an audience. A true magician would, however, always be concerned about the effect each experience has on his audience.

Preparation

Preparation is what you need to have, build, or buy before you can do the effect.

Setup

The *setup* is where everything needs to be and what has to be done before the trick can start. Note that sometimes the preparation, setup, and routine are all balled together and just called the *"method"* or *"modus operandi."* I have also heard the word "secret" used, but it is usually found among amateur circles.

Routine/Performance/Presentation

The *routine* of a magic effect is the flowchart or chain of events. It's the schematic for what method will be utilized, when it will be used, and in what order it will flow to create the desired

Secrets of Success

- Learn the fundamentals.
- Get honest feedback from others.
- Study your own magic.
- Perform as much as you can.
- Share your magic (not your secrets) with everyone.

Thomas Meier won first place in Close-up Magic at Fédération Internationale de Sociétés des Magiques (FISM) in 1997 when he was only 19 years old. You can see that magic is an equal opportunity adventure!

• • •

A Peruvian-born illusionist was very successful in France in the late 1800s performing as "L'Homme Masqué," or "The Masked Man." Jose Antenar de Gago wore a mask just like that guy we know (you know, Valentino). He did this both during his performances and when he was in public.

effect. There are two separate channels for a routine: that which the magician sees and follows and that which only the audience sees. Remember, as the magician, you also have to create a routine for fitting your method or secret moves into what the audience is looking at. The only routine the audience is aware of is the one they see. Both sides of the routine are known to the magician but only one is ever known by the audience. Imagine being behind the scenes of one of those computer-animated, robotic shows at Disney. The backstage crew sees a very different part of the routine than the audience sees out front.

Secrecy, the Magician's Code and You
What's the Big Secret and Why?

The big secret these days seems to be that magic is secret. Magic must be kept that way: a secret. But the secret is not where many people believe they will find it. The secret to magic is not in the gimmicks, boxes, and pockets. Magicians are far too clever to keep secrets where we know everyone will look. The basic rules of magic state that you should never reveal how a trick is done, never do a trick without sufficient practice, and never do the same trick twice for the same audience . . . but the magician's code goes a lot deeper than that.

What Happens If I Tell Anyway?

If you tell, you rob the gift of magic from the very person you have first given it to. With their loss of wonderment will also come your loss—the loss of their respect. Their image of you instantly changes from gifted and clever to charlatan and cheat. There is no way to absolutely be sure anyone will never tell; it just isn't our choice. It's not our prerogative. It's not ours to give or take, only to share or to not touch at all.

What Happens If I Don't Tell?

If you don't tell your secrets, you will continue to enjoy the gift of magic that made you look here for it in the first place. That's why you are reading this. Some people are bound to find it and understand, and others are intended to simply see it and see nothing else. Sure, magic falls into the hands of people who want nothing else but to destroy it, but it is a selfish person who steals the dream from another. These people are the same in every avenue of life and their view of magic is no different than their view of the other things that never stop blocking their paths.

So How Come *I* Can Tell?

Magic, like any other craft or art, has to be passed on. It has always been passed on and I am no different than any other teacher of magic. Secrecy is a controversial concept to debate, and some magicians get very upset about the disclosure of any magic methods and secrets of magic. These magicians also forget that they too learned magic somewhere at one time, probably from a book or a mentor. When the revelation of a secret method is shared for the sake of learning and growing in magic, it is far different than the revelation of a secret just for the sake of revealing it.

Stan Allen

"My take on the masked magician was not that he was giving away the art or that the art was going to go away. To me, he was demeaning the art, reducing it to just 'a secret,' thus there's no art involved. My criticism is that no where does he acknowledge the work it takes to perform magic or that magic is truly an art.

I know how an ice skater ice-skates, I still don't know how they spin around like they do. To me, that's even more amazing! The best audience for ice skaters is the kids that have studied ice skating a little bit. They know when that person is doing unbelievable things. So to me, by just showing the *secret* to how a trick is done, you demean it to, 'that's all there is' or 'if I had one of those boxes, then I would be a magician, too,' and that's not true."

Stan Allen, magician and editor of *MAGIC* magazine

CHAPTER 2

Types of Magic—
Which One Is
Right for You?

As I mentioned in the Introduction, magic encompasses a wide range of "tricks." You may be most familiar with sleight-of-hand card or coin effects. Or, you might favor the mystery that comes along with tricks of illusion. Houdini, the great escape artist, might have been the one that drew you to magic in the first place. No matter what your inspiration for making the journey into magic, you'll need to be familiar with the different types as there is quite a bit of crossover between them all. For instance, Close-Up Magic is employed by nearly all of the great magicians of our time, in some shape or form. Chapter 2 will give you an introduction to magic in all its wondrous forms. From there, you can decide in which area, if any, you wish to specialize.

Close-Up Magic

Close-Up Magic is just that: magic that is performed right under the noses of a small intimate crowd. This form of magic is by far the most personal, pure, and original form of conjuring and the foundation for most other forms. Because Close-up Magic typically does not include many of the technical enhancements—such as staging, scenery, lighting—and there is minimal distance between the performer and his audience, Close-Up Magic can often be considered the magician's magic. It is certainly the magical equivalent to jazz music: raw, crafted, and beautiful to behold. Out of the many types of magic that audiences behold, there always seems to be a smile on the face of and a star in the eye of one who recalls seeing Close-Up Magic performed for them, "right there" in the bare hands of the magician. It conjures up a feeling of being pampered at a private table complete with a serenading violinist. The feeling of awe that comes from being the guest of honor as a magician unfolds miracles right there in your private box seat gives Close-Up Magic its strength.

Dollars and Cents

Generally, under $200 will purchase the equipment and materials necessary for a 30-minute performance of professional-quality Magic.

Who Uses Close-Up Magic?

Close-Up Magic is used by most professional magicians in the world no matter what area they end up claiming as their specialty. Illusionists, escape artists, mentalists, and the rest, usually have a personal collection of close-up favorites. First of all, it's fun to perform close-up, and because most magicians learn Close-Up Magic as a starting block for their magic studies, it's part of their roots, usually from childhood on. Amateurs are also big fans of Close-Up Magic because it shares many of the same techniques and methods used in larger areas of magic. It is also the most inexpensive area of magic to enter and the most convenient to handle because of the simplicity and size of the necessary elements, props, and accessories that accompany it. A deck of cards, a coin, and a ton of time can make real magic!

How Can I Use Close-Up Magic?

Personally

Close-Up Magic is great to get your fingers in good shape, to increase reading skills and comprehension, and to share a sense of brotherhood through a hobby. Learning to look at the illustrations, technical drawings, and schematics that accompany the instructions for performing magic can help familiarize you with this type of printed format. Having this skill can be useful in all aspects of life, from understanding a floor plan for an addition to your home to assembling a new gas grill. Magic is also a great form of exercise for your hands and fingers and can increase manual dexterity while lessening pain.

Socially

Because Close-Up Magic is generally portable, you can take it with you and perform it in social situations. It's a great ice breaker and confidence builder.

Definition Please

A *committee* in the world of magic refers to a group of people brought on stage to inspect a prop or to assist in an effect.

• • •

Telekinesis is the process of moving an object using only the mind and without contact or any other ordinary or physical means.

Professionally

If your profession is in sales, customer service, hospitality, training, or another area of business that deals with people, Close-Up Magic is a great tool. It's easy enough to pull out and perform without it seeming as intrusive or calculating. It's also a fresh way to pep up a meeting that just would otherwise lay there like a wet sock.

Parlor Magic

Parlor Magic, also known as Drawing Room Magic, can be described as: magic that is larger in scope than Close-Up Magic. It usually performed on the same physical level as the audience and is smaller in scale than Cabaret or Stage Magic.

Who Uses Parlor Magic?

Parlor Magic is used by performers with an audience of more than a handful of people. They want the act to be visible and exciting without the need for tons of equipment and special performing situations.

How Can I Use Parlor Magic?

Personally

Parlor Magic helps you gain confidence in front of a crowd and good communication skills by getting you in front of a number of people to present your stuff. This magic makes the prospect of facing a crowd a pleasure instead of a chore. If you're looking to build confidence, the difference between performing Parlor Magic for a sizable audience—as opposed to doing Close-Up Magic for a few onlookers—is significant. Furthermore, if your sights are set on performing Stage Magic, starting with Parlor Magic, which tends to involve a more intimate and relaxed setting, is a good first step.

Dollars and Cents

You can do Parlor Magic for under $300, with typical purchases being silk handkerchiefs, small magic props and secret gimmicks, ropes, playing cards, and a small, portable stand or table.

Socially

You can perform Parlor Magic right in your own living room, or in anyone else's for that matter. You don't have to lug around a truckload full of equipment, and you can perform an entire show for a good number of people out of a briefcase.

Professionally

Parlor Magic is a great tool for training or addressing any group. It's a perfect way to add variety to a presentation. Combined with a valuable message, it is powerful and memorable.

Stage Magic

Stage Magic, Cabaret Magic, or Platform Magic would seem a little too big for your typical living room performance. It is usually performed on a stage or in an area created especially for a presentation. In short, Stage Magic is large enough to be easily seen in a large hall.

Who Uses Stage Magic?

Anyone who wants to perform magic for large groups of people in public settings uses Stage Magic. Most people who perform Stage Magic are either professionally involved with magic or view it as a serious hobby.

How Can I Use Stage Magic?

Personally

Again, Stage Magic gets you used to being on stage and in front of people in a professional and more formal platform setting. It is far less casual than Parlor Magic and enforces the disciplines needed to hold a large group of people.

Harry August Jansen, "Dante"

Oddly, Harry August Jansen became a famous magician through the generosity and vision of magician Howard Thurston. Thurston spotted Jansen at a vaudeville performance and liked him so much that in 1923 he offered Jansen the chance to tour a second unit of Thurston's show. Jansen changed his name to Dante and for four years *Thurston Presents Dante in Thurston-Kellar Mysteries* played across America before going on to draw rave reviews abroad. Dante combined live orchestral music with his magic, which poked fun at the old style magicians. When World War II forced Dante to go back to the United States, his *Sim-Sala-Bim* show developed into the first Broadway revue featuring magic.

Socially

Stage Magic shows command a different rapport with your audience. They require you to get in front of large groups and committees instead of friends and family.

Professionally

Stage Magic can be used to enhance your professional life in a variety of ways, in any kind of hosting, emcee, or platform situation from opening a conference to evening entertainment to product introductions.

Illusions

Illusions are the big box tricks, the stuff you see in a showroom in Las Vegas or on a theatre stage anywhere else. An Illusionist is a Magician who specializes in that area.

Who Uses Illusions?

Serious amateurs and professional Magicians use illusions. Their cost prohibits (or at least discourages) novices from using illusions.

How Can I Use Illusions?

Personally

If you are interested in theater, acting, or performing the big stuff, illusions might be right up your alley.

Socially

Illusions aren't really something that you perform in any situation other than on a real stage or in a showroom. It's not like you are sitting around a bar and somebody yells out, "Hey come over here and cut my husband in half!" Illusions do seem to draw more public attention than any other type of magic. Public attention also means media attention.

Dollars and Cents

For Stage Magic you can invest under $1000, for starters, to purchase such items as silks (many of them); larger props, canes, candles, jumbo or specially made cards, substantial tables, a costume, and a dove (of course). Not only do you have to create your show, you have to support it with a truck, van, or trailer; dry cleaning; carrying cases and cages; and food. Sure, you can do Stage Magic with smaller objects, but if it's not big or exciting enough to play well on stage, don't try it.

Professionally

If you are performing illusions, your professional interest is in magic and in getting booked. If you have the equipment and can perform the jobs, you can get the jobs. If you don't, you can't. I don't think I know too many amateurs who dabble in illusions.

Comedy Magic
Who Uses Comedy Magic?

If you are one of those people who is just wacky, nutty, madcap, and filled with hysterical hyjinx in your daily life, Comedy Magic is definitely for you. Comedy Magic is perhaps the most appealing of all the types of magic. Being amazed and tickled at the same time is just a great feeling. Comedy Magic is a type of magic where miracles seem to be happening while they are subtly being supported by humorous patter, props, and pranks, as with the likes of Jeff Hobson, Tom Mullica, and The Great Tomsini. These types of magicians are obviously skilled performers who combine their magic skills with their own style of comedy and character. Then, you'll find another type of Comedy Magic, where some magic does happen but it is underpinned by slapstick comedy and in-your-face madness. Carl Ballantine and The Amazing Johnathan fall into this category.

People who love to laugh and like to see other people laugh use Comedy Magic.

How Can I Use Comedy Magic?
Personally

Comedy Magic makes you feel good, and that helps. I read somewhere that laughing is good for your long-term health, so Comedy Magic must be good medicine.

David Copperfield

David Copperfield first stepped into show business as a ventriloquist, but by the time he was 12 years old, he had changed his focus to magic. Before long David became known for his ability to blend sleight-of-hand magic with stage magic, theater, music, and dance. An extremely charismatic and handsome magician, David adds romance, mood, and texture to his grand illusions to create some of the most beautiful magic seen today.

Today, the entire world enjoys Copperfield on television as he astounds us with his "vanishing" Lear jet, his "walk" through the Great Wall of China, and his "levitation" across the Grand Canyon.

Siegfried and Roy

By themselves, the names Siegfried Fischbacker and Roy Horn might go unnoticed. But together the names Siegfried and Roy represent arguably the world's greatest stars of magic. What does this duo have that sets them apart from other illusionists? High energy, huge illusions, and lots and lots of big cats!

Both Siegfried and Roy hail from Germany. As a child, Siegfried became interested in magic when he received a small magic kit as a gift, followed by a book on magic, and finally a trip to see Kalanag in Munich. Roy had an uncle who was the director of a zoo and who exposed him to many animals, among them large cats. In 1960, the two met aboard a cruise ship where Siegfried was performing and Roy was a steward. Before long the two had snuck one of Roy's cheetahs onto the ship so that

(continued on next page)

Socially

Hey, what can I say? Funny magicians are just more fun to be around. Would you rather be around a guy who is making you laugh and amazing you, or would you rather be around a guy who is showing you another pick-a-card trick and explaining mathematical odds? That's what I thought—the funny guy.

Professionally

A sense of humor is good in any professional situation if it is used intelligently. It opens doors and creates bonds that would normally take a long time, or never happen at all. Throw some magic into this recipe and you've opened endless possibilities and opportunities.

Mental Magic

Mental Magic is the magic that encompasses mind reading, telekinesis, psychic reading, hypnotism, and that sort of thing.

Who Uses Mental Magic?

Mentalism is most often used by a magician that wants a different kind of act than the regular "rabbit in the hat" or top hat image of the magician. Mentalism is usually a more cerebral and mature presentation of mystery, but it can also be very funny in the right hands.

How Can I Use Mental Magic?

Personally

Mental magic is a challenging proposition for creating an entire act. It requires thoughtful planning, presentation, and understanding of magic principles without using the usual magic props. Mentalism is also a great alternative for someone with physical disabilities or budget restrictions.

Socially

Mental magic rivals Close-Up and Parlor Magic for compactness and ease of preparation. Mental Magic is great for parties of any size and truly amazes even the most skeptical of all audiences. People who hate conventional types of magic often love Mental Magic.

Professionally

Because Mental Magic can be done anytime, anywhere, and often without any visible gimmick, it is perfect to present in business situations. Because of its intellectual charm and challenge, it fits formal settings a lot better than, say, suddenly pulling out a brightly colored silk handkerchief and doing a magic trick.

Escape Magic

Escapes in and of themselves are not really what most people would consider magic. Many times they are performed in a way that not only makes them impressive but also makes them seem impossible. The magician escapes (that's impressive), then he suddenly reappears in the back of the theater (that's impossible)—*that's* what makes it magic. Escapes have become connected with magic, especially when associated with the name Harry Houdini.

Who Uses Escape Magic?

Performers who want something different perform escapes. Usually people who choose a louder, more physical side of magic prefer this form. Escapes fall into the "bad-boy" category of magic. It's noisy, dangerous, and tension filled and it, again, interests many people who would ordinarily never look at a magic act.

Siegfried and Roy

(continued from previous page)

Siegfried could try to use it in his vanishing act rather than the typical rabbit. The passengers loved the act, and Siegfried and Roy continued working cruise ships for the next five years. Following that, they had appearances on German television, for royalty at the Lido in Paris, and a 15-minute act at the Stardust Hotel in Las Vegas. Soon after, they became the star act for Hallelujah Hollywood at the then-new MGM Grand Hotel. In the 1980s the two appeared for seven years at the Frontier Hotel starring in *Beyond Belief.* In the '90s, Siegfried and Roy began performing the biggest of all shows at the lavish Mirage Hotel, known simply as *Siegfried and Roy.* To this day, they wow audiences nightly with their grand illusions and their rare and beautiful collection of Royal White tigers.

How Can I Use Escape Magic?

Personally

Escape Magic can be very theatrical and is a good form for the true showman, especially those who are naturally more agile and physical. A true showman can put an audience on the edge of their seats with a well-planned escape. Escape Magic is also a good option for those who may not be interested in mastering tedious sleight-of-hand manipulations, choreography, and patter.

Socially

I can't think of how Escape Magic could possibly be used socially; well, I can, but I don't like to think about those things. I guess you could do some neat stuff with a packing crate at a pool party.

Professionally

Again, escapes have a certain appeal and they don't fit in every situation. If you happen to be involved with a company that you can theme an escape to, you might have something there. Maybe you can escape from a hardware company's hardware or a lumber company's crate (Houdini used to do that). This is not exactly something you can exhibit out on the golf course unless it's, "Hey who wants to see me get out of that sand trap?"

PART II

Learning the
Magic—
the Tricks of
the Trade

CHAPTER 3

*Close-Up Magic—
Card Effects*

Basic Tool Kit

- Pack
- Cull
- Glide
- Glimpse
- Counts
- Deck
- Key Card
- Lift
- Mechanic's Grip
- Biddle Grip
- Break
- Bridge
- Palm
- Stock
- Pass
- Cuts
- Crimp
- Inside/Outside
- Hindu Shuffle
- Forcing

Some Basics
Deciding on Cards

Do yourself a favor and don't use crappy cards. Good ones cost a few bucks but they are worth it. I suggest using red backed, Bicycle brand playing cards with a white border and a jumbo index (i.e., the value and suit usually found in the left corners). These cards are of high quality and are red, which is beneficial if they are accidentally seen between some fingers when they are hidden. (Trust me, it's a lot better than blue.) The white borders make them good for special counts and the jumbo indexes make them easy to see when you tell your subject to remember a card. You would be amazed at how many people say they have looked at a card and either can't remember it or "didn't really see the whole thing." Cut down your chances for encountering trouble by starting right.

Pack vs. Packet

The deck of cards is just that, usually the whole deck, fifty-two cards—that is, fifty-two without the jokers, advertisements, and whatever else comes with it. A pack is usually the same thing as a deck but a *packet* might be just a few cards. Sometimes card effects are marketed and described as "packet tricks." These are great if you have no intention of ever doing card tricks with a full deck.

Get a Grip!
The Mechanic's Grip

Although it's called the mechanic's grip, it's really not that mechanical. I guess "the natural grip," sounded too easy. It is natural so it will come to you easily like a duck takes to orange sauce. The cards are held face down, comfortably resting in the palm of your hand with your index finger resting against the upper end closest to the outer edge. The thumb is on top of the deck resting at a 45-degree angle with its base holding pressure against the bottom inner edge. The other fingers (three, unless you dabble in woodworking) wrap lightly around the outer edge of the deck **(Figure 3.1).** You can adjust this grip to comfortably suit your own hands but the real trick is, hold them however they fit best as long as it looks natural and you keep it consistent for any move. Change ups are not a good idea because the audience starts to look for the "why" and you don't need those distractions. Also, always try to pull the cards out of the box the same way every time.

Biddle Grip

Hold the deck from above with your thumb on one end and the first, second, and third fingers on the other end. Be sure you are holding it from above. Your index finger will rest lightly on top of the deck **(Figure 3.2).**

Figure 3.1

All the Right Moves
Key Card

A key card is a card that is used within the deck in the same way a bookmark is used in a book, except that the key card is never acknowledged. The magician knows the name of the key card and uses it to mark the position of another card(s) above or below it in the deck. Using a key card is also a great backup in case another method of card introduction, such as a *force,* fails. By having a key card on the bottom or top of the deck, the chosen card can be placed on top of the deck and the deck can be cut any amount of times. The spectator's card will be the card next to it. A key card can also be marked on the back so that it is not necessary to look at the card faces to find the spectator's card.

Figure 3.2

Break

A break is a separation of a card or group of cards usually held open with the fleshy part of the finger (or the meat of the pad) or with the finger tip. In the case of "the little finger break," the pack is held in the mechanic's grip and the pinkie's flesh protrudes in between two cards with the first, second, and third fingers laying along the edge as usual **(Figure 3.3).** The break is usually used to secretly retain a location the magician

Figure 3.3

Did You Know?

Ricky Jay described the art of throwing playing cards in his book, *Cards as Weapons* (Warner Books, 1997) but get this, Jim Karol of Catasauqua, Pennsylvania, threw a standard playing card 201 feet at Mount Ida College in Newton Center, Massachusetts on October 18, 1992.

Figure 3.4

needs to quickly find again. This little finger "meatball" is slid in, again like a bookmark, between the correct cards. The rest of the fingers rest along the sides of the cards as usual, hiding any separation from the front. The top ends of the cards come together by that time and look as natural as can be. If they don't, you have too much meatball in the mix.

Palming

Palming a card means to hide the card with the hand so that it cannot be seen. It is not necessarily held in the palm of the hand but can be held, for instance, behind the hand in the case of a "back-palm." However, a basic palm holds the card in the palm of the hand. There are many different kinds of palms, and for now, you should try to do a simple one and stick with it. If you want to learn more, there are tons of specialized books and videotapes to teach you how to palm a card with sinews, webs, and joints of your fingers you probably didn't even know existed. Here's what I call my "easy-way palm." First of all, find out what a card feels like when it is held in the palm. Place a card on the palm of one hand with one end resting in the crevices of the first joints of the fingers, with the fingers curled slightly inward and the other end pushing against the base of the hand and the fleshy part of the thumb. Now, the trick is how to get it there. With the deck held in a biddle grip perpendicular to the floor, push the cards into the flat palm of the other hand and keep that hand still. Now push the deck in the biddle hand about ½ inch toward the end of the palming hand's fingers. The biddle thumb can make sure just one card stays in the other hand's palm. As soon as it is sufficiently away (about halfway off), turn the palming hand's fingers down toward the floor. The palmed card should now be at a right angle to the rest of the pack in the other hand. **(Figure 3.4)** Pull the gripped deck away and retain the palmed card in the other. Your attention should be toward the deck, and the palmed card can drop to the side aided by this misdirection. This is just one method to palm a card off of a deck but it does work; I use it all of the time.

The Pass

The *pass* moves a top section of the deck to the bottom or vice versa. Most times, the pass is done secretly or it would just be a cut. There are a lot of different variants of the pass.

Cut

A *cut* is the action of removing a portion of the deck, placing it on the table, and "completing the cut" or putting the remaining cards on top of the portion on the table. There are a lot of different cuts too. Some of them truly "cut" the cards, but the most fun ones to perform don't affect the cards at all. These "false cuts" appear to mix up or lose cards to make the audience think that the cards are shuffled fairly and that nothing could possibly be set up.

Crimp

A *crimp* is an up or down bend in some portion of a card that marks the card so it can be identified even by sight. It can also be used as a key card or as a means of locating a selected card.

Cull

To *cull* is group and keep certain cards together, usually at the top or bottom of the deck. A select stock of cards is usually culled while shuffling the entire deck. It is also used to move cards to certain locations.

Glide

The *glide* is a way to switch one card for another, usually while you seemingly place the card down on the table. This is a nifty little piece of business and it's fun to practice too. Hold a small packet (we'll say five cards) from above in what is very much like the biddle grip if you held the cards by their sides instead of their ends. You want to be holding the cards by their sides. Do you see why it's best to learn all of these tools first? They are dependent upon each other and if you learn them from the start, you'll never have to stop in the middle of learning a new trick just

Definition Please

A *packet* is a group of cards that is less than a full deck: usually only four or five. A *pack* refers to a full deck of 52 cards.

Figure 3.5

to learn a basic move. Once you have the tools, you can build. Okay, you've got the cards gripped, but now you have to alter the grip a bit. Curl your second, third, and pinkie fingers around so they are pressing down on the face of the bottom card. By moving your thumb and forefinger ahead a little, all of the packet with the exception of the bottom card, which is held by the second, third, and pinkie fingers, move forward. This reveals the second card from the bottom for the taking. **(Figure 3.5)** If you begin by showing the face of the packet, turn the packet face down and perform the glide. You can seem to be placing the face card on the table but it is in fact the second card from the bottom.

Glimpse

A *glimpse* is taking a very quick peak at the face of the card without the spectator knowing it. This can be performed in a number of ways, including simply looking at the bottom card during a shuffle, bending a card up, or even glimpsing through a reflection such as a knife blade.

Counts

Special *counts* are used a great deal in close-up card magic, especially with packet tricks. These counts allow for cards to be miscounted, or for certain cards to be hidden, added to, or secretly flipped over at will.

The Elmsley Count

If you are going to perform close-up card magic you must learn the Elmsley count, especially for packet tricks. This count lets the magician count four cards while concealing cards that are face up or are different in design such as in color, pattern, or printed image.

We will use four cards to learn the Elmsley count. We will count four cards as four face-down cards, but there will really be one face-up card within the packet. Reverse the card that is the third card down and hold the cards between the thumb,

---

Definition Please

A *block* of cards is just what it sounds like, a number of cards kept together with no partic-ular order or for no specific reason.

A *stock*, also known as a stack, is a group of cards that stay as one, usually at the top or bottom of the deck. These cards are often in a certain order or sequence.

index, second, and third finger of one hand. The reversed card will be hidden during this count. The thumb is on top, opposite the fingers, which are along the inner edge of the face of the cards. There are different opinions about how to hold the cards during any count, but my opinion is that the grip should be as natural as possible. The opposite hand will grip the top card, sliding it off of the packet with the thumb on top, supported by the index finger below **(Figure 3.6).** When the card has cleared, bring the hand back toward the packet as if returning to simply grab the next card. What actually happens is, the original card is placed on the bottom of the packet and the top two cards (including the reversed card) are pinched off together and slid off of the packet with the same grip. To help you prepare to slide these two off, you can pinch the two-card block very slightly to the outer edge when the first card is pulled away. The two actions actually happen at the same time **(Figure 3.7).** The hand with the two-card block returns and places the block underneath, still retaining it but also peeling off the third card. The fourth card is taken the same way to appear as though you have simply counted four face-down cards from one hand to the other. Actually the cards are now three face down on top and one face up on the bottom. Incidentally, this is the set-up position for the next very important count.

Figure 3.6

Figure 3.7

The Jordan Count

The end of the Elmsley count sets you up for the beginning of the Jordan count, three top cards face down and one bottom card face up. The count begins with the same gripping position as the Elmsley count.

The opposite hand will grip the top card, sliding it off of the packet with the thumb on top, supported by the index finger below. When the card has cleared, bring the hand back toward the packet placing the card underneath and peeling off the next card. Once the two cards have cleared, bring the packet back underneath, bringing its outer edge squarely underneath the inner edge of the cards in the opposite hand. Pinch the bottom card away from the rest of the packet and pull the top three away.

This packet contains the reversed card in the middle. Once that packet clears, return the hand to peel away the last card. The order from the top of the packet is now: first card, face down; second card, face down; third card, face up; and fourth card face down. The cards are left in the set-up position for the Elmsley count. One count ends in the set-up position for the other and this makes it great for rehearsal.

Flustration Count

The flustration count lets the magician deal a number of cards onto the table while showing they are all the same. They can in fact all be different but the audience is only seeing the face card over and over.

Hold the packet in the biddle grip. Turn the hand face up showing the bottom card. Turn the hand back down and peel the top card off onto the table. Turn the hand palm up again (apparently showing the next card) and repeat the deal. Continue the count until all the cards have been dealt.

Forcing

Forcing can be a little scary at first but it's all about believing and practicing. You have to believe that it is possible to have an audience member "choose" a card when you know darned well they have no choice at all. You also have to do it quite a few times before you can gain that confidence. I know one magician who tries new forces all the time just for fun. He will have you select a card, "his way" and if he gets it, good. If he doesn't, no big deal; he chuckles and says, "Oh well," and goes onto another trick that he knows he has mastered.

Never use a questionable card force in situations when the selected card absolutely must be a certain card, such as with a mind reading effect where the name of the card has been previously written and is inside a sealed envelope beyond the point of no return. In cases when you just have to find out the name of the card a bit before the spectator does, any force is fine. Never completely count on a card force unless you have some way of getting

---

Definition Please

If you are holding the deck in a *mechanic's grip*, the *inside of the deck* is the side closest to the thumb. The *outside of the deck* is covered by all of the other fingers.

The *top of the deck* is the printed back. The *bottom of the deck* is the printed face.

If you are holding the deck in a mechanic's grip, the *top edge of the deck* is the end closest to the index finger and the *bottom edge of the deck* is the end closest to the pinkie finger.

out of it. Also, never tell your audience what you are going to do before you do it or what is going to happen before it does; that way they don't know what to expect. It sounds simple and it can be, but it takes a little gumption, that's for sure.

Gimmick Deck Force

Probably the simplest, near-perfect force comes from the use of a gimmicked deck. That's the good news. The bad news is that you have to use a gimmicked deck, which can't be passed around for inspection by your audience. This means you can't do any impromptu tricks with someone else's deck, and you forfeit one pocket, pouch, or slot just to haul the deck around. This may sound trivial, but with Close-Up Magic you have to take how many props you use into consideration, especially if you are performing it as you walk around the room.

There are decks that will allow you to force more than one card for more than one effect, but all gimmicked decks have their limitations, and you shouldn't push them or your luck. There are so many great forces, it seems a shame to rely on a gimmick deck. However, if you do decide to use one, choose one that looks like an ordinary deck and matches the cards you will use in other routines after you switch out the gimmicked deck.

Cross-Cut Force

Another simple force comes from simply having the spectator cut a portion of the cards off the deck onto the table. The magician completes the cut by placing the remaining cards not only on top of, but also "across" the already tabled cards **(Figure 3.8).** When the spectator finally sees the cut that he has cut to, it is the card the magician wanted him to take all along. This force is a beauty in its simplicity and psychology. These are two elements that are very important in creating the perfect deception. The cut is real; the selection is fake. Begin with the card to be forced on the top of the deck with the deck face down **(marked by the "X" in Figure 3.8).** Ask the spectator to simply cut about half of the cards onto the table. Now the remaining cards are added by the magician to

Figure 3.8

Alex Elmsley

Just about every magician who has ever studied magic has attempted to do "an Elmsley." If you want to be good, you have to perfect something, and Alex Elmsley perfected the Elmsley Count, a false display (or count) that has become a cornerstone in many card tricks, especially packet tricks. A British inventory and card magician, Elmsley developed the count and introduced it in America in 1958 at a magic convention in Chicago. It has been a staple ever since.

complete the cut but they are laid across the tabled cards. After some by-play, the top section is lifted off to see what card the spectator has cut to. Hmmm . . . did you get that? Something's fishy here. He didn't cut to that card at all! In reality, the card he cut to is on the top of the block that was just lifted off. Don't make a big deal out of this. Just lift up the block and tell him what to do. He will do what you say.

Here are a few pointers. The amount of the deck cut off of the deck (half) is not an absolutely essential amount but it helps establish what's going on. The cards are out of the magician's hands and it gives the participant an interest in "getting it right." It also leaves the two blocks of cards looking that much more similar. Remember, the strength of this force is that everything seems so deliberate and commonplace. When the top block of cards is added across the other cards, spectators forget which block is which, since nothing has happened except that the deck has indeed been cut. The only thing that has been shuffled is their minds. Such fun!

When it's time to look at the card they have cut to, you pick up the top "crossed section" yourself. Las Vegas card guru Frank Zak pushes the section a little closer to the spectator saying, "Take a look at the card you've cut to." This gets the cards even further out of the magician's reach and adds to the confusion of what was where and when. This technique doesn't seem confusing to the spectator. It seems completely straightforward. When he looks at the top card, it is the force card. The cross-cut force works great!

Countdown Force

The countdown force is somewhat gimmicky but if your routine has something to do with numbers or it somehow ties in with counting, this might fit in perfectly. Place the card you want to force ten cards down from the top of the deck. Give the deck to your spectator and ask her to tell you a number between 10 and 20. When she has done that, ask her to count that same number of cards off onto the table one at a time into a small pile. Next, ask her to add the two digits of her original number and deal that number of cards into a new pile from the pile she has just formed.

The card that you originally placed tenth from the top, the force card, will be the last card placed down on that second pile.

Hindu Shuffle Force

The Hindu shuffle goes like this. The cards are held in one hand. The opposite hand cuts most of the cards away from the pack, leaving only a small block behind. The magician asks the audience member to say "stop" any time and then continues to cut cards back into the original hand and onto the original pack. When the helper says "stop," the magician shows at which card he stopped. This card is the one that the magician later names, tames, or maims. At any rate, the card that the spectator sees is the card the magician wants him to.

Start by glimpsing the bottom card; it will be the card that is forced. The hand is over the backs of the cards holding the bottom sides of the cards with the thumb, second, and third fingers. The index finger can rest lightly against the top. The cards are brought over the opposite palm-up hand and a small amount of cards are gripped high with the tops of the thumb, second, third, and pinkie fingers. This hand then pulls away the small packet of cards **(Figure 3.9).** Once away, let the packet fall into the palm of that hand and repeat **(Figure 3.10).** Ask the spectator to say "stop" at any time. When she says "stop," show her the card on the face of the remaining cards and ask her to remember the name. That's the card that you first glimpsed and was there all along. After she says she has it, continue to shuffle the remainder of the deck proving her card to be completely mixed in with the other cards.

Classic Force

The classic force works like this. The audience member is offered the cards as they are spread out in a fan one at a time. When the card to be forced is at the decided position, in front of the audience member's reaching fingertips, the deck moves closer and she latches onto it. It's similar to putting the bait right in front of the fish's mouth. Have the same person put the card back in the deck and mix it up. If you need to take it out

Figure 3.9

Figure 3.10

again, you can do so but reinforce the thought that they have the freedom to pick any card and lose it in the deck before the magician gets his polished paws on it again.

The most necessary elements of the classic force are nerve and practice, in short, confidence, which is essential.

Begin with the force card on top of the deck. You can false shuffle or simply cut the cards maintaining a break above the force card. Move the top portion of the deck to the side so you can keep track of the force card while beginning to spread the cards while you ask the spectator to select a card. When his fingers are near the force card, spread the top cards away from his hand, placing the force card right in front of his fingers. Continue to spread the remaining cards and he will begin to think he is running out of time and will take the force card. This is probably the most difficult force in this book but when done well, it's mighty powerful. Don't rush it; study it. It can be a real doozie!

Shuffles

Hindu Shuffle

The Hindu shuffle is the same as the Hindu Shuffle force except you don't need to control the location of any card. This means that you just do the shuffle until the entire stack is passed from one hand to the other.

Overhand/False Shuffle

The overhand shuffle is your regular looking shuffle. The deck begins in one hand held by the ends with the thumb on one end and the second, third, and forth fingers on the other end. The index finger rides along the top side edges of the cards. One side of the deck faces up. The palm-up fingers of the opposite hand come underneath the cards and a block of cards is allowed to drop into them. This happens again with the next block falling on top of the existing block. This continues until all of the cards have been transferred.

Definition Please

To *force* a card means to lead a spectator to select a specific card although he may think he has freedom of choice. This is also sometimes called "the magician's choice."

• • •

By-play is magician lingo for patter, which is also magician language for chitchat, also known as conversation to a normal person!

To false shuffle, meaning to leave a card or cards on top of the deck, execute the same shuffle but replace the last block on the back (or top of the deck) instead of in front. Do this by bending the receiving hand's fingers in and allowing all of the blocks to fall against the thumb, which leaves the backs of the cards facing up so the remainder can just be plopped down on top of them.

Farrow Shuffle/Riffle Shuffle/False Shuffle

A riffle shuffle is that shuffle people do in card games with half of the deck in each hand gripped by the ends. The index fingers push down to buckle the cards and the thumb allows them to fall toward each other and interlace **(Figure 3.11).** To false shuffle and retain a top stack, simply time it so that the last cards to come down are the ones in the top half of the deck.

Figure 3.11

Lifts

The most popular lift in magic is the double lift. The double lift allows the magician to show a top card, turn it back over, and have it change to another card. It is an extremely useful sleight and there are many favorite handlings. Here are the basics.

The card you want to eventually show is on top of the deck. The cards are in the mechanic's grip. Get a little finger break under two cards (keep it tiny). The opposite hand comes over top of the deck, grabs the two cards as one by the outer corners, slides it off a bit and pivots it around, turning it face up by pivoting it against the fingers that are wrapped around the outer edge of the cards in the mechanic's grip. The index finger buckles the cards slightly so that they stay together, and the cards pivot and slide back into the mechanic's grip still maintaining the little finger break. The face of the second card is what the audience sees. Reverse the two cards the same way and allow them to come to rest on top of the cards without the break. Now all you have to do is pick up the top card and show that it has magically changed.

Figure 3.12

A Couple of One-Card Tricks

Card to Bill

Here's a neat effect I learned as a kid that I still use today.

Effect

A playing card is held in one hand. The other empty hand passes over it and the card instantly changes to a dollar bill. The bill is turned over to show that it truly is a bill on each side.

This is one of those effects that you have to make up, but you can carry it with you and it's quick, simple, and surprising. The workings of this little gimmicked pack are as shown **(Figure 3.12).**

Preparation

Take a couple of very crisp one-dollar bills (or larger if you're a real show off) and cut them to the width of the playing cards you normally use. Now, get an extra playing card such as a 2, 4, or 10 and fold it in half, end to end and face to face. When you fold playing cards, the ink cracks along the crease, especially after repeated use. You should use cards in the values stated above (in any suit) because they have a blank or white area between the two halves. The crease area is very small and the rest of the card has a lot of ink. Using paper rubber cement, glue the bills to the back of the card carefully, making sure that when the card is eventually folded inside of the bill, the bill still looks real. Don't forget to have a front and a back to the "closed" bill and to orient them correctly so it looks just like a genuine green back.

Setup

This is a good little stinger to use to get the audience's attention before performing a card effect using a whole deck. Simply place the gimmicked pack face up on the bottom of a deck. The bill is now where the back of the pack would normally be. When the deck is removed from the box, everything comes out at the same time. Get rid of the cards (all but one of course) and perform your minimiracle. As a note, place the gimmicked pack so the folded end of the bill is nearest the opening of the card box and not the raw edge. It's much easier to get out of the box this way and won't beat up your bill(s).

Routine

In performing, place the card in the palm of one hand as in **Figure 3.13** with the arm to the side and the face of the card toward the audience. Bring the opposite hand up along the arm and over the top of the card. Catch the top of the card with the hand and continue moving the hand downward, closing the top of the card down over the bottom as it moves. You'll have to move the thumb of the hand holding the card out of the way for a moment during the fold **(Figure 3.14).** Because of the way the bill is folded behind the card, as the hand closes the card, it will seem to suddenly change into dollar bill the same size as the card. By just keeping those two ends pinched between the fingers and continuing to pull that "pack" down, the entire bill is extended. With that same hand you can show the bill on both sides. I suggest putting the bill away quickly so no one gets a chance to put his or her mitts on it. I usually pull out my money clip and put the new "bill" with the rest of his buddies.

Figure 3.13

Figure 3.14

Whirling Card

This is not a close-up trick in my opinion but it is great one-card effect. I would say if the lighting is right, you can perform it within 10 feet of the audience but I have seen it done even closer.

I'm not sure who came up with the idea of whirling, hovering, or flying a playing card, plate, credit card, or disk, but the version I first saw was Bob Hummer's Whirling Card marketed by Berland. It is a simplified version of all of the others and is a good little one-card ditty. Again, this is not an effect that I would consider worthy of the title "show stopper," and I wouldn't traipse around Vegas yelling, "All right, Siegfried, you two have really had it now!" It is an interesting little stunt though and I have seen it literally stop 'em in their tracks. Sometimes that's all you want.

Effect

A card is held in one hand, tossed spinning out away from the body, around the body, and back into the waiting hands.

Preparation

First of all you need to set up another gimmicked card. This will be a lot easier than the last job so hang tight. Get the thinnest black cotton thread you can find and cut a length that is about the length of your arm from your shoulder to the tip of the middle finger. Thread one end onto a needle and pull about an inch of it through the exact center of a playing card. Take the needle off and tape that inch of thread to the card. Now you've got a card on a string! Now tie the other end of the string around something not too large that can be put in your mouth and held there—maybe a nylon washer or something soft like a plastic Lifesaver. Yup, you can find them if you have a lot of spare time. Anyway, just find something that won't gag you and hook it up.

Setup

To begin, you want to have the card in a spot you've chosen for it. It can be inside of a box with other cards with the thread run inside with it. It could be in your pocket with its thread running to the "whatchamacallit" in your mouth. When it's time, take the card by the thumb and fingertips of one hand and bring it out.

Routine

There is no real routine per se to this because it is such a quick trick, but here's how it goes. Facing the audience, pull out the card and bring it to the end of the thread. Hold it in one hand by an inner bottom corner with the face parallel to the floor. With the other hand, flick the outside upper corner with the middle finger and it will spin like crazy. When it does, take both hands away and turn your body around in a circle in the direction that it is traveling and spinning **(Figure 3.15).** When you are back to where you started from (spinning that is), catch the card with the

Figure 3.15

hand furthest away. This should be the same hand you held it with to begin. This is a fast effect and shouldn't be repeated or performed too close to anyone. It looks great! Try it.

As an added note, you can get a wonderfully thin "thread" from a pair of pantyhose. It will be made up of several strands; at least six. Separate one strand. These tiny strands are great for any kind of floating effect but be careful that the strand is thick enough to hold the weight of whatever you want to float, fly, or levitate. Also, you might want to make sure that your wife says it's okay to use the hose and isn't actually wearing them when you decide to snip and dissect. No magician is too impressive wearing a finger cast.

A Two-Card Trick

Two-Card Monte

Effect

Two cards are fanned in one hand showing a red queen and a black ace, one face up and one face down. The face-up ace is seen being placed into the pocket and the face-down queen is left in the other hand. When the spectator is asked where the queen is, he responds that it is the card in the hand. Reaching into his pocket, the magician pulls out the queen while telling the spectator he must not have been watching carefully enough. This time he repeats the trick, placing the queen into the pocket. When asked where the ace is, the spectator replies, "in the hand." Again, he is wrong. The magician never loses; he just stands there and smiles.

Preparation

There's a little bit preparation for this trick but you'll have fun with it once it's done. You're going to have to make a couple of gimmicked cards. You'll need a red queen, a black ace and two other cards of any value. Once again, try to make these cards from a deck that is the same kind as the one you will use in the rest of your magic. Using paper rubber cement, glue the queen and the ace together back to back. Glue the other two cards together face to face. There are better ways to make double sided cards but this

Did You Know?

The highest price ever paid for a single playing card was $7,450, for a card dated 1717, and was used as currency in Canada. It was sold by the dealer Yasha Beresiner to Lars Karlson of Sweden in October 1990. Imagine having a deck of those little babies?

will work. If you like the trick, I would suggest purchasing professionally printed gimmicked cards from one of the dealers listed in the Appendix.

Setup

You really can't set this one up wrong. Begin with the two cards held in one hand slightly fanned out between the thumb and the fingers so you can see some of each card.

Routine

Take the two cards out of your deck and hold them as described in the set up. Rotate the wrist to seemingly show both sides of the cards. The illusion of showing both sides of two cards is very good but don't bring to much attention to the fact. There's no reason for your audience to think any different.

Turn the cards until the ace is facing upward. Remove the ace and place it in a pocket, flipping it over when it gets there so it will come out the other way around (showing the queen). Still holding the face-down card in the other hand (the double backed card) and ask where the queen is. When the spectator indicates the card in the hand, you reach into your pocket and pull out the queen telling him that he must have become confused. Place the queen back with the other card and show both sides again. Next time give him a chance to keep an eye on the queen when he actually sees it put into the pocket. Now when you ask where the queen is he will say, of course, "In the pocket." You bring out the ace and say, "No (placing it with the other card again and showing both sides again). The queen is over here." Even if you do it again and the spectator decides that he will try to mess with you by answering opposite to what he should, you never lose by flipping the card over as you reach into the pocket to retrieve it again.

Now, a Three-Card Trick

If you're looking for the obvious answer to a three-card trick, Three-Card Monte, don't worry, I put that one in Chapter 18, *Street Smarts*—Street Magic.

Thrice Is Nice

Here's a three-card mental card effect that is a variation of the first card trick I ever learned. A deck of cards is borrowed from the crowd and the mentalist fairly shuffles the deck. The deck is placed face down on the table and the magician asks the spectator to leave it face down and cut it into three separate piles. Once the spectator has done this, the mentalist begins his focused concentration toward the cards, telling the spectator how he can feel vibrations from the cards and, if the wind is right, he can determine each card's value. (I guess the air needs to be hot!) The mentalist gazes at the cards and points at the first pile saying, "The 5 of hearts" and then picks up the card. With his eyes on the second pile he pauses and says, "The 7 of diamonds." He picks up the card and zeros in on the last pile saying, "The queen of clubs." He picks up the last card, now holding the three cards in his hand. He looks at the spectator and says, "Remember, I chose the 5 of hearts," and he puts the real 5 of hearts down face up on top of the first pile. "The 7 of diamonds," he repeats, placing a face-up 7 of diamonds onto of the center pile. "And finally, the queen of clubs," he exclaims as he places the last card, the queen of clubs, face up on the final pile of cards. A true mental miracle with a borrowed deck and the well-honed mind of the mentalist has just taken place.

Preparation

There is no preparation and the deck can be borrowed. Keep in mind that the three cards will be different each time.

Did You Know?

Muscle man magic monster Ken Simmons was listed in the November 1997 *Linking Ring* as being perhaps the strongest magician known. He can bench press over 500 pounds. He doesn't lift barbells, he lifts "Tarbells." (That was a magic joke, you'll get it later.)

Setup

The set up for this experiment is to take a glimpse of the top card after you are finished shuffling, or a glimpse of the same card first followed by a false shuffle. Either way you need to know what the top card is. Remember that the top card is the face-down card on top of the entire deck.

Routine

For the purpose of this illustration, let's suppose the glimpsed card was the ace of spades. After you are set up from the shuffle, place the deck face down on the table and have your spectator cut the deck into three piles. We know that the last pile made has the ace of spades on the top of it.

Point to the pile furthest from that pile, concentrate for a while and say, "The ace of spades."

Pick up that card with one hand and put it into the other hand, quickly glimpsing at its real identity (let's say it's the 9 of diamonds).

Now move your focus to the middle pile, pause dramatically, and say, "The 9 of diamonds." Pick up that card with one hand, glimpsing at its real identity (let's say the 3 of diamonds) and put it into the other hand in front of the first card you're already holding (closest to you). Proceed now to the final pile (the one you already know has the ace of spades as the top card) and say, "The 3 of diamonds."

Pick up that final card with one hand and add it to the front of the other two cards (closest to the audience). Now you simply need to recap what has happened with the borrowed, shuffled, and cut deck (that's always good in a mentalism effect). Then remind the audience that you felt the vibrations of the ace of spades, laying it down on the first pile (not the one it actually came from), exclaim "the 9 of diamonds" as you lay that one on the middle pile, and finally, "the 3 of diamonds." You are left clean and the audience is in a state of nirvana.

What's More, a Four-Card Trick
Red-Black Transpo

Here's a trick by Frank Zak and Keith Merrill that I first read in their book, *The Magic of Bartending* (1995). You can find more information about Frank and Keith in Chapter 7, Close-Up Bar Magic. This is not a bar trick but its uses a sleight you already know—the glimpse—and it's fast and fantastic.

Effect

Four aces are shown, two black and two red. The black aces are placed on the table and the red aces are kept in the hand. In a wink and with a snap of the fingers, the aces change places. Sounds great right? It is.

Preparation

Get the four aces out of the deck.

Setup

Arrange the aces so that they are from the face, black, red, red, then black.

Routine

Hold the packet in the biddle grip ready for the glide. Show the black ace on the face. Perform the glide and remove a red ace (the red ace was the second card from the bottom). Change the grip of the three remaining cards to the mechanic's grip and reverse the cards by counting them from one hand to the other. Show the second black Ace and perform the glide again (of course, another red Ace was laid down again). Count the two cards again to show that's all you have. Reiterate that you had two black aces and two red aces. The two black aces are on the table and you now hold the red aces. Snap your fingers and turn over the black aces, showing both sides that are now in your hand. With the other hand, flip over the tabled aces showing that they are red. The transposition has taken place in a flash.

Definition Please

A *one ahead* is a principle whereby the magician is one step ahead of what he is presenting to the audience. This is shown nicely in the Thrice Is Nice card effect.

And, Finally, a Six-Card Trick

The Everything® Magic Book Six Trick

Here is a twist on a trick originally created by the late and great Sid Lorraine marketed under the name, "Blank Surprise." I have seen variations on it, one of which is explained here. The effect involves six cards but one card is used as a wand of sorts, making the other five the real stars.

Effect

The magician introduces a packet of six cards that he shows to be blank on both sides. Placing the cards on the table one at a time, and showing them to be blank, he continues until all six cards are tabled. Picking up one card he uses as a magic paintbrush, he lightly strokes the back of each card. When the cards are finally turned over, the first card is magically printed with the letters "EV." The next card is printed with "ER" followed by the third, "YT," then "HI," and finally, "NG." The five cards spell out the word, "EVERYTHING." Finally the wand card is flipped over to reveal "MAGIC BOOK," printed on it.

Preparation

You'll actually need seven blank cards (six that the audience know about). The cards are printed as explained and one card is left blank. Do the following:

1. On one card print "EV" with a marker or transfer lettering. In the bottom right corner of that card ("EV" oriented upright), draw a light pencil line about ⅛ inch long on the bottom right corner to represent the number 5. This is a marking to help reset the trick and a line is easier to see than the difference between four dots and five dots, especially when it's dark in the room.

2. On the second card, print "ER" and mark two pencil dots (representing the number 2) in the corner.

3. On the third card, print "YT" and mark four pencil dots in the corner (representing the number 4).

4. On the fourth card, print "HI" and mark one pencil dot (representing the number 1) in the corner. On the back (blank side) of this card put one pencil dot centered along the bottom edge (the same edge but on the opposite side of the printed side with one dot).

5. On the fifth card, print,"NG" and mark three pencil dots in the corner.

6. Leave the sixth card blank.

7. On the seventh card print "MAGIC BOOK" (or your own groovy message). This card is kept aside to switch in place of the blank card at the end of the routine.

Setup

All that pencil marking was to make this set up quick, easy, and accurate. Place the first card, "EV" with one dot face up on the table with the dot farthest from you so the letters are upside down to you but read correctly by a spectator. All cards will be oriented in the same direction.

On top of that card put card number 2, then 3, 4, and 5 (with the straight line). The blank card goes on top. Now, turn this entire pack over and you will see the single dot to tell you which side is the correct side to start with and which direction the cards need to be pointed in. The dot should always be toward the spectator when dealing. I usually put a rubber band or clip around the cards so they don't get goofed up before it's time to make the magic.

Routine

Spread out the cards and get a break between the top two cards and the bottom four. Lift the two top cards off with one hand and openly turn the other four-card block over in the other hand.

Put the two cards back on top of the overturned block, turn the entire stack of six cards over one more time, and deal the top card onto the table to your left and to the spectator's right (stage left). All cards will be dealt to the right of that card.

Joseph Dunninger (1892–1975)

Joseph Dunninger began as a vaudeville magician and developed his specialty in mental magic at about the same time radio was just beginning. Although magic is typically not an art featured on radio, Dunninger found that he could successfully combine phenomena of spirits with mind reading and hypnotic challenges on his radio show. In 1943 he had a Sunday night radio program, "Dunninger, the Master Mind," which was broadcast from coast to coast. Five years later Dunninger shifted the showcase of his talents to television and he appeared on the three major networks until 1953. During the 1950s, when mind reading became a popular phenomenon, Dunninger gained even more fame. His ability to deny any special powers seemed to make the public believe in him that much more.

Turn the cards over and deal another card right beside the first tabled card. Turn the cards over again and deal another card. Repeat this turning over and dealing until you have laid down all of the cards. When dealing the final card, you can even turn it over on its way down to the table because it really is blank. This ingenious setup of cards makes everything appear blank so far. Now you pick up the last card again and use it as your wand, paintbrush, or printing press. Wave or brush along the row of tabled cards turning it over after passing each card so that the audience continues to see both sides as blank. Using the card as a flipper, turn over the stage right card revealing the first part of your finale. Move on down the line until all the cards have been turned over and the audience can read the message revealed.

While they are reading and computing what they have just seen, drop the wand card down and switch it out for the "BOOK OF MAGIC" card. As you explain why the cards spell out "EVERY-THING" bring the card back into play with the blank side showing. When you're ready, turn over the card for the kicker and the only thing left blank will be the expressions of the spectators. If you prefer, you can simply leave the wand card blank and print a finale on the last card that is turned up.

Effects Using a Regular Deck
Final Attraction
Effect

After the spectator shuffles a regular deck, the magician removes two cards and tables them face down as his prediction of what is to happen in the very near future. The deck is given back to the spectator, and he is asked to deal a number of cards onto the table which he can deal from the top, bottom, middle . . . anywhere. When he feels the urge, he is to stop dealing and is given the option to deal more if he likes. Once he is completely satisfied, the magician asks him to put the remainder of the cards aside and to deal his chosen cards into two piles, first in one, then the other, and so on until the cards are all used up. The magician reviews what has happened thus far and asks the spectator to turn over the top two cards in his two piles. When the magician turns over his two prediction cards, they match in both color and value. If the spectator's cards, for instance, are a red 9 and a black king, so are the magician's!

Preparation

Yippie! There's no preparation for this one! Zero, zip, nada, nothing—just an ordinary borrowed deck and a secret.

Setup

The setup for this takes place right in front of the spectator so it's extra sneaky. You really have the spectator shuffle the deck and return it to you. While you look for the prediction cards, you first of all have to figure out what they need to be. This trick uses two key cards that don't move around but that keep track of other important cards. They simply tell you what those important cards are and stay put so your spectator can "find" them. The cards she eventually "selects" are the top two cards of the deck. While looking at the faces of the cards to find your prediction cards, you secretly glimpse at them and you are ready for action.

Routine

After determining what cards you need to remove from the deck for your prediction cards (the two that are alike in both color and value to the top cards), you remove them and place them down on the table. You then table the rest of the deck for the spectator to work with. The two cards the spectator will "choose" are on top of the deck. You ask the spectator to start dealing cards face down onto the table. After she has dealt the first two (her cards), you remind her that she can take them from anywhere in the deck. Don't say that too soon, though; you have to wait for her cards and maybe one more to be down on the table first. When she has finished, offer her the option to deal more or even take a few away.

Placing the remaining cards aside, you instruct her to start dividing her pile into two piles by dealing them face down, alternating

(continued on next page)

back and forth. When she has done so, her two cards will be on the tops of the piles. All you need to do is have her turn her top two cards face up, explain about cards having a natural sympathetic attraction for their favorite pals, and you reveal your amazing prediction. A "final attraction" and an amazing piece of magic!

Self-Working Effects

Yes, there are card effects that are "self working"; in fact, there may be too many, but that's another book. This does not mean that you just get a special deck push a button and it starts to "magic" on it's own. It doesn't even mean that you need a special deck at all. Any magic that is worth it's salt has some degree of practice that is necessary. Many self-working effects are mathematical so they rely on an interesting presentation to make it a winner. After all, an audience shouldn't know that it's taking a lot of work to make the magic happen. Magicians make magic and you are a magician.

The Not-So-Crazy Clock

Effect

The magician asks a spectator to take a deck and shuffle it. He then shows the faces of the cards to be thoroughly mixed and tables them face up. He turns around and asks the spectator to picture the face of a clock, think of one number on the face, take that number of cards off of the face deck and hide them from him. The magician turns around, takes 12 cards from the deck and deals them on the table to represent the face of his clock. After concentrating on the clock's face, the magician reveals the number on the clock and therefore the number of cards the spectator has selected.

Preparation

There is no preparation or special deck for this self-working trick.

Setup

Have the spectator genuinely mix the deck. As you take them back and show that they are indeed mixed, count and remember the 13th card from the top. This will be your key card. You can do this in your hands as you fan the cards or as you spread them on the table and count while delivering your patter. Don't forget it or you'll look like the crazy one.

Routine

After asking your spectator to imagine her clock and remove the cards while your back is turned, you determine the 13th card and remember it. Deal off 12 cards face up onto the table and put the rest of the cards aside.

Now, create the face of a clock by redealing them onto the table as your clock face. This reverses the order of the cards. Start with one o'clock and continue clockwise until you finish at 12 o'clock. Along the way you will see your key card again and its position on the clock will tell you the number that she thought of and therefore what number of cards she has concealed.

Add some great patter to this and you'll have a card effect that you can perform anywhere you find a deck of cards, except at a blackjack table. Those dealers have no sense of humor when it comes to the Not-So-Crazy Clock effect.

Cards with Props and Gimmicks

Card Box

There are a number of props that can be used during close-up card magic. One of the best known is the card box.

Effect

A card box is used to exchange or switch playing cards or other flat items.

You can easily make a card box yourself if you don't need a totally professional looking prop. Sometimes it's better if the prop doesn't look like a purchased piece of magic anyway. It allows the credit of the miracle to go to the magician and not to the pretty thing.

**Harlan Tarbell
(1890–1960)**

(continued from previous page)

national lecture tour with his newfound fame. He also continued to illustrate his own works and the catalogues and magazines of other magicians and magic dealers. In 1940 Tarbell struck a deal with Louis Tannen of the world-famous Tannen's Magic in New York. This partnership allowed *The Tarbell System* to be republished in a seven-volume set of books, now called *The Tarbell Course in Magic,* offering tricks, routines, insights, and illustrations for everything from sleight-of-hand magic and mentalism to Comedy Magic and large-scale illusions.

To make a simple card box, get two small boxes just large enough for a playing card to fit into. A small jewelry box with a top that fits over the bottom can be used. What happens in the working of a card box is that the top of the box conceals a card in its lid. The card is under an insert or flap that, when shown, appears to be just the inside of the box. Because the card and the flap are thin, there is no hint of a false panel.

Preparation

The flap can be made by carefully cutting the top out of the matching box. This flap will be inserted into the top of the box to be used. Because the flap needs to fall into the bottom when the top is put on, it will need to be cut back to be slightly smaller so it is loose enough to fall but not bind. By carefully applying some white glue with a cotton swab to the edge of the cut panel, the edge will be prevented from wear and distortion. You can smooth away any rough spots with a fine emery board.

Setup

Before your performance, load the card above the panel into the top of the box. The lid will be set down separate from the box or set face up on top of the bottom section where the original card is to be placed.

Routine

After showing the card you want to change into another, place it inside the bottom of the box, face down. Place the top onto the box, allowing the flap and the secret unknown card to drop into the bottom. When the lid is lifted the card appears to be the original card until it is turned over and is seen to have been magically transformed.

A blank card can be turned into a chosen card, one card can change into another card, the possibilities are endless. You can even place a threaded needle into the load compartment. Place a needle and thread in the bottom and when the top is placed on

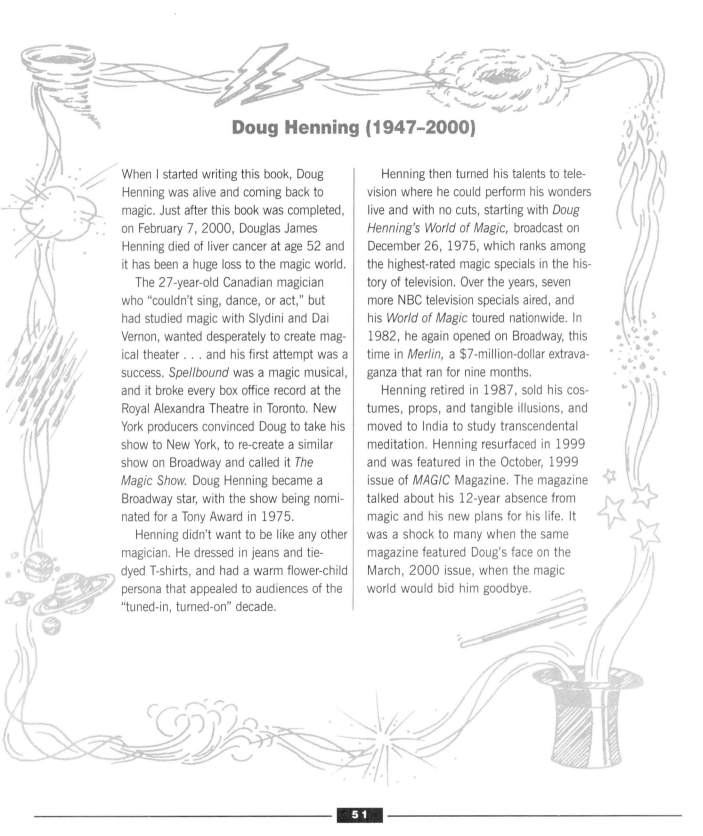

Doug Henning (1947–2000)

When I started writing this book, Doug Henning was alive and coming back to magic. Just after this book was completed, on February 7, 2000, Douglas James Henning died of liver cancer at age 52 and it has been a huge loss to the magic world.

The 27-year-old Canadian magician who "couldn't sing, dance, or act," but had studied magic with Slydini and Dai Vernon, wanted desperately to create magical theater . . . and his first attempt was a success. *Spellbound* was a magic musical, and it broke every box office record at the Royal Alexandra Theatre in Toronto. New York producers convinced Doug to take his show to New York, to re-create a similar show on Broadway and called it *The Magic Show*. Doug Henning became a Broadway star, with the show being nominated for a Tony Award in 1975.

Henning didn't want to be like any other magician. He dressed in jeans and tie-dyed T-shirts, and had a warm flower-child persona that appealed to audiences of the "tuned-in, turned-on" decade.

Henning then turned his talents to television where he could perform his wonders live and with no cuts, starting with *Doug Henning's World of Magic,* broadcast on December 26, 1975, which ranks among the highest-rated magic specials in the history of television. Over the years, seven more NBC television specials aired, and his *World of Magic* toured nationwide. In 1982, he again opened on Broadway, this time in *Merlin,* a $7-million-dollar extravaganza that ran for nine months.

Henning retired in 1987, sold his costumes, props, and tangible illusions, and moved to India to study transcendental meditation. Henning resurfaced in 1999 and was featured in the October, 1999 issue of *MAGIC* Magazine. The magazine talked about his 12-year absence from magic and his new plans for his life. It was a shock to many when the same magazine featured Doug's face on the March, 2000 issue, when the magic world would bid him goodbye.

and taken back off, the needle appears to be threaded by magic. Play with this; you'll have a lot of fun.

Card Wallets

Card wallets are commercially available and they are all different. Some wallets allow you to switch cards and flat objects. Other wallets allow you to have a selected card vanish and appear inside of a sealed envelope, which is inside of a pocket in the wallet. This is a dealer item and is worth looking into if you are serious about card magic. Ask about Himber or Eclipse style wallets or variations of them. There are a lot of different varieties, sizes, and working options, and clever new wallets seemed to be devised every day.

Other Props and Gimmicks

Outside of the myriad of gimmicks made for individual card effects, such as floating, rising, spinning, and throwing gimmicks, there are props to use in conjunction with cards that will make a small deck of cards play for a larger venue. I will talk about these in Chapter 10 when we learn about Stage Magic.

Dollars and Cents

Under $10,000 will purchase enough equipment for a 30-minute Illusions show. This won't do it if you want the biggest and the best but remember that not every successful illusion needs to be that flashy. As the old adage goes, "It takes money to make money," and this is true of magic acts also. An act with big rigs and fancy props is bound to attract a larger audience in a big venue.

CHAPTER 4

Close-Up Magic— Coin Effects

T. Nelson Downs (1869–1938)

T. Nelson Downs worked on his sleight-of-hand coin effects during the long, lonely evenings spent as a railroad telegrapher in Marshalltown, Iowa. Working small-time vaudeville, by 1895 he got a booking at the Hopkins Theater in Chicago where he featured his production of silver coins from thin air called The Miser's Dream. The specialty coin act became an overnight success. Eventually, Downs incorporated cigarettes, silks, cards, watches, and even ropes into the act. He also sampled work with cards and billiard balls and even used illusion, but he was always known as "The King of Koins."

Working with coins entails learning a number of skills—from the palm to the pass to the vanish—all of which are discussed in this chapter. This basic tool kit will prepare you to work your Close-Up Magic with coins, which will also help your game with cards and other props, what have you!

Palming
Finger Palm

Probably the easiest and most popular palming technique used with coins is the finger palm. Because you practice until it isn't noticeable anymore (and then it becomes very second nature), it is an underrated utility: an unsung hero in the basic tool kit of close-up coin magic. The finger palm is mighty deceptive, stealthily strong.

Stand in front of a full-length mirror to see what your hands look like when you are standing naturally with your arms at your sides. The fingers of your hand curve in a little (they are not straightened out). The backs of the hands should be turned slightly inward. Now it's time to add the coin to one of those hands, and things shouldn't look any different. If they do, analyze what is different and really do your best to adjust it. This is the foundation of a good "hands at the side" finger palm position and it's used all of the time, not only for coins. It's important that you really study and master this one.

Start by holding the coin you will use in most routines in your preferred hand. I use a 50-cent piece or a quarter. The coin should be positioned on the second and third joints of your second and third fingers of the palm-up hand **(Figure 4.1).** The coin can also be palmed in cahoots with other fingers, but start learning the finger palm like this first and you can get fancy later. You should be able to use at least the index finger and the thumb of the same hand to pick up another coin, playing card, or snack. Knowing how to do this is a matter of survival in Close-Up Magic. Once you are at home with the feel of the coin at your side, try moving the hand around and see how you do. You'll find that if you lift your hand up and across your chest, you'll need to bend the fingers in a little more. That's okay because it's natural. Gravity does the same thing when the hand is empty. Different actions necessitate different reactions.

The Clip/Cupping/Front Palm

Clipping is another way of palming with the fingers, but instead of the hand being curved, the back of the hand can be shown flat and natural. The coin is held between the inside edges of two fingers for this example (two finger clip)—the index finger and the third finger **(Figure 4.2).** In this illustration the coin is being "clipped" closer to the palm. I have found a smaller coin can be clipped easier if it is closer to the tips of the fingers where a large coin would hold the fingers open too far and the coin could be seen through the cracks. On the other hand (good pun, eh?), there is more meat in the fingers nearest to the palm and larger coins seem to snuggle right in there a lot easier.

Figure 4.1

In the case of large coins, a clip using the outside fingers works pretty well. Your first and fourth fingers grasp the coin. This allows a coin to be clipped closer to the tips of the fingers and is useful in some routines. To position the coin properly you might want to invest in a close-up pad. A pad allows the first and fourth fingers to get "under" the coin a little bit, and that's necessary to get to the edges. Try it on a table and it's almost impossible. Try it on your leg while you are sitting down and the leg acts like a close-up pad would. (This is the magicians excuse for never having to go on a diet, if you ask me.) It's a lot easier, but unfortunately, there isn't a lot of coin magic performed on the leg. Instead, consider a close-up pad. Refer to the Appendix for suppliers who offer a variety of them. It's a good investment.

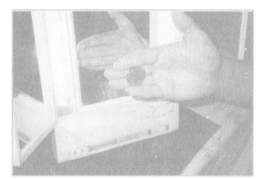
Figure 4.2

There's not a lot of sense in telling you that the coin should be right on the joint, or exactly where it should be. You'll find out where your coin needs to be. If you don't, someone will tell you, don't worry. What I really mean is *do* worry. Practice the clip. It doesn't feel as natural as the finger palm and it's easily put down because it is awkward. Remember to use a mirror, video, or honest friend for feedback.

Figure 4.3

Figure 4.4

The Classic Palm

To me the classic palm is the most fun. Maybe it's just the name. "Yeah, look at that . . . I've got a 1962 'Classic' palm with extra chrome . . . expanded, double header!" Unfortunately, you really can't show off a classic palm. The classic palm is also one of the toughest moves to master. I have seen a lot of people, yes even practiced magicians, who perform a classic palm with a coin so that you would have no idea they were trying to hide it. That's because they looked more like they might be hiding a Buick or something even larger. Doing a classic palm with a coin can put the muscles in your hands through some weird contortions. The natural look of the hand is the name of the game when it comes to this palm. If your hand looks like you are being cramped by high voltage while you are palming, you're doing it wrong **(Figure 4.3).** If your hand looks, acts, and moves naturally, it's ready **(Figure 4.4).**

Start with the hand palm up and the coin lying near the middle of the palm of that hand. Now, bring the thumb and little finger toward the coin but do not curl them in, around, or on top of the coin. The other fingers might need to adjust inward too, but most of the pinching work is done by the thumb and little finger. You are trying to pin the coin between the fleshy bases (the meat) of the little finger and the thumb. Your hand will be in a position that some of my Italian friends use as a gesture after a good meal or when they are bothered. I'm not sure what it means in Italian but it means "classic palm" in coin language.

If the coin slides upward when you start to pinch, you have to start again until the little devil is secured. One good way to stuff the coin into the classic palm is to bring the second and third fingers around onto of the face of the coin first and give it a power push into the palm, as if you were trying to push your fingernails through the coin. Once in position, go into the palming and release the death grip. Your hand can now be turned palm down without the coin falling out. Your fingers should be able to move and should straighten out a lot, but they won't be as straight as they might be with, say, the clip. Hey, don't worry. It takes a lot of practice.

The Pass

A pass is when you sashay up to someone and say, "Hey there, haven't we met somewhere before?" The pass in magic, however, is much subtler but equally as deceptive. A simple coin pass looks like this.

A coin is placed into the hand, and the fingers of the hand are closed around it. When the hand is opened, it's gone. Sound impossible? Nah, it's just magic!

Hold a coin between the thumb and middle finger of one hand. Have the other hand empty, open, and to the side. Place the coin high against the palm of the empty hand **(Figure 4.5).** Close the fingers over the coin one at a time from the bottom (little finger) to the top (index finger). Make the fingers look tight. The closed fingers should still be facing the spectator. To the spectator, it appears as though the coin has been trapped by the fingers. That's true, but the thumb and middle finger of the opposite hand are also still in there and they've got the goods. Now for getting the coin out of there. Keep pinching the coin but rotate the wrist of the "pincher hand" toward you so that its index finger comes around and touches the middle of the closed index finger of the closed ("with coin") hand. This forces the pinched coin to be pulled out of the fist. This is exactly what you want **(Figure 4.6).** Use the pointing index finger (with clipped coin in tow) as a misdirection tool as you slide the finger down across all of the closed fingers, still pointing at the closed hand as it is moved away **(Figure 4.7).** Remember to keep your attention (and eyes) on the hand "where the coin is" and just let the right hand fall to your side. Don't rush it or it will look very unnatural . . . like you're trying to hide something. Also, remember to let your pointing index finger go into a natural position as it drops to the side. You don't want to be standing there looking like you are ready to "stick 'em up."

The fact that the coin is seen right up until the point when the last finger closes on top of it lets the spectator assume you must really be trapping it because they still see it. A larger coin will also help because more of the coin is seen and it flashes

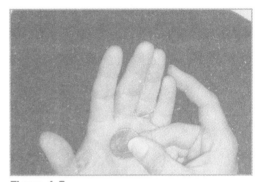

Figure 4.5

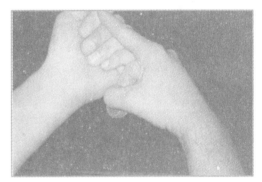

Figure 4.6

Figure 4.7

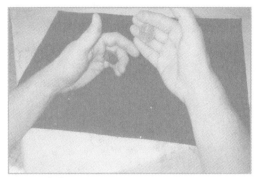

Figure 4.8

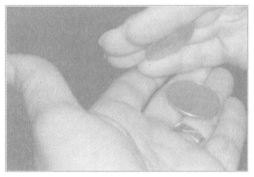

Figure 4.9

right until the very end. This ghosting or retention of the object in the spectator's eye really works and is a proven physiological effect that benefits every good coin worker.

Once you have the coin safely away, you can secretly regrip it so it's in position for whatever your next step might be. I'll bet a pinched penny you'll want to make the coin vanish from the other hand and have it reappear somewhere just about now. Hey . . . just call me part of the Psychic Network!

There are a lot of variations on the pass, and I think you should check out all of them. Find the ones that fit you and use those. I have a couple of favorites that I use, continue to practice, and know will work in any situation. You will too.

Now that you have the basic tool kit for performing Close-Up Magic with coins under your belt, let's put some of them to use.

The Shuttle Pass

The shuttle pass is one method for changing one coin into another or for another. Here's a simple exercise to help you understand the whole thing. Let's say you have a routine where you need to switch one coin for another, as in the traveling coins routine later in this chapter. Maybe it's a different situation where you need to exchange a coin that has just been secretly marked with a scratch by a spectator for a duplicate that looks the same. Hold the unmarked coin in a palm in one hand, palm down. Have the spectator place the marked coin on the table. Pick up the marked coin with your empty hand and put it in prime position for a clipping. You can use the thumb to help you, but don't make it obvious that the coin needs to be in any specific spot. Now move that hand toward the other hand (the other hand has the coin in a finger palm), and just as they are about to meet, begin turning up the finger palm hand as if it's receiving the marked coin **(Figure 4.8).** So, you are turning both hands over during this move. One is getting turned down (that's the one with the clipped coin) and one is getting turned up (that's the one with the finger-palmed coin).

Because the previously finger-palmed coin is now covered by the hand with the clipped coin **(Figure 4.9),** when the hands separate again it appears as though one coin has simply been transferred from one hand to another. Obviously, the one hand can't take the coin if it is still facing down and the other hand can't pour the coin into it if it is facing up. That's the reason the hands need to flip. If the coin is being moved to the left, the hands will flip over to the left. If you try to turn them the wrong way, you will break your wrists. Don't worry; it's not really that dangerous. You can't really flip them the wrong way. Once "the marked coin" is placed into the other hand, the true marked coin can be palmed off to be used further on in the effect, as below with the ball of string.

Look at what it looks like "for real." Try placing one coin from the palm of one hand into the other. That's what we're looking for. Now add a secret coin, insert the shuttle pass, and "presto," you've got yourself a dazzling deception.

The French Drop Vanish

The *French drop,* sometimes called the French vanish or the tourniquet vanish (although I haven't heard it called that since Napoleon was a cadet) is a staple of magic. It's overused but it's still a building block in Close-Up Magic, so learn it.

The French drop has gotten some bad press and here's why I think that is. The original French drop looked pretty weird, pretty unnatural, and no one ever thought to change it a little bit. That's odd, considering that almost all of the moves in magic have to be adopted and changed to fit each individual's hands and needs. Here's a general description of what the French drop looks like and how I recommend approaching it. When it is used correctly and artistically choreographed, this vanish can be a very elegant piece of magic.

A coin is held in one hand between the first two fingers and the thumb. The other hand approaches, reaches over and around the coin, and carries it off. The coin is rubbed between the fingers and it seems to vaporize, to vanish into thin air.

Step 1 All you need is one coin, which is held by the edges in one hand between the tips of the first two fingers and the tip of the thumb. The coin is facing the audience and, in fact, can slant toward them a little bit. The palm is facing up, and the third and

Quintino Marucci, "Slydini" (1901–1991)

Tony Slydini was born in Italy and raised in Buenos Aires, Argentina, but he was always a hero in America. In 1930 he began playing fairs and carnivals in New York, followed by a seven-year stint in Boston, working various venues until friends finally convinced him to return to the Big Apple.

Slydini performed Close-Up Magic as an art form. His attention to microscopic details, his sense of timing, and his natural mannerisms allowed him to create magic of a new level, using such props as cigarettes, cards, silks, coins, paper napkins, newspaper, ropes, and rings.

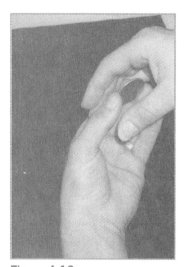

Figure 4.10

forth fingers are held in a natural line with the first two, which hold the coin.

Step 2   The opposite hand approaches, reaches over and around the coin **(Figure 4.10),** and while hidden by the fingers, falls down into a finger palm position. The hand now moves away, with its fingers and thumb held together holding "the coin," and the wrist is gradually turned so that the fingers are pointing up.

Step 3   By rubbing the fingers and a swirling thumb together in that same gesture sometimes used to communicate money or "dinero," the fingers are gradually separated to show that the coin is gone. Practice letting the coin drop from your fingertips to the finger palm position. It's important that once the coin lands, it is controlled. Sometimes I close the fingers around the coin in the finger palm, turn the hand toward my body, and point to where the audience thinks the coin is as it is moved away.

Remember to treat this vanish softly. Don't bang and crash through the thing or it no doubt will look bad. Just because it doesn't have a bunch of knuckle-busting moves to get the job done doesn't mean it's not strong. Real magic shouldn't bust a person's knuckles, remember? The French drop will serve you well if you treat it with the respect, time and that "je ne sais quoi" it certainly deserves.

Dilly of a Vanish

Here's a neat little utility coin vanish from coin monster, Dean Dill. It's a strong contender to replace the French drop for a simple coin vanish. It's always a good idea to have a couple of different methods.

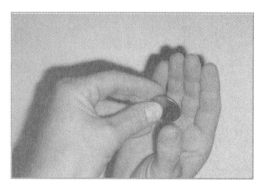

Figure 4.11

Holding a coin very gingerly between the extreme fingertips and thumb of one hand, the opposite hand comes up from the bottom and side and pretends to take the coin away **(Figure 4.11).** Notice that the coin is tilted back toward you a little bit so that if it is pushed forward even slightly, the coin will drop in the slot between the fingers and the thumb. Let the thumb contact and push the back of the coin, and it will drop right on into your hand. The approaching fingers complete the illusion by closing together (but not curling in) and carrying "the coin" away. The palmed coin is dropped to the side in a favorite palm, and sooner or later the coin vanishes; simply, slowly, and cleanly. That's the way Dean works.

Appearing Coins

If there's any close-up coin effect that's more popular than producing a coin out of someone's ear, I can't imagine what it is. Children's eyes open like saucers and jaws drop to floors. Adults chuckle, remembering their first time, and smile as if as grown ups they now "get it"; they don't, it's magic!

Pulling a coin out of an ear isn't exactly in the chosen repertoire of the magic elite. That's probably because it's easy and usual, too usual for a cutting-edge professional. But it still has all the wonderful ingredients of a keeper, and it's been around a long time for a good reason—it works *and* it works well.

Coin Holders

Bag, clip, sleeve, pocket, pail, purse, dropper, catcher, stand, slide . . . sounds like the parts of a new country and western dance doesn't it? Well, these are a few of the devices magicians use to store coins before, while, and after they are used. Since this section deals with performing coin magic close up and not on stage, huge amounts of coins don't need to be concealed or handled but they do need to be controlled. Wherever you keep your coins, keep them handy. Looking for the coins you need for a routine looks really bad. It also looks as though you are looking for specific "magic" coins drawing attention away from the intended routine. Have you ever watched and waited as someone set up a deck of cards before they presented their amazing card trick? It didn't seem much like magic did it? It probably seemed more like a clever stunt or a neat puzzle, but magic, no. If you were really doing magic, you wouldn't have to prearrange anything; you'd do that by magic too. Remember, an effect starts even before the

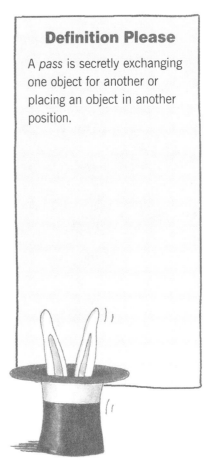

Definition Please

A *pass* is secretly exchanging one object for another or placing an object in another position.

Dean Dill

Dean Dill is the best teacher of magic I have ever had the privilege of studying with. Dean has been doing magic for about 30 years. He joined the Famous Magic Castle in 1975 with his beloved friend Monte Smith. His long line of credits include performer at the Magic Castle and consultant for David Copperfield. He taught Copperfield to do the hundred-dollar-bill switch, which David performed on his TV special and national tour. Dean then met Johnny Carson at Hollywood Magic and was fortunate enough to become his magic teacher for a few years. Johnny then asked him to be on the *Tonight Show,* and from that point things began to change. A lecture tour through Japan with his friend and fellow magician Doug Malloy opened up a whole new world for him. For the next few years, Dean created his

(continued on next page)

actual trick. It's the whole picture that is taken into consideration. Don't let the audience see backstage before the curtain rises.

Keep particular coins in certain pockets if that works for you. There is nothing wrong with reaching into your pockets, pulling out a handful of change, and using the four half-dollars for a routine. I do however think it makes a whole lot more sense to use four quarters. Half-dollars aren't exactly regular pocket change unless you happen to enjoy walking around with your pockets dragging your pants down. Whichever you choose, don't pull out a handful of change and select one specific coin from the pile—that's red flag material.

You might also consider using different holders for your coins. I am presently working on a coin assembly routine that uses a leather sack to hold four coins and a secret gimmick. The sack is rolled inside of a mat that acts as my close-up pad. All of those elements are used in the patter and are part of the entire picture. The mat sets the stage and creates a setting and time period and rolls to reveal a sack. They both look old and intriguing. The sack reiterates the period, characterizes the coins as precious, and provides the stage and support properties for the patter. It also keeps my coins and the gimmick in the correct position when they are poured out; setting, script, stage, props, and of course the characters—you and the coins. The subtle nuances of a solid routine are what separate the good magicians from the great ones.

Sometimes you might want to obtain a coin secretly and introduce it magically. This means the coin has to be held where it can't be seen and where it is easy to steal when it's magic time. One of the neatest holders for this is a magnet sewn into a hem or even placed in a pocket (not the one the coin has to be removed from or you'll reach in and pull out a pretty weird looking coin and have a lot of explaining to do). There are rare-earth magnets available now that will just about suck the fillings out of your teeth if you're not careful. Look in the Appendix at the back if you need help locating them. Remember, all coins are not magnetic so it won't solve every problem, but when they can be used, they're great.

One particular coin has its own holder, the hook(ed) coin. These used to be available from magic dealers but they might be too old-fashioned today. You can make one or have some handy friend make one for you. The hook coin simply has a hook made from a pin soldered onto the coin. This means you can hook it anywhere you want: inside of a jacket or hanging off of a pant leg. I have even seen the coin hung on the spectator, then magically plucked and produced by the magician with a completely empty hand. Pretty tricky, eh?

Traveling Coins

Effect

Here's a simple routine for traveling coins. Similar routines, called *coins across, flying coins,* or *flying eagles,* have a very similar plot with a very simple routine, great for getting started.

Preparation

Obtain five of the same type of coins. Make sure the spectator is aware of only four of them.

Setup

In collecting the coins, you could have nothing else in one pocket except the coins you need. Another possibility is to put your hand into the pocket and palm one of the largest coins as your hand is removed with the rest of the change in it. Keep that palmed coin a secret and look for four coins to use, perhaps all four from your hand, or perhaps using some from the audience. If you borrow one from a spectator, it helps the audience focus on the fact there are only four coins in play; the illusion is established before the routine begins.

Routine

To make things clearer for you, the moves for the right and left hands are described below.

Step 1 Start by taking out four coins and laying them on the table (five really, but one is in your right hand using the classic palm). You should be able to use the fingers of the right hand to pick up the coins, giving the impression that the right hand is empty. Pick up the coins with your right hand and place them haphazardly

Dean Dill

(*continued from previous page*)

own tricks mainly with coins. His first coin video, *Intimate Coin Miracles,* made his name stand out throughout the world. He went from a rather unknown coin guy to one of the main attractions in the world of magic. He began lecturing and selling his products at conventions and finally wrote his first book *Intimate Miracles.* Johnny Carson wrote the foreword to the book. He worked on the movie *The Grifters* as a consultant and was on the "Greatest Magic of Las Vegas" TV special for the Fox family channel. In the day he works as the Magic Barber in Glendale, California. His shop has become a mecca of magic, the jam capitol of California. Magicians from all over the world must stop by and experience the magic of Dean Dill. He resides in Eagle Rock, California with his beautiful wife Denise and his son Jamie.

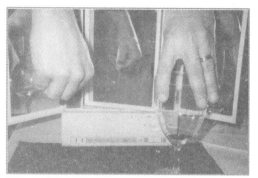

Figure 4.12

into the palm of the left hand while counting, "One, two, three, and four coins."

Step 2 Now, apparently transfer the coins back into the right hand but perform a shuttle pass and keep one (any) of the coins back in the left hand with either a classic palm or finger palm. If you use the finger palm, you'll have to eventually transfer it from the finger palm to the classic palm under cover of the misdirection of showing the coins now in the right hand. Show the three coins that were just transferred and the one coin already in the right hand (still in the classic palm sweet spot) as the same four. Now you are "one ahead."

Step 3 Pick up the glass with the left-hand fingers and thumb, palm down over the mouth of the glass. The palmed coin is still in the classic palm position, but the fingers will be able to move enough to allow you to hold the glass.

Now, close the right fingers over the four coins and turn the hand with the closed fingers down and bend the back of the hand toward the spectator **(Figure 4.12).** Now you are in position to let the first coin "fly."

With your attention toward the right hand, shake the hand a little, lessening your grip and then tightening it again to make a sudden "click" noise. Just a split second later, release the coin in the left hand from the classic palm and the coin falls into the glass with a "ping." One coin has magically traveled to the glass. Shake the coin in the glass with the left hand and let three of the coins in the right hand fall onto the table. One coin remains in the right hand using the classic palm.

Step 4 With the right hand (one coin still palmed) pick up the three coins and place them into the left hand one at a time just as in Step 1. Transfer them into the right hand as in Step 2, palming one off again and keeping it back. Pick up the glass and the one coin with the left hand as in Step 3 and continue.

Do the "click" in the right hand and the "ping" into the glass with the left and the second coin flies. Shake the coins in the glass with the left hand as in Step 3 and let two coins in the right hand fall onto the table. Again, one coin remains in the right hand in a classic palm. Now you have two coins in the glass and two coins on the table.

Step 5 With the right hand (one coin still palmed), pick up the two coins and place them in the left hand again as in Step 1. Again, do the transfer into the right hand as in Step 2, keeping one coin back. Pick up the glass and let 'er rip. That makes three coins in the glass and one falling to the table.

Step 6 Now you are ready for the final coin to fly and by this time your audience knows the rhythm and the routine of how things happen. If you want, you can just finish the routine as in the last five steps. The shuttle pass will seem kind of "empty" when you transfer/switch one coin for the other but you can do it that way. A better idea is to do a change-up for the final flight. This gives the routine a little variety and takes some of the heat off of two hands with one coin. If you prefer to keep on keepin' on, you might want to pour the four coins into the right hand from the glass (added to the fifth) after the final flight, as you are putting them away; no one will notice there is an extra. Of course, you don't want to hold the hand out flat then either. Don't ever challenge an audience to a contest of hide and seek; they will oblige and conquer. If you prefer to pour them into the right hand and drop them on the table for examination, just keep the fifth coin palmed in the right and drop the others. You can ditch the extra coin as you put the glass aside.

Did You Know?

A lot of walk-about close-up performers wear vests with inside and outside pockets, special belts or aprons, or just assign certain coin sets to certain pockets of a jacket. I use a portable close-up table with separate storage compartments to keep everything organized. You can only carry so many effects on your person. Unless it's okay to repeat some of your effects, you might consider this option.

CHAPTER 5

Close-Up Magic—
Effects with Cups
and Balls

Michael Ammar

Michael Ammar is a teacher, lecturer, and champion of Close-Up Magic. In 1982 he won the Fédération Internationale des Sociétés Magiques (FISM) Gold Medal. A year later, he became the youngest magician to win the Academy of Magical Arts' Lecturer of the year Award.

Michael has an ability to mix the necessary elements and nuances of Close-Up Magic with different kinds of teaching aids, such as books and videos. Most recently, he created perhaps the most complete guide for the cups and balls routine. Michael's books, tapes, and lectures are some of the most valuable instructional methods currently available for students of magic.

The cups and balls is an "oldie but a goodie," as they say. I've never been sure who "they" are but I know they say it a lot. There are a ton of different routines to be found in and around the cups and balls, but generally, there are three cups and one or more balls. The cups can be just about anything, from the size of a coffee creamer to a 50-gallon, galvanized garbage can. I'm not making that up either . . . you'll see. The balls can vary just as much. From foam rubber to cork to crochet, from fresh fruit to foul, they have all appeared, disappeared, multiplied, and mystified those who have witnessed some version of this effect. Familiarity walks hand-in-hand with surprise to make the cups and balls effect one of the most recognized and loved themes in magic.

Palming

Palming is one of the most important aspects of the cups and Balls. Balls are palmed before, during, and even right up to the finale of most routines. I think in using the palm, the magician gets an advantage in the cups and balls because there are other interesting distractions, directions, and expectations—the cups, different styles of balls, the wand, and surprising climax items. Palming is in good company. I have always felt much more comfortable palming something in a cups and balls routine than any other situation in magic. That's because the audience isn't always trying to burn your hands, and there are objects to be picked up, moved, and transferred while you are palming or setting up to palm. Think of a coin. Usually, it's just you and the coin, naked and being stared at. In a coin routine, the magician puts a coin in one hand, waits a while, and opens the hand to show the coin has disappeared. Where do you think most audience members think the coin might be? Bingo . . . in the other hand. Now, compare that to the same scenario in a cups and balls routine. The audience might first think it's in the other hand, but they also have the chance to think that it might have flown to the cup like the last time. Or maybe it went into the pocket. Maybe it is with the first ball under the middle cup. You can see there are a lot of directions that not only the cups and balls routines can take but also the guesses of the spectator.

Two palms, the finger palm and the classic palm, are most used in cups and balls so if you learn these two palms, you should be able to get through most routines. The great news is that you are already familiar with them from when we were working with coins in Chapter 4.

Finger Palm

The finger palm is used often in routines with cups and balls because it looks and feels natural. It also can be initiated from a lot of different positions, which fits well with the ever changing style of the cups and balls. For instance, if the ball is placed into the finger tips by the other hand, no problem. If the ball is picked up with one hand, it still works. If the ball is stolen from the pocket and just needs to sit in the hand before making its magical entrance—perfect. Sitting, standing, still or in motion, the finger palm will work for a ball, a coin, a match, a napkin, an olive, or a small cocktail onion. Recently I was in a very remote area in Mexico. With the finger palm and the classic palm I was able to put smiles on some children's faces by showing them how the acorns they had collected could magically jump from one hand to the other; they could vanish and even come right out of their ears. The children were delighted and I realized my coin routine worked just as well with acorns.

You already know all about making your hand look natural, how to move it around, and what the finger palm looks like. My most important note here would be that with a ball you have no edge, no hard angle to anchor into a finger joint. You do have the natural curve of a ball though. One of the hardest parts about finger palming a ball is to not let fingers placed around the ball curve in too much. This doesn't look natural, even if it feels right. Use the mirror, take a peek at how it looks and adjust. Try to use the finger palm on any small object. This will give you great practice; you never know where it will come in handy.

Classic Palm

The classic palm is the other indispensable tool for cups and balls. You know the drill on remaining natural, smooth, and subtle so

Definition Please

Burning occurs when a spectator is fixated upon figuring out the magician's secret. He will resist eye contact and defy attempts by the magician to misdirect or distract him. In short, he seems to stare so intensely at the magician's work that he might burn a hole right through it!

I'll get into just a few ways that the classic palm will differ when used with a ball rather than a coin. Just as with the finger palm, one of the challenges with using the classic palm with a ball is that there are no edges, hard angles, or anchor points on a ball. If you find edges, hard angles, or anchor points, gee whiz, no wonder you're having trouble! On the positive side, balls do come in rubber, sponge, lacquered wood, croquet, cork, and even hard plastic. That really helps the palming situation. Real coins don't come in so many different finishes, so you have to take what you get. With a ball, you can choose one that fits well with your routine—and in your palm.

A Cups and Balls Routine

Here's a basic routine that uses all of the following elements:

- Appearances
- Finales
- Loads
- Penetrations
- Steals
- Transfers
- Vanishes

Cups of Tea(se)

Effect

The magician begins with three cups and three balls on the table. After one of the balls is placed on top of one cup, it is covered with a second cup. When the two cups are lifted, the ball is seen to have penetrated through the original cup. This happens over and over in a couple of different ways and when the audience finally thinks they understand where the routine is going and what is happening, the magician lifts all of the cups and they each have one large object under them.

Preparation

You'll need three stackable cups and four balls (Shhh . . . the audience only ever know about three. You are one ahead.) Concerning the cups, you don't need to purchase professional

Definition Please

Palming is the art of concealing an object or objects with your hand. Palming doesn't necessarily need to have anything to do with the palm, such as in a back palm.

magic cups at first, but there are a few things to consider. I would suggest that the cups or tumblers be unbreakable because you're going to be handling them a lot. Another thing, they have to be able to stack one on top of the other, and the space between them when they are stacked needs to be enough to accommodate at least one ball. Professional cups will often hold three balls. Look in the Appendix for a supplier if you end up doing a lot of cups and balls routines and can't live without a professional set. They are a good investment and cool looking prop to whip out. That is, of course, if you prefer to look as if you are using a magician's property and not just making miracles with ordinary objects. I have seen distressed magical cups used for medieval themes, wine goblets for romantic themes, and a million other variations. Use your imagination and do whatever makes sense for your style.

Setup

The beginning setup for the props is as follows. This is done secretly unless you want to become "The Amazing Mr. Obvious." Place cup #1 mouth down on the table and rest a ball on its bottom; not the ball's bottom, we'll call this "on top" of cup #1 to make things simpler.

Cover the ball and cup #1 with cup #2 then cup #3. Place the three balls beside the stack and you are in wowing position. Depending on how you look at it, you have a ball on top of cup #1 or in cup #2. The cups are in a stack with one ball loaded mouth down on the table, and the balls are beside the stack **(Figure 5.1, ball is marked by dotted circle).**

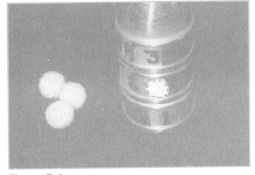

Figure 5.1

Routine

Using Two of the Cups
Step 1. To begin, pick up the stack of cups in one hand with the mouths facing up. Make sure the audience sees inside of cup #1 to show it is empty, even though you will be dealing with cup #3. Pull off the bottom cup (cup #3), turn it over, and place it down on the table.

Step 2. Now, you have to do the same thing again with cup #2 but remember, you have a ball in there, so . . . listen up! You might want to just flash the inside of cup #1 again to reinforce the fact that the audience saw an empty cup twice. Here's the neat part: if you move cup #2 in an arc and with enough speed as you turn it over, inertia will hold the ball in the bottom and it will look as if you are putting down another empty cup. The trick is to make sure that you put the cups down on the table the same way each time. That means you have to *think* of cup #3, cup #2, and cup #1 as *each* containing a ball. You don't, however, want the audience to think anything except that you are unstacking some cups and placing them mouth down on the table. Don't rush this or you'll raise suspicion; smooth continuous action is the key. Don't chop or pound the cups down like you are trying to catch a bug (unless you actually have a lot of bugs around, in which case you are performing like Penn and Teller).

Step 3. Cup #1 remains and you turn it down just like the others. So, you have cup #3, cup #2 (loaded with a ball), and cup #1 separated and resting mouth down on the table. Now, for the balls (that the audience know about anyway.)

Step 4. Pick up one ball and place it on top of cup #2. Take one of the other cups (let's say it's cup #1 since it will probably be to your right if you are right handed) and stack it on top of cup #2. You now have one ball trapped between the cups and one ball secretly beneath cup #2 **(Figure 5.2).**

Step 5. Make the magic moment happen and lift both cups together to show the ball they just saw on top has penetrated through the bottom of cup #2 and is now on the table. That's magic! Remember, you still have a ball secretly trapped between the cups since the audience believes it just penetrated.

Step 6. Turn the two-cup stack in the mouth up position again (flashing the inside of cup #2) and remove the bottom cup (cup #1 with ball) and cover the ball that just penetrated to the table. Now there are two balls under cup #1, but the audience is only hip to one of them.

Pick up another ball from the two remaining and place it on top of cup #1. Take cup #2 and stack it on top of cup #1, just like you did in Step 4 (except that the cups are in a different order).

You now have one ball trapped between the cups and two balls (one secretly) beneath cup #1.

Summon your powers again and "presto" (use a different word though)—when you lift both cups, the second ball has penetrated the bottom of a cup and now there are two balls on the table. Are you getting the picture of what's happening now? No? Then slap yourself and do it again. You'll get it . . . don't worry.

Step 7. Turn the two-cup stack mouth up, and do the deed again. This time cup #2 will be holding the secret gem and will add its ball to the two on the table making three.*

Figure 5.2

Using the *regular method,* pick up the last ball and plop it down on cup #2. Cover it with cup #1. When you lift the cup, "Shayzaam-Shayzaam," it's Jim Neighbours! Just kidding, it's ball three, lying in a pile with the other soldiers **(Figure 5.3).**

The *alternate method* for doing this is to back up to the * in Step 7 and try this instead.

Pick up the last ball and perform the French drop that you learned in Chapter 4. Whichever hand the ball is to vanish from, it can seem to be tossed invisibly into the cup. When the hand is finally shown to be empty, move the same hand over to cup #2 to pick it up. The third ball has joined the others. The other hand should be palming the ball in a finger palm position and it simply moves naturally into its final resting position (to the side if standing or at the table's edge if seated). There's just no way that ball could have gone from this hand (which is now empty) to under that cup (which now has three balls under it) *except* by the expert handling of a powerful magician. Hey, that's you!

Figure 5.3

Now let's start some trouble

Using the Third Cup

The rest of this routine is based on the fact that you just performed the alternate method for the third ball. This means there will be no ball between cup #1 and cup #2.

Picking up from Step 7, continue with the following:

Step 8. Place cup #2 back down on the table and lift cup #1 off of it and put it beside cup #2. Keeping the ball from the French drop finger palmed, pick up the three balls from the table with that hand. This keeps the hand from getting too "hot" and

Figure 5.4

Figure 5.5

puts it to work in a natural transition. Picking up the balls, count and say, "One, two, three balls." Continue with "And one" (while you put a ball under cup #3), "two," (now you put a ball under cup #2), "three" (putting the remaining *two balls* under cup #1), "three cups" **(Figure 5.4).**

Go back over that until it is clear. You should be looking at three cups mouth down on the table in the order of cup #1 (with two balls but only one the audience is aware of,) cup #2 (with one ball) and cup #3 (with one ball.)

Now go back and do it again. Please, you'll thank me later.

Step 9. Now, here comes the tricky business where all the fun happens!

You need to get the ball out of cup #3 and into your hand. Here's how.

Slide cup #2 and cup #3 forward but start moving cup #2 first. This puts the attention more toward that cup and less on where the action will be. As cup #3 follows, lift the back edge of the cup a little to let the ball sneak into your hand. For me, the ball ends up rolling into a cross between a finger palm and a clip in the second joints of my third and pinkie fingers. It's really more like the ball is caught between the fingers while it is behind the cup, and if the hand rests naturally on the table, the curved first and second fingers cover the ball when the cup is laid to rest **(Figure 5.5).**

Step 10. Now, lift up cup #2 with the empty hand as you announce and reconfirm that there surely is one ball under each cup. As soon as the cup is lifted, transfer the cup into the fingers of the other hand with the mouth of the cup toward you so you can secretly load the palmed ball inside. If you need a little extra time for the load, you can adjust the ball that is on the table with the free hand, then recover the ball(s) again. If you need stronger misdirection, you can roll the ball toward the spectator as you lift the cup, by tilting it back and nudging it with the inside of the back lip of the cup. This will appear as accidental and is a good misdirection. Don't throw the ball however like I have often seen; it's distracting instead of subtly misleading. Adjusting the ball also gives a natural reason for transferring cup #2 to the other hand so that your "good hand" is free to fix the ball. Yeah, you just had a little tidying up to do and, this time, neatness counts. To the audience, all of this should seem like you just moved two cups forward and have shown one ball to be under cup #2. Now you'll go to show them that there is a ball under cup #3.

Step 11. When you lift cup #3 to show the ball, it is gone, much to your confusion. You just saw one ball under cup #2 so everyone knows there is only one under that cup. You probably should look under cup #1. Lift cup #1 and another miracle has taken place. The ball has traveled from cup #3 to cup #1 without you even touching it!

Pick up one ball, put cup #1 back down on the table again (but not on the ball, just let the ball sit in front of the cup), and perform the French drop. This time, pretend to push the ball right through the bottom of cup #2. Use the three "Ps" for this: *push, pause,* and *pierce.* This means that you don't just toss the ball into the cup. Your hand goes on the bottom of the cup with the ball (not really), it pushes the imaginary ball into the bottom, pauses, then suddenly the ball seems to pass as the hand flattens out on the cup. If you think of it like that, it will help you imagine and demonstrate that it's not easy to push a solid through a solid.

Lift cup #2 and (harp sound) an incredible penetration; there is that amazing ball! Wow, this guy is:

(a) good

(b) "making me berry berry angry" or

(c) a woman, and she's good too!

You still have a ball palmed.

Now for the set up and the big finish.

Step 12. Keep the ball finger palmed from your French drop and you're going to pick up the balls again just like in Step 8. Just so you don't have to look back, here's a little review. Okay, the ball is palmed, and you need to pick up the three balls from the table with that same hand. Remember, we are keeping the "suspect hand" looking naturally busy.

"One, two, three balls" (four really, you know how this goes by now). Now, you are going to put a ball back under cup #1, cup #2,

Definition Please

When something in magic is said to be *hot,* it means you have called too much attention to the secrets behind your effect. It's also referred to as *heat*—or unwanted attention—for example, "By moving the first cup forward with one hand, you take the *heat* off of the second hand."

and cup #3 again, but *this* time, you won't put two balls under cup #3. You'll obviously sneak something away. When I say "obviously sneak something away," I don't mean that the audience actually "sees" a ball. It's just that the hand appears to sneak something out and go to the pocket.

"Hey, you did something sneaky right there, Mr. Magic!" This makes the audience think they have finally caught you. That's funny, considering a ball has never been found inside of a pocket yet, but that's just the beauty of rearranging someone's senses; it's senseless.

It's funny to play the shifty-eyed paranoid at this point. People love to outsmart the magician and don't they really deserve to catch on a little about now?

When you took the one ball from under cup #3 and put it into the pocket, the hand came right back with a load. The load can be anything from a citrus fruit to a steel ball bearing to a live chick. Whatever the load is that you decide to steal, it's now in your hand. You went into the pocket with a ball and came out with the load.

Step 13. After some fun with your audience thinking you have taken the ball from cup #3 away, lift it up with the free hand and show them the ball is there just like you were telling them all along. They will think you were just teasing them. They won't know that you really did do something. You just got rid of your extra (one ahead) ball and picked up a load. They will think you were just miming. Transfer cup #3 to the other hand and load the matzo ball. Then you pick up the ball that was under the cup and place the loaded cup down.

Step 14. Openly announce that you will really place the ball in the pocket this time. Place the ball into your pocket but on your way out, steal the live gecko! That's your second load. For your information you don't really have to have a matzo ball or a live gecko. My wife just read this and said that you might not understand that. I was just trying to be funny and let you know that you can use any object that will fit in the cups and they don't have to be all the same. There, is that better, Dear?

Definition Please

Clipping is a specialized form of palming. Generally, with palming a number of areas of the hand work together to anchor the object. With clipping, the object is usually pinched between two fingers.

And Now Cup #2

Lift the cup, load the toad, place cup #2 back down, and pick up the ball. Announce the placement of the second ball into the pocket. Do it but on your way out, steal the Vienna sausage.

And Finally, Cup #3

Lift cup #3, load the Vienna, hide the sausage, and pick up the final ball. With some kind of flair, make sure it gets to the pocket.

Step 15. There are variations to the ending of a routine like this. Some think it is necessary to give some time for the audience to rethink what has just happened. All the balls have been put away and all of the cups are empty. The magician might play a little "Let's Make a Deal" shell game by asking, "If there was a ball in any one, which one do you think it would be in?" He might even try to magically show and pass each ball back under the cups. I prefer to shock 'em. Keep it moving. Lift up the cups and reveal an amazing array of "Matzo, Gecko, and Sausage."

It doesn't matter what you decide. When you turn over those cups, people are going to go crazy. Some might get hungry but most . . . they'll love it.

Wands

If you want to, you can utilize a wand during your cups and balls routines. This illustration shows how a ball can be secretly loaded into a cup under the guise of simply picking up the wand. You could load cup #2 at the beginning of this routine in this manner if you like. It will allow you to really show all of the cups empty and just three balls in the beginning of the routine **(Figure 5.6)**.

Figure 5.6

CHAPTER 6

Close-Up Magic—
Restaurant Magic

Bread
Gosh, It's a Nosh

The floating bagel is a fun impromptu piece that is cuter than it is amazing. It's one of those tricks you can do during a dinner that will make people think, "Yeah yeah, that's cute, now stop playing with your food, shut up, and eat!" It's good to feel that kind of love at the table.

Effect

The magician holds up his napkin between two hands. There is some movement behind the napkin, then a bagel floats gracefully above the table's edge, back down, over the table, and finally back down into the magician's lap.

Preparation

You need a knife or fork, whichever is the lighter one, a dinner napkin, and a bagel. A dinner roll will work too but a bagel works better visually, and it's a lot funnier.

Setup

Stick the knife or fork, we'll say a fork, into the edge of the bagel as close to the edge as possible so that it can be lifted. Now hold the fingers behind the napkin with the bagel to the center as shown **(Figure 6.1)**. Keep this set up in your lap until your are ready to float the nosh.

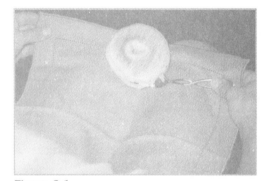

Figure 6.1

Routine

Bring the napkin in front of you and move the handle of the fork to make the bagel rise above the edge of the napkin **(Figure 6.2)**. Bring it back down and let it hit against the inside of the napkin by pushing the thumb against the fork.

To make it float out over the table, push the thumb against the fork and with both arms act as though you are trying to hold the runaway bagel from going too far. Here's a nice added touch. While the napkin is draped over the top of the bagel, you can briefly let go of the napkin corner that isn't controlling anything

Figure 6.2

(as if it was pulled out of your fingers by the power of the bagel). It seems to be getting away. Quickly grab the "dropped" end and bring it back toward you and under control. Play a little tug of war with the bad bun and finally capture it back. Have it do a few more peeks over the edge of the table until it floats down into your lap, where you can "unrig" it and bring it back up onto the table. Don't bring the fork back up right away, since this will show everyone how you did it. Of course, the napkin is supposed to be in your lap anyway so you're all set.

Napkin and Toothpick

It's a Snap

Effect

A toothpick is laid into a dinner napkin and the napkin is folded up around it. The spectator is asked to feel the toothpick through the napkin. He is then asked to bend the toothpick until it breaks. When the magician unfolds the napkin, it is seen to have been restored to its original state.

Preparation

Two toothpicks and a napkin with a hem.

Setup

Hide one toothpick by slipping it inside the hem of the napkin at one corner.

Routine

Take your napkin and lay it on the table. Toss a toothpick on top of it. Lift the napkin up as if you are bringing the toothpick underneath and into the center, but as you do, hold onto the corner that has the extra toothpick in it and place it into the center. The extra toothpick can be either palmed or just bunched up in the napkin.

Let the spectator feel the toothpick through the cloth and ask him to break it in half. You will hear the snap. Now either just let

---

**Max Malini
1873–1942**

Max Malini was born in 1873 in Ostrov, located on the border between Poland and Austria. Although he certainly knew how to make a name for himself with his constant self promotion, not too many people outside of magic circles recognize his name. Malini also looked different than other magicians. He was short, with tiny hands—what a perfect foil for a skilled magician. Malini was known as a conjurer who was always ready for the opportunity to amaze an audience. One such story is when Malini was seated at a stylish restaurant and, just before the chicken was to be carved for the table, he waved his hands and caused the bird to get up and run back to the kitchen for cover. One can only imagine the ruckus he caused throughout the restaurant.

the napkin fall open (if the original toothpick was actually placed inside) or unfold the napkin, letting the duplicate drop out of the hand and into the center as you open it up. No one will ever know what happened but you! It's a snap!

Cutlery
Switch Blade

If you eat in some of the nicer culinary establishments like I do, then you know that the cutlery is often a part of the beautiful presentation. Usually, my favorite restaurants offer a "spork" (that's a spoon and a fork in a plastic bag) but sometimes I end up in a place that actually has the knives and forks made of genuine metal and rolled up in real linen. In this case, it's a perfect opportunity to perform the following effect.

Effect

The magician lays his fork on top of his napkin and rolls it up so it's inside. When he unrolls it, the fork has changed to a spoon.

Preparation

All you need is a fork, a spoon, and a cloth napkin.

Setup

Lay your napkin on the table diagonally with one corner pointing toward you and with the spoon underneath, lying horizontally under the center of the napkin. The spoon's "bowl" should be pointing up. Don't lay the napkin too smoothly or the spoon will make a lump that will show.

Routine

While you explain about the service you usually get at your favorite haunts, and that you love using "sporks," you have learned to put up with the more refined cutlery that does only one thing at a time too. Make up some patter that fits your personality. Then, hold up the fork. The good news is that you are a magician and no matter what utensil you have, you can still make it work for you.

Put the fork down horizontally on top of the napkin on the opposite side of the spoon. With your thumbs and fingers, begin to roll the napkin around the fork and the spoon (hidden underneath) at the same time, by rolling everything away from you **(Figure 6.3).** Keep rolling until the end that was toward you (and is now on the top of the roll) flips over and is now against the table. Essentially, what has happened is that the napkin has been turned over and so has everything with it. When what was the top layer has been flipped over and becomes the bottom layer, the bottom will also be rolled up and be on top of the roll. It will appear as though you have simply rolled the fork into the napkin. Now, if you pull the ends in opposite directions, the napkin will unroll and be flat on the table and the spoon will be on top of the napkin (with the fork underneath).

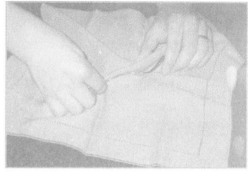

Figure 6.3

Variation

You can also vary the routine by exchanging other items this way. How about a pack of sugar for some sweetener, or try changing a red lighter into a white lighter. You can think up a lot of ways to use this.

See You Ladle

Effect

The magician grips a normal spoon by the handle and with great strength presses it against the table until the handle is severely bent. When he thinks the spoon has had enough, he tosses the spoon back on the table and it is as good as new.

Preparation

Zero.

Setup

None of that either.

Figure 6.4

Figure 6.5

Routine

Place the spoon on the table in front of you, showing your audience that it's totally normal. Explain that you will bend and unbend it with your own wimpy strength. Keeping the spoon on the table, grab the spoon handle with your hands overlapping. The pinkie finger of the hand underneath wraps around the base of the handle, near the bowl. This is the only grip you'll have on the spoon. The other hand overlaps the other and hides the rest of the handle, appearing to add strength to the grip, but actually it just rests over the other **(Figure 6.4).** Now the bending begins. Press the bowl firmly against the table with the pinkie holding on and rotate your wrists and fingers forward, allowing the spoon handle to slowly slide out of the back of the hands and lay almost flat on the table (except for the space you'll need for your pinkie) **(Figure 6.5).** It is "bent." Now ease up on the pressure slightly, and let the spoon tilt back up again, but before you are all the way back to normal, release the grip(s) and toss the spoon onto the table. Wow! What strength! This is a quick table trick and if you do it at the right fancy feast, it will really make people nervous, just ask my mother.

Variation

I have seen a couple of people perform this trick by pinching the edge of a nickel between the thumb and second joint of the index finger so that it looks like the end of the spoon. This allows you to make the spoon look like it's bending even further because the top hand can continue bending and make the spoon appear to bend in half. You might really like this variation but, to me, it looks a little *too* good and therefore not quite so impromptu. I like just being able to walk up to the table, bend the spoon, and be on my way.

Creamers
Eye Scream

Here's a disgusting little table gag that isn't for everybody, but it gets such a good reaction. Sometimes it's just hard to resist.

Effect

The magician complains about having something in his eye and pulls the bottom of his eyelid down to see if he can blink it out. He reaches for a fork to help and brings it up to the eye. All of the sudden the hand slips, the fork pokes into his eye, he screams the names of people he doesn't even know, and a bunch of white eye goo runs down his cheek. He takes his napkin and rubs the eye, wipes the cheek off, and continues as usual.

Preparation

You'll need a creamer, a fork, a napkin, and a table full of people with hearty stomachs and even greater senses of humor. If you're on the fence about whether to do this or not, don't. It might be a good thing to do when it's getting really late, and the rest of the table thinks it's a good time to arm wrestle or build fires in the ashtray.

Setup

Pick up a creamer and finger palm it in one hand with the opening to the foil cover pointing down away from the thumb.

Routine

When things start to get a little too quiet, suddenly go into hysterics and claim that you have something in your eye. Pull the bottom lid down with the index finger of the hand that has the creamer palmed in it and try to get whatever it is out. With the finger still holding the lid down, look down your nose, spot your fork, and pick it up. Holding the handle of the fork and with the tines facing up, bring the fork up under the bottom of the hand and puncture the foil top of the creamer. Squeeze the creamer and you've got yourself some shootin' goo. Scream some expletive and drop the hand with the creamer down to your lap while you pick up your napkin. Leave the creamer and bring the napkin up to clean things up. "Ahhhh, that's much better. Sorry . . . you were saying?"

Finally, *be careful*. It's dangerous and I am warning you right now. I don't want anyone to get hurt, but I just know some of you people won't be happy until somebody puts an eye out.

Uri Geller

Uri Geller was living in Israel and wowing audiences with his mind-over-matter routines by age 23. He moved to the United States with the hope that television audiences would appreciate his gifts. He bent spoons, stopped watches, turned pages of books—all apparently with the use of nothing more than his mind. The scientific world was excited by his abilities, but many magicians were angry at his claims that this was real ESP and not simply magic. There is one thing that everyone did agree on, however, and that was that Uri was certainly getting much attention and press with his mental tricks. This made the world, including magicians, realize that Mental Magic, real or not, is entertaining and memorable to audiences everywhere.

Salt Shakers
You're Charged with a Salt

This is a classic effect in Restaurant Magic, but not a lot of people have seen it. Every magician has seen it but most audiences aren't filled with magicians. It's worth learning and is a great example of how to use misdirection.

Effect

The magician explains that he will now show a magic classic, "The Coin Through the Table Trick." He borrows a coin, puts the coin on the table, places a salt shaker on top of it, and covers the salt shaker with a napkin. He explains that he will be pressing the coin through the "soft spot" in the table, causing the coin to fall to the floor. The magician moves the coin, shaker, and napkin to several different locations, trying to find the soft spot. He then thinks one particular observer to focus on. He puts the coin and covered shaker back down and "slam," he smashes his hand down on top of the salt shaker, and the napkin flattens on the table. The magician quickly lifts the napkin and the coin is still there, but the salt-shaker is gone. A loud knock and scraping noise is heard under the table, and the magician brings out the salt shaker. The audience is completely fooled.

Preparation

All you need is a saltshaker, a paper napkin large enough to cover it, and a borrowed coin.

Setup

You will need to be sitting at a table that has been partially cleared. The real setup happens during the routine. The only other thing you have to do is make sure that your knees are together. You are going to be dropping the salt shaker in your lap and you don't want it to fall and break all over the floor. I don't care how good your magic has been up until that point. Once you have some sort of accident, it's over, you are back to mortal level.

Routine

1. Borrow the coin and place it 8 to 12 inches in front of you on the table. Carefully place the salt shaker on top of the coin and then cover the salt shaker with the napkin, sort of wrapping it around so the folds are somewhat flat against the sides the shaker. Depending on the thickness of the napkin, you might have to fold it in half or quarters. The main objective is for the shaker not to be seen through the napkin, especially the top of it, which is usually chrome and shiny. The other important point is that you need to practice covering the shaker with the napkin so that when the shaker is taken away, the shape of it remains in the napkin.

2. Explain to the audience that you're looking for the "soft spot." Not the one in your head . . . the one in the table. Explain how the napkin will keep any salt or glass from flying out in case you overdo it (or it happens really fast). Now place one hand around the salt shaker and put the other hand on top of it. Showing great concentration, hit the top of the salt shaker with your open hand to "push" or make the coin penetrate through the table.

3. Lift the hand that's holding the still covered shaker and discover that the coin is still there. "Nope, that must not be the place," you say. Now, temporarily rest the shaker on the table near you as you reach the other hand out and move the coin to the right. Replace the shaker thoughtfully and hit again, making a noise of effort, and shaking the table a little. This establishes the fact that the shaker is still a solid object under the napkin. And now the misdirection happens.

4. This time when you lift the shaker to show that the coin is still there, bring the napkin and shaker toward you over the edge of the table and for a *brief* moment. Loosen your grip on the shaker just enough to let it fall into your lap with the shape of the shaker still visible in the napkin. The illusion is perfect. Meanwhile, the other hand is reaching and moving the coin closer to the spectator **(Figure 6.6).** To do so

Figure 6.6

means you almost have to raise up a bit to get all the way over there, which means it's also a very natural time for the opposite hand to draw back for balance. Also, because the coin is very close, the spectator intently keeps her eyes on it. Place the shaker-shaped napkin back over the coin and just before you hit it, appear to have a quick second thought. Lift it again and move the coin to one side, just a bit you say, "There's the spot I think," as you hammer it flat, "Yup!" As soon as it happens, your opposite hand creates misdirection so you can make your next sneaky move.

5. While you're enjoying the look on all the faces, locate the shaker in your lap. Lift up the napkin and say, "Oh, no! Wrong object!" The spectator will look at you as if, "Really, you didn't mean to do that?" because she is too stunned to reason. At that moment you reach as far as you can under the table with the hand that's holding the shaker and bang the salt shaker against the bottom of the table. Things will get silent because suddenly the feeling of "What just happened there?" changes to "Could that be the salt shaker?" As this happens, drag the shaker against the underside of the table, making a scratching sound, and continue dragging it up and over the lip. This is a weird and unusual sound and creates a tension like the sound of a bowling ball rolling down the floor before the final, "pwockatock." Think of the entire table, except for the very top, as being a high-powered magnet. When you get the salt shaker over the lip, the "magnet" turns off and the arm jumps up as it's released from the force. Raise the shaker into the air and set it down in the area it supposedly passed through. The spectator will never forget seeing this great piece of magic. It's got intrigue, great misdirection, a surprise ending, and lots of "in your face" theatrics.

Another important tip I can give you here is to watch your angles and sight lines. Don't perform this if the person next to you can see in your lap. If they can, they will tell everyone just to soothe the looks on their faces and you will be busted— charged with a salt!

CHAPTER 7

Close-Up Magic— Bar Magic

Frank Zak

Frank Zak has exhibited his bartender skills for 11 years. His magic has delighted patrons across the country. Zak, a long standing member of the International Brotherhood of Magicians, uses his vast knowledge of the magic industry to accent the needs of all bartenders, from the novice to the expert. He is also a good friend and always willing to share his card expertise.

Bar Napkins
Hairy the Haunted Hank

I learned this little trick when I was but a young conjuror. I used to love an illusion performed by the late and great master magician, Harry Blackstone, Jr., in which a borrowed handkerchief was made to come to life, to fly and dance. It is a classic illusion, and that's just part of the reason I like this little stunt. I would put it in the category of "cute and entertaining," which is okay because not all magic has to be a trick, but all magic does need to be entertaining.

Effect

The magician takes an ordinary bar napkin and unfolds it. Taking it by one corner, he strokes it until it stands up while held by one hand. The napkin mysteriously stays upright, seemingly held rigid by some unknown force. Then he plucks out an imaginary hair and wraps it around the top of the napkin. By pulling this "hair," the napkin moves back and forth or in any direction that the hair is pulled.

Preparation

All you need is a regular bar napkin. It works with any size or weight. In fact, you can even do it with a tissue.

Setup

The entire setup is done as part of the performance, in full view of the spectators.

Routine

Unfold the napkin and hold it by one corner with the left hand. With the right hand, stroke the napkin downward until you reach about two inches from the bottom where the right hand squeezes the napkin between the thumb and first and second fingers. Give the tip in the left hand a twist between the thumb and index finger and let go of the left hand. The napkin will stand by itself held up by only the strength of its diagonal and radial support. You might have to experiment a little with it; you want to have as much of the napkin standing up as possible. It becomes a cross between strength and balance.

Now, pretend to pluck a hair from your head (if you could see my hairline, you'd see I've practiced this a lot). Continue to pantomime, twisting the hair around the upper, twisted end of the napkin and then feel around for the loose end of the hair. When you find it, wink, pull it slowly until it's "tight" and then pull it to the left, following the motion with the napkin by squeezing the right thumb and fingers. By moving the thumb and fingers very slightly, you'll see the motion is exaggerated at the top, enough to make it move quite a bit. The billowing of the napkin at the right fingers covers some of the movement, but there really shouldn't be much at all if you practice. Also, keep in mind that the attention of the audience is at the top of the napkin and the moving hair, not down below where you're "just holding it still." If the napkin falls over too easily and won't come back up, you have too much napkin above the right fingers and you'll have to readjust it. Once you try this a couple of times, you'll know which kind of napkins will give you a certain kind of stability. Just make sure that the left hand and the napkin move in sync with each other so the illusion is at its best.

Soda Straws
Caterpillar Straw

I first learned this as a trick (more of a stunt) to make a snake out of a soda straw wrapper, but in fact it looks more like a caterpillar so that's what I call it. I guess it bugged me.

Effect

A soda straw wrapper is ripped at one end and stripped and compressed to the other end until it is a small wrinkly tube about $1^1/_4$ inches long. The magician claims that this is a caterpillar egg and that he can add the secret ingredient of life to turn it into a

Did You Know?

caterpillar. As he drops the ingredient onto the egg, it begins to grow, wriggle, and seemingly come to life. It's soda creepy!

Preparation

No preparation is needed and you don't even have to practice much. You need a soda straw that is dry and has a wrapper on it. You'll also need a glass of water or other liquid that you don't mind parting with a drop or so of.

Setup

Take the wrapper off of the straw by opening one end and stripping it down to the other end. Rip the other end too and compress the wrapper as tightly as you can on the straw. Now, slide the wrapper off of the straw and place it in its compressed "egg" onto a waterproof, slick surface, such as a bar top or table top.

Routine

Explain about the metamorphosis that takes place when a caterpillar's pupa or chrysalis rests inside of a cocoon waiting to become a butterfly. But how does the caterpillar come to life? Well, it's one of these, a caterpillar egg. Place the egg down on the bar and explain that for all life to begin you need three things. Oxygen (or smoky air), light (or Bud light), and of course beer (or water just in case). Take the soda straw and put it into a glass of water and extract a small amount by placing your index finger over the end of the straw. Bring it over top of the egg and allow a small amount of water to drop onto the table along the bottom of the egg. It will begin to expand in a creepy-crawly way. Try it and they'll ask you to show them some more bar magic. Now try to wriggle out of that one.

David Bamberg, "Fu Manchu" (1904–1974)

Theo (Okito) Bamberg's son also adopted unusual stage names as soon as he started doing magic. As a teenager, David performed as "Syko, The Beetle with a Superhuman Mind," and much later adopted the stage name of "Fu Manchu," the fictional villain he'd read about in Sax Rhomer novels. After completing his education in England, he worked as chief assistant on the Okito show, but it wasn't until he toured with "The Great Raymond" that he envisioned his own magical extravaganza. He chose to tour South America to make his mark as the formidable Fu Manchu. David already knew from experience that a Chinese character had an

(continued on next page)

Swizzle Sticks
. . . Without a Paddle
Effect

The magician shows a bar swizzle stick with the logo of the bar embossed on each side. He waves the opposite hand over the stick and the printing vanishes. He shows the other side and it is blank too. The Magician then reaches into the air and plucks some "magical embossing" dust out, and rubs it on the under side of the swizzle. Now, when he turns it over, the printing is back. Waving the hand again over the swizzle stick, both sides are shown to back to "normal." As a finish, the magician rubs the bottom printing off, this time showing it to be printed only on the top side. The swizzle stick is handed to the spectator for examination.

Preparation

A swizzle stick and knowledge of the *paddle move* as explained in the routine.

Setup:

Get a swizzle and get ready to sizzle!

Routine

First you need to use a swizzle stick that is only printed on one side. That's most of them. You should also use one that is symmetrical so that if it is turned over it is exactly the same shape on the other side. If the design is not a circle, rectangle, diamond, or square, when you flip it over it will look funny during the paddle move. To get a better idea of what I mean here, let's look at it.

The Paddle Move

The paddle move allows you to turn the swizzle over so that it appears the same on both sides, even though each side is different.

1. Begin by holding the shaft of the swizzle with the design up, between the thumb and first and second fingers. The head

---

David Bamberg, "Fu Manchu" (1904–1974)

(continued from previous page)

element of intrigue that would draw theatergoers. But unlike the silent act of Okito, he wanted to add patter, comedy, and drama to the show of his dreams. David always fully scripted his productions—extravaganzas of scenery, costumes, music, and lighting effects. Being a consummate writer, David Bamberg contributed countless articles on stage presentation and magic production in many magical periodicals.

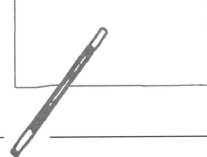

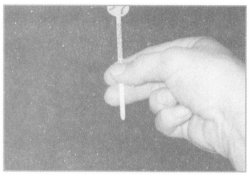

Figure 7.1

of the swizzle should be facing the spectator. **(Figure 7.1)**. Rotate the wrist back toward you so that the head of the swizzle stick is moving back toward you. While you are making this movement, you must also twist the shaft so the stick flips over. To do the twist, move the thumb in one direction and the first and second fingers in the other. It doesn't take very much finger movement to twist the thin shaft around, and the rotation of the entire wrist hides it as all being one smooth motion. Now, the spectator will believe that he is seeing the other side and that both sides are printed. Reverse the motion and show the first side again, then back. *That's* the paddle move.

2. Wave the opposite hand over the swizzle stick and cover the entire stick with the outstretched palm as it passes over top of the swizzle hand. When it is briefly covered, perform the twist on the shaft again as the hand continues the wave. It will appear as though the printing has suddenly vanished.

3. Perform the paddle move and show that there is no printing on the other side either. The swizzle stick has been magically erased! Leave the stick pointing toward the spectator.

4. Reach into the air to grab the "magical embossing" substance and rub it onto the underside of the paddle.

5. Now, simply turn the wrist toward you but this time, don't perform the paddle move and one side is back to its original embossed state again. Point the swizzle back toward the spectator.

6. Wave the hand over the stick again and do the twist (not the Chubby Checker thing—the move). The top of the swizzle is back to normal too.

7. To erase the bottom side of the swizzle stick before handing it to the spectator, simply leave it pointed toward the spectator with the printing up and pretend to wipe off

the bottom-side printing with the fingers of the opposite hand. Bring the fingers up and blow the dust off of them and once again show the swizzle stick on both sides (without performing the paddle move). This leaves the stick in normal condition so that it can be handed out for examination.

Variation

You can use the paddle move for a lot of different small items, including matches, pencils, pens, and even a popsicle stick, which will be explained in Chapter15, Magic for Children.

If you want to get fancy, you can use two swizzle sticks at a time (one in each hand). By rubbing the printing from one onto the other, it seems as if the design is jumping back and forth. It's great fun. Because both hands are busy and you can't do the wave movement with an empty hand, I strike one swizzle stick on top of the other with a "click." When they hit, I do the twist and it looks as though the design just jumps onto the other stick. The striking hand causes misdirection so the audience isn't burning the twist. It happens very quickly and it looks like magic.

Paper Matches

You can also perform the paddle move with paper matches. Matches are about the right width and you can mark dots on them with a pen that will appear to jump on and off just like the embossing on the swizzle sticks. You can also show a match on both sides by holding the match by both ends, with the head and the base of the match touching the pads of the thumb and the first fingers. Don't put too much pressure on the match or it will buckle. With a dot drawn in the middle of the match, cover it with the thumb and fingers of the opposite hand just like you did in the "without a paddle" routine. The difference is you will turn the wrists of both hands at the same time (joined at the match). Now, you have to lift the index finger to show the dot. When you reverse again, you have to raise the thumb or simply remove the thumb all together. Once you start using the paddle move, you'll try it on everything. It's a sickness.

Channing Pollack

In the early 1960s, no one seemed to want to book magicians. Enter Channing Pollock, whose dashing good looks and sophisticated dove act won him great acclaim and did wonders for magicians as a whole. His act is perhaps the most mimicked of all the styles of magic: black costumes contrasted with beautifully colored silk scarves, creating a dramatic backdrop for his live white doves. As a Hollywood actor, Channing created a character of supreme elegance and style. After serving it well, he retired from performing magic in 1969.

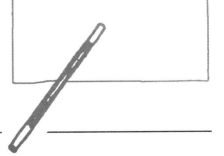

Cocktail Swords

The "X" Caliber Files

Effect

The magician has the spectator examine a cocktail straw and a plastic cocktail sword to make sure that they are both solid and have no cracks, splits, or trapdoors. He has the spectator pinch each end of the cocktail straw between her fingers and places a bar napkin over top. Picking up the cocktail sword, he places it under the napkin and counts to three. When he pulls away the napkin, the cocktail sword is seen swinging by its handle on the cocktail straw. Somehow, it has penetrated onto the straw without the spectator letting go of the ends.

Preparation

You'll need a napkin, a cocktail straw, and two cocktail swords of the same color.

Setup

Secretly palm one of the cocktail swords before beginning the effect. The sword should be palmed with the handle down, in the first joint of the second finger and with the end of the sword against the palm **(Figure 7.2).**

Have the cocktail sword, straw, and napkin on the bar.

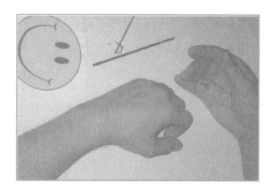

Figure 7.2

Routine

Pick up the cocktail straw and ask the spectator to take a good look at it to make sure it is solid and has no cracks or splits or holes. Tell her the hole in each end is one she might miss so you should remind her. Take the straw back and ask her to examine the cocktail sword. This is your misdirection so you can do some dirty work.

While she is looking at the sword, you'll need some time, so tell her to make sure that the handle is solid and doesn't pull away from the sword. Ask her to be positive that it doesn't fold up in any way—any way to get more time. While her attention is on finding something, you need to get the palmed sword threaded onto the straw. To do this casually, pick up the straw and insert it into your very loose fist so it runs against the insides of your fingers and into the handle. Your thumb of the palming hand can help: put the handle in a good position to "receive." Make sure that it does get inside. Sometimes, it feels as if it is but you really can't look, so wiggle the straw back and forth a little to make sure it is trapped. Push the straw through the hand and let it come out the other side of the palm-down hand **(Figure 7.3)**.

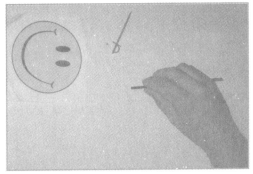

Figure 7.3

When she has finished her examination, ask her to put the sword down on the table and pinch one end of the straw between her first finger and thumb. You might want to call it the index finger to avoid a lesson on digits. With the fingers of the fist closed a little tighter, and with your index finger and thumb holding the straw toward her, offer her an end. The sword remains palmed, with the straw running through it, and she pinches tightly.

Leave your hand over the straw and ask her to pinch the other end. When she reaches for it, slide your hand and the palmed sword toward the first end she pinched so she can see a lot of the straw. In her eyes, she has just seen the entire straw, first one end and now the other. Once she is approaching the end, reach for the napkin with the other hand and place it over everything so nothing can be seen. Keep the right hand in position and don't let go of the palm. If you do, the sword might hang down and hit one of her fingers and she will know that there is something else down there. The napkin might also fall off or blow away and that would be bad too.

Leave the napkin on top of everything and pick up the sword. Show it to her and take it under the napkin. While you are looking underneath, you need to let go of the palmed sword and place the loose sword back in the exact same palm. The switch has been made.

Bring the hand with the palmed sword to the edge of the napkin with the thumb on top and the fingers (and the palmed sword) hidden by the napkin. Count to three and pull the napkin away from her hands quickly, being careful not to drop the palmed sword. Amazingly, the sword is now hanging from the straw.

If you pull the napkin off correctly, it will hit the handle of the straw on its way and cause the sword to spin around the straw when it is revealed. The strong misdirection gives you plenty of time to lap or drop the sword. Bring the napkin back up on top of the bar and everything is clean.

Most spectators won't even look up for quite some time. They'll really give the props a good going over after this, expecting to see something that they might have overlooked and thinking that you'll probably take the props back to switch them.

This effect is one of my favorite impromptu pieces of bar magic.

CHAPTER 8

Close-Up Magic—
Bar Bets, Gags,
Stunts, and Scams

H ere is a collection of some of my favorite bar bets, gags, and stunts. You really don't have to do them at a bar, but the props you need will be there.

Match Stunts
Slick Eddie

Here's a slick way to light a match with one hand. Take the match pack in one hand with the top (flat) edge of the pack pointing toward the floor. The staple end is pointing toward the ceiling with the cover flap away from you. Use the fingers to draw the cover down and bend a match so that it's sticking straight up over the stapled end **(Figure 8.1).** Reach up with the thumb and bend the match head down onto the striker. Pinch the match head and the striker between the thumb and the finger and use the other fingers to flip the cover back up. You have to close the cover before striking; apparently that's some sort of law I just never knew about. Now, with the fingers holding the closed pack firmly (in sort of a finger palm position), flick the head to the side with the thumb and it will light. Make sure you get your thumb out of there in time or you will scorch yourself. The match can even be laid onto the bar with the pack as a little presentation stand.

Figure 8.1

Juicer's Staple Diet

If you'd like to have some good natured fun with a friend at the bar, try this trick. Take a regular straw through the top opening of a matchbook, and ask a barmate if he'd like to try to learn some magic. Have your helper, "Juicer," hold on to each end of the straw. Drape a bar napkin over the straw and matches, then reach under the napkin and come out with the matches. Pull away the napkin and Juicer is left holding just the straw.

Even Juicer will think that he's figured it out and will respond, "Well that's easy magic boy, even I can do *that* stupid trick." So you let him try. You put the matches back on the straw and when Juicer tries it, he can't get the matches off the straw.

After he begs for the secret, you say, "OK, Juicer, it might have been easier for you if the matches weren't stapled shut."

You have to set this up before you even get to the bar. Staple one matchbook closed (through the cover) and have a second, unstapled matchbook with you also. When showing him the trick the first time, use the unstapled one. When you have him try it, switch the regular matchbook with the stapled one. Since you could do the trick and he couldn't, Juicer will think you're amazing and probably offer to buy you a glass of Ripple.

Edgy Does It

Bet someone that they can't drop a match from 18 inches above the bar and make it stand on its edge. They can try and try until you show them how to do it. Simply bend the match at its center before you drop it and the bent match will stand on the edge every time.

KaBomb!

When you shake a match out after using it, toss it into the ashtray and poke your fingers in your ears. It's funny but don't do it in front of airport security.

The "Lighter" Side— Tricks with Lighters
The Flame Thrower

Light your butane lighter and pretend to wrap your fingers around the flame. In reality, let go of your thumb and the flame stops. Pretend to keep squeezing on the flame and carry it away from the lighter. Toss the imaginary flame into the air toward the hand with the lighter, following its arc and catching it again on the lighter. To catch it, you just relight the lighter at the moment your mimed "flame" would seem to hit it. This doesn't fool anyone but it makes you look so cool! People will go "tisk tisk" at this, but you will see them doing the trick to someone else later.

Did You Know?

Cigars Work Too!

Here are a few things you can do with cigars:

1. Place a wrapped cigar on a napkin, roll it up, and have it magically come out of its shell.
2. Push a wooden match into the end of a cigar and pretend to light it like a giant match on a matchbook.
3. Pick up a salt shaker and salt the end of the cigar saying, "Gee whiz, these things taste terrible!"
4. Perform the paddle move using the cigar band while it's on the cigar.
5. Smoke them and annoy people.

Sticker Shock

Get one of those lighters that has a warning sticker on the side and turn it over so that the sticker is on the bottom. Holding the lighter by the action end, perform the paddle move, showing both sides to be the same solid color. Place the lighter in the palm-up hand and squeeze a fist around it. Turn the fist upside down, and while the thumb pushes inside of the hand causing the lighter to rise from the other side, the opposite hand covers the thumb's action by wiping the back of the hand in circular motions. It looks like you actually print the sticker on the lighter while it comes out of the other end of the hand. Perform the paddle move again and show that the sticker is on both sides.

Cigarettes

Butt How?

By placing a cigarette under the cover of a match book and holding it shut with two outside matches **(Figure 8.2),** you can keep the setup in your pocket until you are ready to perform this little piece. Ask somebody if they happened to see the special matches that this bar has. They are make-believe matches; you don't even need cigarettes. Bring out the setup with the cigarette pointing down into your hand. Take one of the matches, light it against the back of the cover, and bring the hands together as you would to shield the flame as you are lighting the cigarette. As you do this, bring the cigarette into the lips and as you pull the hands away a cigarette seems to appear between your lips.

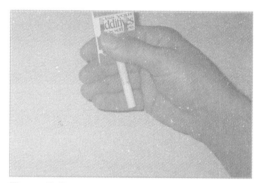
Figure 8.2

Two-Butt-Too

When you put the matches back into the pocket, pick up another cigarette and palm it in the hand between the second finger and palm the way you did for the cocktail sword in Chapter 7 **(Figure 7.2).** As you bring the hand up with the index and second finger open to nab the cigarette, the second finger loads the filter of the palmed cigarette into the mouth beside the first one **(Figure 8.3).** The fingers tighten on the

Figure 8.3

first cigarette and the lips tighten on the one just loaded in. Pulling your hand away makes it appear as though you have pulled one cigarette out of the other. Of course, the second butt isn't lit, but if you pull in a mouthful of smoke just before you do this, you can let it come out at that time.

Figure 8.4

Match This

Bet a spectator to pick up a pack of matches that is set against a pack of cigarettes as shown **(Figure 8.4).** The matches must be held between the index and third fingers while keeping the middle finger planted on the bar **(Figure 8.5).** the spectator just can't seem to do it now, can he?!

The secret is to bend the second finger down first, then put the tip of that finger on the bar just behind the cigarette pack. Lift the matches with the index and third fingers, pivot the hand back on the middle finger, and as you straighten, lock the joints of the middle finger. Pivot the hand back toward the cigarette pack and the matches can easily be lifted onto the edge **(Figure 8.6).** With practice, you can do this very quickly and even place the matchbook on its edge.

Figure 8.5

Tumblers
Shot Right Through

You can perform a version of the vanishing salt shaker with a shot glass too. If you have forgotten how, check Chapter 6, which discusses the effect, "You're Charged with a Salt."

Straws
Light Beer

Bet someone that you can lift a soda or beer bottle by touching it with just a single soda straw. To do this, you just have to bend the straw about two inches from one end. Push the bent part of the straw down into the neck of the bottle, continuing

Figure 8.6

with the rest of the straw until the bevel of the bottle's neck allows the end of the straw to fold downward. When the end is just about horizontal, stop and try to lift the straw back out. The straw will bind in the neck of the bottle and the entire bottle can be lifted **(Figure 8.7).** Bring the bottle back down, push the straw even further into the bottle, allowing it to straighten out, and the straw can be pulled out. Be sure not to ever lift the bottle too far, it can fall and that could mean trouble!

Souper Straw!

Take the very end of the paper rapping off of a straw and blow into the end of the straw. The paper "skin" will fly with amazing accuracy right into the hair, ear, or soup of someone at the bar. What the heck is somebody doing eating soup in a bar anyway?

Figure 8.7

Numbers
Roman Charge

Tell your spectator that you can prove half of 11 is six. When he disagrees, take six matches and form them into the Roman numeral "xi," which is 11. By taking the three top matches away (the top half), you are left with "vi," which is six.

Roman Around

Place 11 matches on the bar to form x + i = ix or, as we would read it 10+1=9. Bet that you can correct this roman equation in Roman numerals without moving or doing anything to any of the matches. The answer is to view it from the other side of the bar where it will read, xi = i + x or 11= 1+10.

Coins
Ear It Is(n't)

Tell a spectator you're going to make a coin disappear from your hand by using a magic wand. Turn so your left side is toward them, and place the coin in your outstretched left palm. Using a straw as a wand, dramatically wave the "wand" from beside your face down to the coin saying, "One" as the wand taps the coin. Raise the hand back up and down, saying, "Two." Now, raise it up again but this time hide the straw behind your ear and bring your empty hand down saying, "Three." Laugh, saying you were just kidding and turn your right side toward the spectator, so she can see the straw behind the ear. Now remove it. Meanwhile, pocket the coin and turn back around with the hand in the same pose but positioned high enough so the spectator can't see the palm. Do one more wave, saying, "Three" and the coin vanishes. This is misdirection at its finest; you can't beat that with a straw.

Two Hole Bits

Bet that you can push a quarter through a quarter-inch hole in a piece of paper. The taker will try every which way and fail. The secret is in the wording, "Push a quarter *through* a quarter-inch hole in a piece of paper." The answer is to take a straw, push it through the tiny hole in the paper, and then push the quarter with the straw (*through* the paper!).

Liquids
Liquid Hatsets

Bet the skeptic that he can buy you a shot, place it under a bar napkin, and that you can drink the shot without touching the napkin. Have him order (and pay for) the shot and cover it up. Take a soda straw and carefully place it under the edge of the

---

Servais LeRoy
(1865–1953)

Servais LeRoy was a magician from Belgium who first came to the United States in 1897 as part of a multiple person act. He eventually settled in the United States in 1918. LeRoy created a fantastic illusion known as the "Asrah" levitation. This illusion, originally called "Mystery of Lhassa," was a levitation where LeRoy's wife Talma was hypnotized and made to rise beneath a lightweight sheet. Eventually, the sheet was pulled away and Talma vanished in midair. Talma was a magician in her own right and was billed as "Talma, Queen of Coins." LeRoy also created the "Duck Tub," a version of the "Hindu Rope" and "The Duck Vanish." Servais LeRoy retired from magic in 1930 and died in 1953.

Figure 8.8

Figure 8.9

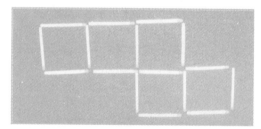

Figure 8.10

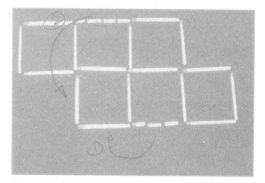

Figure 8.11

napkin. Use another napkin to cover the straw and lean down to make some slurping noises. When you are finished, toss the straw down and tell him you are finished. When he lifts the napkin to see, grab the shot and toss it down. You have drank the shot without touching the napkin all right.

Challenge Shot—An Anti-Heckler Device

Here's another kicker from magician and bartender Frank Zak. Bet a heckler that he is unable to follow a simple, follow the leader test. Of course, he will accept. Bet that if he loses, he pays for two shots. A shot of the challenger's favorite grog is put down for each player. A match is put down on both sides of these shots. Take the matches and move them one at a time and let "Mr. Thorn" do the same. Finally, pick up your shot, down it, and set the empty glass down on the bar. He will do the same. Now you spit your shot back into the glass and "oops," he just can't do it. You win. In fact, you win twice! Drink up.

Brain Teasers
Olive a Go at That!

Four matches are arranged to represent a martini glass with an olive (a piece of rolled-up napkin) as shown in **Figure 8.8**. The bet is to move two matches so that the martini glass is still intact but with the olive left outside of it. The answer is in **Figure 8.9**—the dotted lines are where the matches used to be.

What's the Five Four?

Sixteen matches are set up as shown **(Figure 8.10)**. This forms five squares of the same size. The bet is to move two matches and make four squares that are the same size. The answer is shown in **Figure 8.11**, with the dotted lines indicating where the moved matches started from and the arrows indicating where they are going.

Scams

Bob Farmer's "Scam to the Future"

Here's a scam courtesy of Bob Farmer, magician, lawyer, writer, guitar player, and a bigtime fan of the scam!

The Hook: I've written a prediction on this 20-dollar bill. Now, I'm either a fraud or a real psychic who can see the future. If you're right about me that 20 dollars is yours. I've also written a second prediction on this 50 dollar bill, but we'll come back to it in a minute.

The Bet: If you think the first prediction is right, then you think I'm psychic. If you think the first prediction is wrong, then you think I'm a fraud. So how do want to bet: *fraud* or *psychic.* If you're right, you win the 20 bucks; if you're wrong, you pay me 20 bucks.

The Outcome: You lose, I win.

The Secret: I write the following on a 20-dollar bill and fold it in half: "You will call me a fraud." Though this appears to be a 50/50 win or lose proposition, you will lose no matter which way you call it. If you say that I'm a fraud, you're saying the prediction will be wrong. But the prediction is right (since I predicted you would call me a fraud) and you're wrong, so you owe me 20 bucks. If you say I'm a psychic, then you're saying the prediction will be right. But the prediction is wrong (I predicted you'd say I was a fraud) and, therefore, you're wrong (so you pay me 20 bucks).

Here I remind you about the second prediction I made on the 50-dollar bill. If that prediction proves to be correct, you will pay me another 20 dollars. If it proves to be wrong, I will pay you 50 dollars. If you take the second bet, you will lose again. The prediction reads: "You will lose the first bet."

References: This is based on a version of "Brain Popper" by Martin Gardner, which appeared on page 577 of IBIDEM (Howard Lyons Publisher, March 1961). Martin's version was much more abstract and cerebral, and he didn't use a second prediction. Farmer's version is to write on *two* pieces of paper, "You are a fraud, your prediction is wrong," and "You are psychic, your prediction is right," and then having the spectator hand him either one to indicate his bet.

CHAPTER 9

*Parlor Magic—
the Audience
Grows*

Max Scott

"Magic really has been my life for such a long time and it still is today. I enjoyed helping Greg grow up in magic, and I still get a big kick out of helping people like my grandson Brian learn about the art that is such a big part of me. Magicians hold serious secrets, that's true, but they also hold a wonderful brotherhood and open their arms to anyone who shows a sincere interest in magic. I'm also very fortunate that my wife Edna enjoys magic so much too. We plan for magic conventions just like other people plan for vacations and they really are vacations for us. It's fantastic to rub shoulders with all of the greats, and I've made lifetime friends that I look forward to seeing over and over. Magic really does last forever."

Max Scott, Magician and my magic mentor

Parlor Magic, also known as drawing room magic, can be described as magic that is larger than Close-Up Magic, is usually performed on the same level as the audience, and is smaller in scale than Cabaret or Stage Magic. Imagine Parlor Magic being performed in the parlor or reception area of a home, with no special staging, no usual seating, and no required lighting. Parlor Magic is a collection of magic that bridges the gap between Close-Up and Stage Magic. For instance, Cabaret Magic leans much more toward the theatrical edge—utilizing more routines, characterization, music, lighting and accepted specialized stage properties—whereas Parlor Magic is often a little more intimate and not quite so grand in scale. Although Cabaret and Parlor Magic are often thought of as one in the same, I believe the two can be separated by performing the following test: If the magic is a little too "big" for the living room, it falls into the Cabaret or Platform Magic category, not the Parlor Magic one.

Silks

Dyeing the Silks

Here is an effect that can be performed for Parlor, Cabaret, or Stage Magic. This is a routine for dyeing one silk from red to yellow and back to red again. The magician says he will explain the trick to the audience and in the middle of doing so, he fools them again. It's a sucker ending that you'll be "dyeing" to perform.

Effect

The magician shows a red silk and his two empty hands. Making a fist, he pushes the red silk into one end of his hands and it comes out the other end as yellow. Showing the yellow silk and the two hands again, he reverses the process and the silk turns back to red.

Now the magician explains that the trick is really done with two silks and that he hides the yellow silk in a "surgically made hole" in his hand before he begins the trick. Sure enough, he reaches into the hand and produces the yellow silk. He goes on to demonstrate that when he pushes one silk in, the other comes out and appears to change color and that it's just an illusion. He also reminds the audience that during that time he can't open the hand, because if he does, it destroys the illusion. When he opens the hand to prove it, the silk has vanished which fools the audience even more.

Preparation

This effect uses a gimmick called the "dye-tube," which is commercially available through magic supplies retailers (see Appendix). You can also make up the gimmick yourself. I use this effect almost every time I appear in front of an audience. It's really worth the time to make up and learn. Here's how:

1. Cut a two-inch length of one-inch copper tubing. You can also use a copper fitting for plumbing that is already cut to the correct size.

2. You'll also need about six inches of flesh-colored satin ribbon. Don't use pink; it's too bright. If you have to, you can color white ribbon with permanent makeup to match your skin.

3. Using a hack saw, cut a slot into each side of the center of the tubing. This slot needs to be long enough for the ribbon to pass through (plus a little more to make your life easier).

4. Thread the ribbon through the tube and trim it so the ribbon ends stick out of each slot about $5/8$ of an inch and so there is a loop inside that will hang down with just a bit sticking out **(Figure 9.1).** Tape the ends of the ribbon down to the outside of the tube so it can't slip before the next step. One end gets taped up and the other gets taped down.

5. Wrap the entire outside of the tube tightly with one inch of flesh-colored, cloth, adhesive medical tape. Mine is Elastoplast, a brand made by Smith-Nephew, and is perfect.

6. You'll also need to purchase two silks. I use two 24-inch silks that have been cut on the diagonal and refinished on the edge. By cutting the silks diagonally they still hang from the corner to look large but they use up half the amount of space inside of the dye-tube.

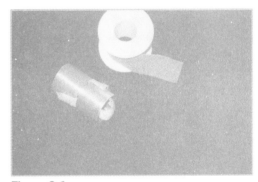

Figure 9.1

If you don't feel like making this is something you can do, feel free to order a dye-tube from me.

Setup

The tube is first loaded with the yellow silk, starting with the corner and leaving the opposite corner on top. Then put the red silk on top of it and load it the same way, as far as you can. Usually, about 5 inches of the red silk sticks out of the end.

Place the dye-tube into your right pocket and you are set. I like to iron all of my silks before a show but after you put them into a dye-tube they will definitely look like they need ironing again. I just make a joke out of it, there's not much you can do about it and at least they are both in the same wrinkled condition.

Routine:

1. Reach into the pocket and bring the dye-tube out in the following position. Your hand goes around it and gets into the finger palm position; however, the middle finger is pushing inside of the tube on top of the silk that is sticking out (the red one). The index finger and thumb are on each side of the silk. They don't really hold it; it's more like they guide it. The mobility of these two fingers further enhances the idea that the hand is empty. The middle finger pushes in, forcing the bottom of the dye-tube against the base of the thumb **(Figure 9.2).**

2. As soon as the silk is brought into view, the left hand grabs the tip of the silk and pulls it out of the tube to the left. You control the speed with the right thumb, the index finger, and the reduced tension of the middle finger. The misdirection caused by a waving silk takes the heat off of the right hand and its load.

3. Now comes the placement of the silk. The left hand whips back in front of the body to the right and back to the left again, causing the silk to fishtail. During this movement to the right, the index finger and thumb of the right hand open up wide so that when the silk comes back left, it can easily get in between them. Of course, the back of the right hand is to the audience and conceals the dye-tube. When the silk is between the finger and thumb, close them and allow the silk to glide between them and ride across the top of the third finger, which is still stuck down in the dye-tube **(Figure 9.3).** When the silk is pulled about half way out, the right thumb tightens against the index finger to stop and anchor the silk for the next important move.

Figure 9.2

4. This transfer move is probably the most difficult move in the entire routine. It gives the impression that both hands are empty by secretly transferring the tube from one hand to the other. Practice this slowly and speed up when you finally understand it. Let's break it down further:

    a. *Setup.* The left hand lets go of the silk (which is still in the hand from the previous step), and the open thumb and fingers come up underneath and get the silk into the crotch of the thumb. Again, the side of the thumb tightens against the index finger to stop and anchor the silk. The backs of both hands should be facing the audience and, under the cover of the hands, the transfer move happens.

    b. *Transfer.* The fingers of the right hand open up as to regrip the silk and, in the process, the third finger (which is inside of the tube) transfers the dye-tube into the palm of the left hand **(Figure 9.4).** Opening all of the right hand fingers together helps this movement. The fingers of the left hand close around the silk and the tube and hold it firmly. The silk should be against your left fingers, then the tube on top of that, followed by the squeezing left thumb.

Figure 9.3

    c. Showing the Hand. The right hand (still back toward the audience) now slides along the silk to the right and off of the silk, leaving it held by the left hand. To show that the right hand is empty, the palm of the right hand turns toward the audience when it reaches the end of the silk. The left hand is hiding the dye-tube with the silk held about halfway along its length.

5. The right hand now grabs the right-hand end of the silk, pulling it out and away from the left hand (and the dye-tube). To do this you have to loosen the grip on the left hand so that the silk slips between the dye-tube and the fingers of the left hand. Don't worry about the tube in the left hand. Your attention (and theirs) will be on the waving silk, and the misdirection doesn't have to last for long.

Figure 9.4

The right hand immediately brings the silk back to the left hand, and the left wrist turns so the back of the hand is facing up. The ribbon of the dye-tube should be right there waiting for you with the silk behind it. Of course, it's only visible to you because to the audience it just looks like you are holding a fist waiting for the silk to be pushed in. Start pushing the corner of the red silk into the top of the dye-tube, keeping the left third and pinkie fingers clenched tight so that the silk can't come out before it's time. Alternate pushing it in with the index and the third fingers of the right hand. When there is only about six inches of the red silk remaining to be pushed in, release the pressure of the left third and pinkie fingers. The yellow silk should pop out or, at least, be seen. Turn the left hand over (counterclockwise and fingers up) and pull some of the yellow silk out. Turn it back over and continue poking the red silk in, but holding the left bottom fingers tight so the yellow silk doesn't just fall out. When the red silk is all the way in the tube, turn your body so the back of the right hand is toward the audience and turn the left-hand thumb up, so you are poking the red silk into the top of the tube (they see it as your fist). Now for the last tricky move.

6. The steal is probably the most brazen move in the entire routine, and it allows you to show the entire yellow silk (the red silk dyed to yellow that is) and that the left hand is empty. But how can you show the left hand as empty if it's holding the dye-tube? Easy, you take it out!

After poking the red silk into the top of the dye-tube with your right hand, the back of the hand is to the audience. On your last poke, you bring the thumb of the right hand in and pinch the edge of the dye-tube against the second finger, which is inside of the tube holding the red silk down. On the upstroke of the final poke, you just pull the whole tube up and out **(Figure 9.5).** The back of the hand hides the tube and the left hand raises the silk into the air to display it. This steal often also pulls the other end of the yellow silk out of the top of the hand when the dye-tube leaves—good bonus! Your attention toward the left and the moving yellow silk causes needed misdirection. The audience figures that the red silk must still be in the left hand.

Figure 9.5

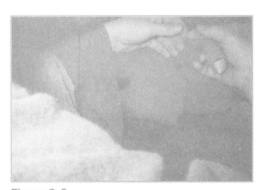

Figure 9.6

On its way back down, from it's final upswing, the right hand grabs the bottom corner of the yellow silk and, with the open index finger and thumb, it latches onto it and pulls it out of the left fist. With your attention toward the closed left fist and your right hand dropping to the side, you now open your left hand. Wow!

You have just dyed a silk from red to yellow in your bare hands! Now, you want to turn it back to red.

7. Bring the right hand up, whip the yellow silk to the left, grab the end of it, and you are back in the same position (but with the opposite color) that you were in the beginning.

8. Repeat Steps 3, 4, 5, and 6, which will place the silk, transfer the tube, dye the silk back to red, and allow you steal the tube away again.

9. Now, here's the sucker setup. You need to get the tube back into the left hand again so you can tip the trick by admitting to the use of two silks as a setup to explaining how this trick works (fake as the explanation will be). Repeat Steps 3 and 4 to get it back to where you need to be.

While explaining that the trick uses two silks, you reach into the bottom of the dye-tube and pull the yellow silk straight out to the right, about halfway. Turning your left wrist so it is thumb up, perform the steal (Step 6), and some of the yellow silk should pop out of the top while you are pulling the dye-tube away. This time, instead of grabbing the corner of one silk as the right hand comes back down, you grab both of the silks and with the same hand, point with the index finger into the middle of the left palm to show that there is a "surgically made" hole in your hand!

Now, take the right hand (dye-tube still held) and flip both of the silks over the left arm like a wine steward holds his towel **(Figure 9.6).** With the right hand, take the yellow silk off of the inside of the arm, whip it to the right, and back into the left hand. Perform Step 3 and 4 so that you have the dye-tube and the yellow silk held in the left hand.

Perform Step 5, but this time there is no silk in the dye-tube. You are simply loading it in so you can steal it away neatly for the finale. At the same time, you are also explaining how you keep one

silk hidden inside of the "surgically made" hole before the show starts so that when you place the red silk on top of it and push it through, it appears to change color.

Once you have the silk loaded in, you tell the audience, "After placing the yellow silk *into the hand,* before placing *the red silk* on top, the only thing you have to remember is to never open that hand."

When you say the words "into the hand," you make the steal (as in Step 6) and the right hand drops down to grab the end of the red silk. By the time you get to the words "the red silk," you should be taking the red silk off of the arm and just dropping it to the side. Everyone's attention is of course on the left hand.

10. Now for the sucker ending. The left hand (with the yellow silk?) is left in a high position as you say, "If you do that, it *does* ruin the trick." As you accept your applause, place the red silk and the loaded dye-tube into your right pocket.

Ropes

You need all the help you can get when you start learning rope effects, so do yourself a favor and get some decent rope. Ropes are sold by magic suppliers (see Appendix) who can tell you what's best for your needs. Magic rope is generally woven, very soft, and has a core that can be removed to make things easier if you need to use it as a gimmick or do other sneaky things to it. I have used an off-white cotton rope for a long time but some of the pros have changed to a very white "super rope." Although it's easier to see on stage, I don't like it for everything. I like it for special uses, such as for stage effects where the rope doesn't really need to be supple but does need to be visible. Try both types and you'll soon discover which type is good for what. I also usually wash the rope before using it. This takes the stiffness out of the rope and eliminates shrinkage if they are washed again after they are cut to the correct lengths.

Treat the ends of your ropes with white glue, tape, or thread to prevent ropes from fraying too much. I use bright red vinyl tape most of the time, because it clearly marks the end of the ropes for you and your audience. The tape also adds a measure of physical misdirection and is useful when you don't want to attract attention to parts of the rope, especially if the rope has been gimmicked. Some effects will demand that the ends come together and be grasped and covered with your fingers to appear as one piece. In these cases, the glue or other invisible means are the only option. Also, consider the fact that a piece of rope that has been taped is no longer an unprepared or innocent piece of rope. A couple of times my red taped ends have become suspect and people have asked, "Hey, what's up with the red tape?" I explain that it keeps the rope from fraying, that's all.

To Knot . . . or Not Two Knots

Here's a cool little piece of magic that is fun to fool people with and is easy to learn. It also is easy for an audience to follow. Adding some fun patter is also a possibility.

Effect

The magician begins to form a simple single knot in a length of rope but when he separates his hands, the knot dissolves. The magician repeats the process, but this time a knot is formed. The magician can form a knot . . . or not . . . anytime it is desired.

Preparation

Get yourself some magician's rope from one of the suppliers listed in the Appendix. Don't do rope tricks with regular, hardware store rope—it's just not made for magic. Magician's rope is soft, easier to cut, and shows up well on stage.

Setup

You don't have to set up anything. Just have a piece of magician's rope about 3 feet long, memorize the following positions and moves, and you are in business.

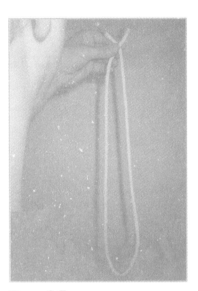

Figure 9.7

Figure 9.8

Routine

1. Start with the ends of the rope in each hand pointing toward the sky. Leave about 3 inches of rope sticking up out of the fingers. Grip the ends as if holding the stems of two wineglasses. Don't hold the ropes like you are holding two beer bottles. The rope should now look like a letter "U," the end of a water ski, or a horseshoe for a horse with really long hooves **(Figure 9.7).** Move the right hand and rope to the left and place it *under* the left rope. Hold the right rope securely against the left rope with the fingers of the left hand where the two cross each other, forming an "X." The right hand is free to move toward the bottom of the loop. Pull the loop down and diagonally to the right, with your right fingers inside of the loop pointing toward yourself. Now, straighten things out a little.

Raise your right hand up and place the bottom loop (fingers pointing to the left) over the end of the rope that is on top and pointing toward the right. The loop will be hanging over your finger, your thumb, and the "X" formed by the ropes. Leave it there **(Figure 9.8).** Grasp the end you just placed the loop over and pull your hands apart. It will appear as though a knot is about to form, but it won't knot. You'll have nothing. Sometimes in magic, learning to look like you are doing nothing is the hardest part.

2. Now that you have learned how to manipulate your rope and do nothing, let me show you how simple it is to do *something*. Start again as shown in **Figure 9.7** but this time place the right rope *over* the left rope. Everything else is exactly the same except that the left rope will now be on the bottom and the outcome actually produces something. This time when you pull your hands apart, you will have a single knot in the center of the rope.

If you need a little help in remembering all of this, try saying this little memory code to yourself: "The KNOT . . . is

RIGHT . . . OVER there." To make the knot, the right rope is placed over the left rope.

3. Here's a variation that allows you to change the final outcome (knot or nothing) no matter what your initial starting position is. This means you can start out with "The KNOT . . . is RIGHT . . . OVER there" setup to create a knot and change it so that *no* knot will be produced. In reverse, you can start with the right rope under as the setup to create nothing and change it so a knot *will* be produced.

The secret to this change-up happens later on in the game than the previously explained over or under positioning of the rope ends. It's a great alternative or "way out" for a routine. For clarity, let's start as if we are positioned to make a knot (right end over left end). If you lift the right hand and loop up in the usual manner, the expected thing will happen—you'll get a knot. Here's the subtle difference that allows you to reverse the outcome. Instead of simply placing the bottom loop over the end of the rope that is pointing right, the loop needs to make a 180-degree twist inward. This is done secretly. **Figure 9.9** shows a different hand position that will take care of this, but I think a change in hand positioning is an obvious tipoff to an audience. Once you understand exactly what has to happen, try it another way. As you are explaining what will happen, turn the loop with your fingers. Immediately return to your original hand position to hold the loop (right fingers inside of the loop pointing toward yourself). Of course, when you pull your hands apart, the opposite of the "usual" will happen—you will have nothing.

To produce a knot from a *"nothing"* setup, begin as in Step 1 and add the Step 3 change-up. When you pull your hands apart, the opposite of the "usual" will happen—this time it will be a knot.

Figure 9.9

CHAPTER 10

Stage Magic

Figure 10.1

Card Manipulations—
An Introduction to Card
Handling by the King of Cards

Although Jeff McBride is a well-known stage magician, he also possesses proficiency in Close-Up Magic. He generously helped me with his insights and expertise with card handlings that you can use either on stage or for your close-up. It's sort of a double bonus! Contact Jeff at *www.mcbridemagic.com* or by calling Tobias Beckwith, manager, at (702) 697-7002.

Charlier Cut or One-Hand Cut

I use this in my close-up routine and also for an onstage flourish. Hold the deck at the sides by your fingertips and thumb (I use my left hand). The thumb is positioned at the side of the deck very high up, not low, or else you're not going to get much clearance. Now, I bend my thumb slightly toward the fingertips and let about half of the deck fall onto my palm **(Figure 10.1).** Then, just my index finger pushes the outer edge of the deck (of the bottom deck) back up so that it glides along the bottom of the cards of the top deck. The bottom deck is now moving toward the thumb **(Figure 10.2).** Continue until the bottom deck slides under the top deck and lets the top deck fall. Then, I clear my finger and let the bottom deck fall in the other direction on top.

Figure 10.2

The Thumb Fan

Almost everyday of my life I walk up to a group of people and say, "Would you please select a card out of the center of the pack?" I have found that a thumb fan is a much more attractive way of presenting cards to a spectator for selecting a card than just pushing the cards forward. The way I make my thumb fan is to start with the deck held vertically in one hand, facing the audience. The back of the deck rests against the first, second, and third fingers, with the bottom of the cards just

Figure 10.3

above the pinkie **(Figure 10.3).** The side of the thumb pushes into the face of the deck about ½ inch from the bottom, creating a pivot point for the fan. Now, the opposite thumb will bevel the cards and push them in a circle. This makes the fan.

While maintaining the grip, bring the opposite hand across the face of the deck and with the thumb, bevel the inside edge of the deck (the inside edge being the edge closest to the web of the thumb). Bevel the cards in the direction and angle that the thumb naturally follows **(Figure 10.4).**

Move the thumb in a circular motion following in the arc created by the anchored thumb, and the cards will fan out **(Figure 10.5).**

Figure 10.4

Closing the Fan

To close the fan, I create a pivot spot with my middle finger by moving it down, pushing the cards and then pulling them around with the other fingers.

Begin with the cards held in a fan in one hand. Move the middle finger down so it's about even with the first joint of the other fingers and create a pivot point by pushing the middle finger tip into the cards **(Figure 10.6, rear/upstage view).** Now, the index finger pushes the back of the fan up to the other fingers and they pull the cards down until the fan is shut.

Figure 10.5

Springing the Cards

We've seen it in all of those gambling sequences in the movies and it's something that no card manipulation sequence is complete without: springing the cards from the tips of your fingers. Other magicians prefer springing the cards off of the thumb. I'll tell you my method.

I hold the cards by their ends at the extreme tips of my right fingers. The thumb curls around the back. The cards are bent inward creating bevels in each end. My left hand creates a sort of "catcher's mitt." The cards are gradually released from

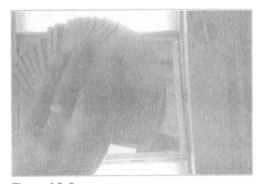

Figure 10.6

Figure 10.7

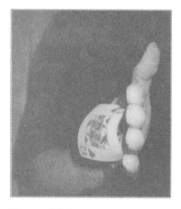

Figure 10.8
"Off stage right" view

Figure 10.9

the left hand toward that mitt. When you start, start small, not too far apart. Just let the cards off one at a time. Try to get it smooth and even. Try not to get chunks of cards sporadically. By just practicing and releasing the pressure, moving the fingers back, you'll get the hang of it. After you get the basic move, you can build up your distance and your speed **(Figure 10.7).**

Back Palm Productions

Now it's time for back palming. We learned some fans, flourishes, and springing, now it's time for back palm production. Back palming starts with the card on the back of the *hand* (though it's called back *palm*). It's done by clipping the card between the index finger and the pinkie. One corner of the card is clipped between the index and second fingers and the other corner is clipped between the pinkie and third fingers. The middle finger and the ring finger hold the card just like in the offstage illustration. **(Figure 10.8, offstage right view).** The corners of the card may peek out the front from between the fingers, but you don't want too much of the card showing, so bring it back a little bit, away from the finger tips.

To bring the card into view, bend your fingers inward and the card comes against the middle finger; the thumb grabs the card and the rest of the fingers release so it's held just between the thumb and the middle finger **(Figure 10.9).** To make the card vanish, we just reverse the procedure, bringing the pinkie underneath, the index finger on top reclips the card, and the fingers are straightened while making the motion of throwing the card up into the air. Learning this is your first step on your way to producing many, many cards.

The Roy Benson Move

The hands are shown empty, very cleanly, and the card is produced. With this, you don't have to do a whole lot of gyrations because the movement of the hands gives the impression to the spectator that you're showing both sides of your hands. Again, the card is clipped in the back palm without the edges showing. The hands hinge at the blades **(Figure 10.10),** they shut, and now they hinge at the thumbs **(Figure 10.11).** With perhaps one more time down, you produce the card the same way you did in the back palm production. You reach up and you produce the card and then you bring your fingers back to the position in **Figure 10.12.**

The card stays in one place when the hand swings down. The hands come together and now they hinge up on the thumbs. There are a few methods for producing the card. You can produce it just like in the back palm production, by pulling it up with your thumb and then getting your hands back into position very quickly. Another method, which is a little bit easier for beginners, is to simply bend your fingers in and push the card out straight. It looks very nice if your thumbs don't do a whole lot of moving around during this production.

For the more advanced who have mastered the other two ways of doing it, you can try to produce the card at the finger-tips, straight up and down. This is done by crossing the fingers, much like you would to say good luck, and it is done very fast. When I produce the card, whether it be in the Roy Benson move or just pulling it out of the air, I always give the impression to the audience that there's a pocket in the air. This is my inner dialogue—that I'm reaching into an invisible pocket in the air and pulling that card out so that it doesn't give the impression that the card is just springing off the back of my hand. And that pull creates the illusion that the card is coming out of the air. Oh, and one more thing. This is a great way to present your business card. Again, be very careful of your angles. At a social gathering, when you are just about to meet someone say, "Wait I have something for you . . . my card." It's just a nice little touch to use when making a business connection.

Figure 10.10

Figure 10.11

Figure 10.12

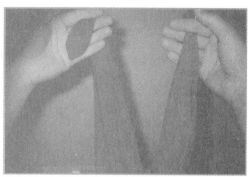

Figure 10.13

Figure 10.14

Silk Effects

Here are a couple of effects for silk magic that work very well for Cabaret or Stage Magic.

The Speed Knot

With the left hand palm facing toward you, clip one end of the silk between the second joints of the index and second fingers with the silk coming from the back (that is, through the fingers into the palm side). The other end is clipped between the same fingers of the right hand, but the silk is coming from the front. Allow about two inches of the tips of the silk to stick outside of the fingers. If you have a hard time remembering which way the silk goes in each hand, try saying, "I'll be *right outside.*" This is where the right-hand silk goes—*outside* of the hand. The other is just the opposite with the silk inside of the hand **(Figure 10.13).**

With the index and second fingers held together holding the silks, open the other fingers and bring the right hand behind the left hand (closest to you). The back of the right hand will slide against the fingers of the left hand. You will be trying to clip the opposite ends between the second and third fingers of the hands.

Place the right hand silk between the second and third fingers of the left hand and visa versa. It will help you align correctly if you think primarily about placing the end of the right-hand silk into the opening between the second and third fingers of the left hand **(Figure 10.14).** If you think about making sure the right-hand fingers grab the left-hand silk, the right-hand end will be too far up. Think about giving, not getting.

Once you are there, clip the ends of the silks between the second and third fingers of both hands and release the holds in the first and second fingers. Now, pull your hands apart again and the silk will tie into a single knot. This is a very professional and attractive way to tie a knot in any silk.

Dissolving Knot

Start out by holding a silk in each hand between the thumb and the first and second fingers with about three inches of the silk tips above the fingers. Bring the silks together and cross them to form an "X" with the right-hand silk closest to the audience and the left-hand silk closest to you. The fingers of the left hand will rest against the right hand's thumb. The third and forth fingers of both hands will wrap around the silks below. Now, release the holds with the fingers and thumbs and regrip the opposite ends of the silks, keeping the third and forth fingers below, gripping firmly.

Then, you pretend to tie a knot in the silks by turning your wrists, and when the silk tips are pointing toward you or better yet, pointing slightly downward, you again switch the ends so one silk wraps around the other. If they don't wrap around each other, you did it backward. The right hand needs to go around front. There's one knot tied (well, that's what it looks like to the audience). The silks will actually be as shown in **(Figure 10.15).**

Now, you simply tie a regular knot on top of that and pull the knot tight, still maintaining the hold with the third and forth fingers below. Try to duplicate the rotation of the wrists for the real knot just like you did with the fake one. Keep things consistent and nobody will know you're trying to pull the silk over their eyes. When pulling the knots tight, it looks like you are tightening the knot but you are really just doing a little tug of war between the two hands. If you let go of any fingers, the knots will fall apart.

You can now hold the two silks by one end and the other will remain "knotted," If you don't pull on it or move it too fast, it will hold. You can drape the silks somewhere or dangle them into a clear glass and when you are ready for the magic to happen, just pull them out with a little tug and they melt apart. If you do it just right, they'll even seem to separate in midair and you can expertly catch one in each hand. Now that's pretty!

Figure 10.15

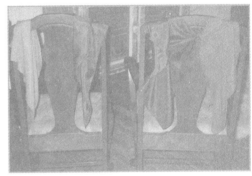

Figure 10.16

Jeff McBride

Jeff McBride has received countless awards celebrating his innovative fusion of mask, myth, drama, and illusion, including the prestigious French award, "The Golden Mandrake," the "Best Stage Magician" at the International Magic Awards, the "Grand Prix Magiques de Monte Carlo," the "Magician of the Year" by *both* the Magic Castle and the Society of American Magicians, and the International Brotherhood of Magicians' "Star of Magic." Jeff combines a lifelong study of the multicultural roots of magic with his sheer artistry and masterful manipulations to create a magical and mystical experience. Jeff also shares his knowledge through lectures, workshops, and personal instruction.

Variation

As a variation, you might try to perform a variation of the "sympathetic silks" with the silks lying as shown over the backs of two chairs **(Figure 10.16).** The chairs should be as far apart as possible. The knots on the set of silks on the right are covered by the center back support. From the front they appear to be two silks side by side just like the silks on the left. Perform the dissolving knot with the silks on the left and put them into a tumbler while they are still "tied." Simply take the two seemingly separate silks on the right and put them in another tumbler on the other side of the stage. At your command, the silks that were untied are now seen to be firmly tied, and the silks that were tied are separate.

Balls, for Stage

The use of balls for stage performance is very popular. Balls show up well on stage, and the most commonly used colors are red and white because they read best of all.

The Props

The main props for ball manipulation for stage are logically the balls themselves. You can use any type of balls, really, but I recommend that if you are truly interested in this area of magic, you go out and purchase a professionally made set of billiard balls from a magic dealer. These offer a gimmicked solution to many different types of performance, such as multiplication of balls. Since we won't be able to cover everything in this book, I will touch on that only briefly at the end of this section. Billiard balls also offer a variety of colors and finishes, which helps them be visible and gripped easily.

Palming

The palming of a ball we discussed in Chapter 5 for Close-Up Magic, and the Cups and Balls routines are good preparation for what you'll need onstage. The finger palm and the classic palm are the two favorites and they will be performed onstage in much the same way as in Close-Up Magic, except that the balls for Stage Magic are generally larger in size. Larger balls for Close-Up Magic are usually only seen during finale sequences. Also, larger balls, oddly enough, are sometimes easier to palm than the smaller ones.

Vanishing

Here are a few ways to make a billiard ball vanish and appear again.

Finger Palm Vanish

Begin holding the ball in the fingers of one hand with the palm face up and your thumb pointing toward the audience. You are trying to give the illusion that you are placing the ball into the opposite hand.

Bring the hand across the chest toward the other hand, which will also be palm up but with the fingers pointing toward the audience. You can slightly clip the ball between the index and pinkie fingers during its travel so that the ball doesn't roll or drop. When the ball reaches its destination, turn the hand toward you (thumb up) so the ball comes down on the opposite hand.

Begin to curl the fingers of the receiving hand upward (as if to take the ball) and, at the same time, curl the second, third, and pinkie fingers of the hand with the ball into the palm. Make sure the hand that is supposed to be receiving the ball closes as if it has a ball in it. Trying to "overclose" the hand by bending the fingers in to the base of the thumb is much better looking than closing it as if making a fist. It should look as if there is something as large as that ball inside of it. As the fingers of the opposite hand continue to close, pull the finger-palmed ball away, leaving the index finger pointing toward the "ball in the hand" **(Figure 10.17).**

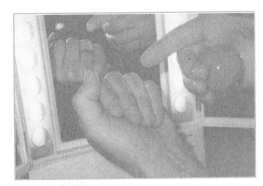

Figure 10.17

You can drop the finger-palmed ball and hand down to the side with the back of the hand toward the audience, or you can use the three palming fingers to roll the ball into the classic palm position. The classic palm will give you better mobility and fewer problems with sight lines. The hand that is supposed to have the ball can perform a flourish to vanish the ball, such as blowing on the hand or wriggling the fingers until the hand is finally opened to show the ball gone.

Figure 10.18

Reappearance

To make the ball reappear, simply reach behind the knee, under the arm, or anywhere with the ball still concealed. Bring the palmed ball out of the palm, into the fingertips, and visibly display it.

Classic Palm Vanish (Top Position Placement)

This type of vanish uses the classic palm. It contains many of the moves of the finger palm vanish, but the ball starts out in a different position and is moved into the classic palm during the move. This means the hand can immediately drop to the side after the ball is "placed into the hand."

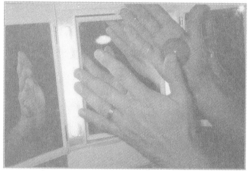

Figure 10.19

Begin holding the ball on one hand as in **Figure 10.18.** With the back of the hand toward the audience, the tip of your index finger is placed into the first joint of your thumb, forming a circle. The fingers below follow the curve of the index finger. The ball rests on top.

The hand moves to place the ball into the opposite hand, which is palm up with the fingers toward the audience. When the base of the hand with the ball is just about to touch the open hand, it quickly opens, closes, and opens again. This lets the ball drop (open), pushes it into the classic palm (closed), and opens again (classic palm with hand appearing empty). This happens fast and it sounds tougher than it is. You just have to slow it down, look at the steps, and then speed them up to real time. Now, the fingers of the receiving hand begin to curl upward (as if to take the ball), and the hand with the palmed ball drops away and to the side.

Another of the many options for the vanish might be to let the palming hand drop only about one foot below the hand that apparently has the ball in it. Turn your body to that side, and with an upward tossing motion, open the hand. The ball in the classic palm can be opened as well and it will appear as though the ball vanishes in midair **(Figure 10.19).**

French Drop Vanish

We learned the French drop with coins in Chapter 4, and it will also work with a larger object such as a billiard ball. The ball will drop down as usual and go into the classic palm position.

Doves

Doves can be a beautiful addition to any magic act, but first consider the commitment to these animals and what you will need to keep them as healthy business partners. Consider these factors:

- Cages
- Foods, grits, and minerals
- Knowledge of illnesses and cures
- Knowledge of grooming and clipping
- Care of the doves when you are away
- Problems with neighbors due to the noise (yes, they coo)
- Loss of the animals from sickness, cats, or dogs
- The time to tame or train them

EZ Doves It

Learning to "produce" a dove like Channing Pollack or Lance Burton takes quite a while as well as some very special equipment. If you like the idea of working with livestock (doves in particular), here is a simple dove production that can be used with

Did You Know?

Eliaser Bamberg, Holland's court magician and great-great grandfather of Theo Bamberg, was known as a great magician who performed seemingly impossible miracles. The truth was that he had lost a leg in a war and had his artificial limb fitted with secret compartments, allowing him to perform amazing magic effects.

one of the illusions described in Chapter 12. Purchase a 24-inch silk, set a dove diagonally on the center of the silk, and wrap the side of the silk up and around the dove. Mark the position of the silk where the two halves would come together to hold the dove like a tube. The rest of the ends of the silk would go beyond those marks. Now you need some loop fasteners the same color of the silk. Place them at three intervals along each part of the silk where you have marked it for size so that when it is closed it holds the dove. It looks like the dove is in sort of a sling. The dove can easily breathe and the harness is very soft and will not harm the bird in any way. This is your dove harness. When you are ready to produce the dove, reach into your container and produce a couple of silks, showing them freely. Place them in the palm-up hand and reach into the container with the other hand to get another silk. This time you pull out the silk with the dove harnessed in it. Obviously, you won't wave this one around. Simply drape it on top of the other silks and, without pause or attention, reach back in to get the last silk. Move away from the production prop, waving the final silk, and put it on top of the harness. To the audience you simply have four silks. Bring the silks together, move the final silk to the front, and the three closures will be pointing at you. Rip open the three fasteners by peeling the silk off each side of the dove and then thrust the dove forward. The movement will cause it to flap its wings and you have produced a beautiful, live dove.

CHAPTER 11

Comedy Magic—
Hocus Yukus

The Amazing Johnathan

The Amazing Johnathan, dubbed "The Freddy Kreuger of Comedy," is fast becoming known as one of the most original and bizarre magic acts today. Tricks like "The Knife Through the Arm" are his takeoff on more traditional illusions, such as sawing a woman in half. He's instantly recognizable, with black headband and outrageous lounge-lizard clothing. He's been on a record number of appearances on Fox's *Comic Strip Live, Showtime, Late Night with David Letterman,* and *Comedy Central*. His home is Los Angeles half the year and Australia the other half, where he is one the country's biggest comedy stars.

If you are one of those people who are seen as wacky, nutty, madcap, and downright hysterical, Comedy Magic may be for you. If you've ever purchased a whoopee cushion, a joy buzzer, cigarette loads, or pepper gum, all the more reason to consider Comedy Magic. I don't know if there is anyone who doesn't like to laugh. Laughing is fun, it's good for us, and when mixed with magic, it is the best medicine!

Gag Magic
Watch This!
Effect

The magician shows a large cloth on both sides and says, "Watch!" His hand goes underneath the cloth and some long, pointed object is seen underneath. When he pulls away the handkerchief, the spectator sees just his pointed index finger.

He puts his hand beneath the cloth again and says, "Watch, Watch!" This time, he pulls away the cloth and his arm is held up with the other index finger pointing toward his watch as he says, "Watch."

Preparation

All you need is a cloth and to be wearing a watch. The cloth can be a napkin, a rag, towel, or anything that's handy and that you can see the finger through.

Setup

No setup is required.

Routine

The routine is the same as the effect. The first time you go under the cloth, you stick up your finger and pull the cloth off to the side sliding over top of the finger. Don't worry, nobody cares about your watch yet, even if they see it. They don't know what you are going to do. The next time you go under the cloth, you make a fist with your watch turned toward the audience. You really whip the cloth off, immediately pointing at the side of the watch face saying, "Watch."

A Paper Thin "Rowlecks"

Effect

As a gag, show the beautiful watch you just bought while you were on vacation in the islands. You unstrap the watch and tell the audience that it isn't a real watch, it's just one that you cut out from one of those pretty brochures they had. You drop the watch and it flutters to the ground. It is obviously paper.

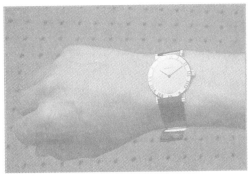

Figure 11.1

Preparation

Get some high-quality watch brochures. I started doing this on cruise ships where we were going to ports that sold expensive jewelry and a lot of high-end watches. The brochures all had thick, glossy paper stock with pictures of watches in their actual size. Some of these brochures are even created with a process where they add metallic ink as a spot color in the printing. These look amazingly realistic. Cut those out and you got your self a "Rolex!"

Cut the watches out carefully and fold the band sides where they meet the watch casing, just to give it some dimension. For a closure, cut a piece of black electrical tape to fasten between the two sides of the band and don't pull it too tight. You want the watch to have some looseness and some dimension. Double a piece of tape on itself for a courtesy tab so you have an end to grab when you want to get it off **(Figure 11.1).**

Setup

Put the cut-out watch on your wrist as you would a normal watch. I have actually done entire shows and forgot that it wasn't a real watch. I guess that also explains my show going 15 hours too long. I thought it seemed like I had been up there a long time!

Routine

Treat the watch the same way you would a real watch. Turn your arm to look at the time, polish it with the sleeve of the other arm, listen to it tick, make it *seem* real. It already *looks* real. When you drop the watch, the weight of the electrical tape will pull one end down and the rest of the watch will flutter like a maple leaf.

The Playing Card

When you start a card routine, explain that the cards are playing cards. Pick up one card and blow in it and it plays music. This is done by palming a miniature harmonica and holding it under the edge of the card. The card is tilted toward the audience so they can't see it. Steal the harmonica away and continue on with your trick. These tiny harmonicas can be purchased from novelty shops, music stores, or one of the suppliers listed in the Appendix at the back of this book.

Handy Wipes

Effect

The magician has someone from the audience up to help him but says that before he begins, he wants the person to wipe his hands on a clean towel, which he holds up to the crowd, showing both sides. The person does this, and when the magician turns the towel back around, it is seen to be covered with greasy hand stains.

Preparation

You need to make up a gimmicked towel. For clarity, let's assume that the towel is a rectangle and that we hold it by the corners of the shorter side, which we will call the top.

Purchase two linen hand towels, preferably with a checkered pattern. Cut one towel in half and sew a seam in the bottom half that runs horizontally along the center of the whole towel, creating a flap panel. Actually, sew it about $1/8$ inch below the center, so the flap end hangs slightly off of the towel.

Now, paint your palms with some black latex paint and place your hands on top of that folded-down panel. You can also go to a craft store and buy black fabric paint, which is water-based but can be set with an iron. With one hand, start with the fingertips down and drag them to make streaks, finally placing the entire palm down. This will make it appear as though whatever the black stuff is, perhaps grease, it was slippery. Be careful not to let too much paint soak through the cloth or it will be ruined. The audience shouldn't be able to see any darkness on the other side. Let the paint dry thoroughly.

If you then flip the painted flap up, it will be ⅛" shorter than the regular, hemmed top edge of the towel **(Figure 11.2).** This allows you to control the flap with your thumb and fingers. Iron this seam down so it lies flat. It will still have tension on it because it flips over on itself, but this stiffness helps the flap fall downward when it is time. Again, if you don't feel as though you can complete this yourself, you can purchase one.

Figure 11.2

Setup

Place the towel on your table until your are ready to use it. Fold it so you can get to the control corners without looking for them. I do this by holding the towel with the flap up (no hand-prints showing) and folding it in half side to side and toward me.

I then fold the towel in half lengthwise and fold it in half again. Now the action corners are on top and you can fold back the top two layers so that the corner is separate from the other two layered corners. If you grab these two corners to lift the towel, it will unfold correctly with the flap toward you.

Routine

Simply pick up the towel when you want to use it as previously described. Show both sides of the towel by crossing your hands. Have the spectator wipe his hands on the towel from the front but to the side a little so the audience can see him. Look at the spectator and say something like, "You know, this is kind of embarrassing . . . I had no idea or I would have never asked you." Move thumbs up and let the panel drop. Look at the audience and turn the towel around by crossing the hands again **(Figure 11.3).** "Gee, your hands were a little dusty!"

Figure 11.3

Sucker Tricks
The Sting
Effect

This is a sucker trick that I first heard of as "Stung, Stung Again." It can be tailored to fit any application and therefore you can make it fit well with your Comedy Magic.

Three cards and an empty pail are shown to the audience. The cards are orange, green, and purple, and the magician asks the spectator to remember all three colors. The cards are placed into the hat. The magician pulls the purple card out, followed by the green card, and now he asks the spectator which card is left. He answers that the orange card is left. The magician reaches into the hat and pulls out a white card with the word "sorry" written on it. He also holds up the cup to show that it's empty. The spectator knows that the orange color must be on the other side so he asks the magician to flip it over. The magician flips the card over by turning it upside down. The spectator asks him to turn it around. The magician holds the card and turns his whole body around. Finally, the card is turned over and the other side of "sorry" says "really sorry." The spectator has been suckered.

Preparation

You'll obviously need to make up some special cards. Get four colors of poster board—orange, green, purple, and white.

Cut four cards out to whatever size you want. If you want to use this for Stage Magic, you can make larger cards or use a larger container.

The purple card is not gimmicked. About one third of the orange card has been cut off and glued onto the face of the green card. The white card has the words "sorry" and "really sorry" printed on it.

You'll also need some kind of container to put the cards in.

Setup

The cards are held vertically in one hand with the purple card on the face and the orange part of the green card showing next, followed by the green card, which of course is attached to the orange piece.

The white card with the words printed on it is hiding horizontally across the backs of these cards **(Figure 11.4)**.

The pail is set to the side on a table.

Figure 11.4

Routine

1. Begin by showing the three cards and the empty pail. Place all of them into the pail and pull out the purple card. You can casually flip it as you put it in the pocket so that the audience sees both sides. Now reach in and pull out the green card (with the orange strip on the back) but don't flip it over. The audience will assume it is normal, just like the purple card.

2. Now all you have left to do is ask a spectator which card is left and he will answer that it's the orange card. Pull out the white card showing the word "sorry," and show the empty pail.

3. He will ask you to turn the card over. Turn it over end to end.

4. He will ask you to turn it around. Turn your whole body around covering the backside with your front.

5. He might say, "The other way." Just turn your whole body around in the opposite direction.

6. When it's time (just as he picks up something to throw at you), turn the white card over and show the words "really sorry."

Clown Magic
Nutty Gloves

Make up a set of gag gloves by purchasing a pair of white cotton gloves and leaving one untouched. With the other, make a tube out of white cotton and sew it to the cuff of the glove, making a very long glove. The tube should be about six feet long. Wearing a jacket, put both gloves on and put the excess tube under one sleeve. During the beginning of your magic, carefully and majestically take the first glove off, finger by finger, and then pull the glove the rest of the way off. Place it into your hat. Do the same with

the other glove but when you start to pull, the glove will become longer and longer and longer. This is a very funny piece of slapstick and is perfect for clowning.

Squirting Ketchup Bottle

Purchase a flexible plastic ketchup bottle and cut the top to receive a piece of red cord. Don't allow too much space between the cord and the inside diameter of the tip. Tie a knot on the cord inside the bottle and one on the cord outside of the bottle. Thread the majority of the cord into the bottle and twist the top on.

Now, if you aim the bottle and quickly squeeze the sides, the cord will squirt out as if it were ketchup. This creates quite a surprise! Make sure not to frighten anyone with it so they jump back and hit something or someone!

Flower/Stem

Purchase an artificial flower and cut the stem about four inches from the bud of the flower. When handing the flower to someone, hold the separation between your thumb and fingers. Offer the bottom of the stem to your helper and when she gets it, walk away, sniffing the flower and leaving her with the stem.

Creating Comedy Magic

If you are up to it, look in joke books and try to see how a joke could fit into a trick you already know. Maybe the shape of part of one of your magic tricks reminds you of something else. A tube could be made out of an oatmeal can with a mustache painted on the Quaker Oats guy. A box might be decorated to look like a safe or a ball might become a bomb with a birthday candle wick. Think of funny words or descriptions and make 'em laugh, make 'em laugh, make 'em laugh!

Comedy Patter

There are many good books on the market with comedy patter. They contain pieces of patter written for stock magic effects. This may help you get your Comedy Magic rolling a little easier.

CHAPTER 12

Illusions— the Big Rigs

Illusion or Magic Trick?

Is there a difference between an Illusion and a Magic trick? Is there a difference between an Illusionist and a Magician? Well, yes and no. A mirage can be an illusion but it isn't a magic trick. Sawing a lady in half can be said to be both. In the magic world, an illusion usually means a stage illusion, or what is now being called a theatrical or grand illusion. Illusions are the big-box tricks; the stuff you see in a showroom in Las Vegas or on a theater stage anywhere else. An illusionist is a magician who specializes in producing these big shows. It's usually the physical size of the props that differentiates the magician from the illusionist. A magician creates illusion and an illusionist performs magic.

Black Art

Black art has nothing to do with the occult or any dark nastiness like that. Black art is a specialized area of magic that utilizes the color black as its primary strength. There are a few performers who really do make it an art form.

Did you ever drop a dark object on a dark floor and have trouble finding it? That's black art, in a way. By placing black (especially *flat* black) objects against other black objects, the ones closest to you seem to disappear. You'd be amazed at how well this works, and it's one of the strongest tools a magician can learn to use. In the next effect, we'll put black art to work.

The Square Circle Production Box

This is a classic standard effect in magic, and with a little imagination, you can use this same idea for many other applications. This is an illusion that you can make yourself and that will serve you well, no matter where you perform it.

Effect

The magician displays a box on a flat tray. Through cutout openings in the front of the box, the audience can see a brightly colored tube. The box is lifted off of the tube and the magician openly shows that it is empty and has no top or bottom. The box is placed

---

Harry Kellar (1849–1922)

You could say that Harry Kellar became known as America's favorite magician in 1896 when his rival Alexander Hermann died. His career from that time remained solid and prosperous. Kellar was very interested in fulfilling the hunger for mystery in the minds of his audiences. Kellar was known as a magician who performed large illusions and was known for effects such as the "The Witch, the Sailor, and the Enchanted Monkey" and "The Levitation of Princess Karnac." This levitation became more famous when it was passed on to Kellar's successor, Howard Thurston. Thurston took the idea and expanded it to the point where he could float the assistant out over the audience. Kellar did perform one more time in 1917 when Houdini talked him into appearing at a World War I benefit.

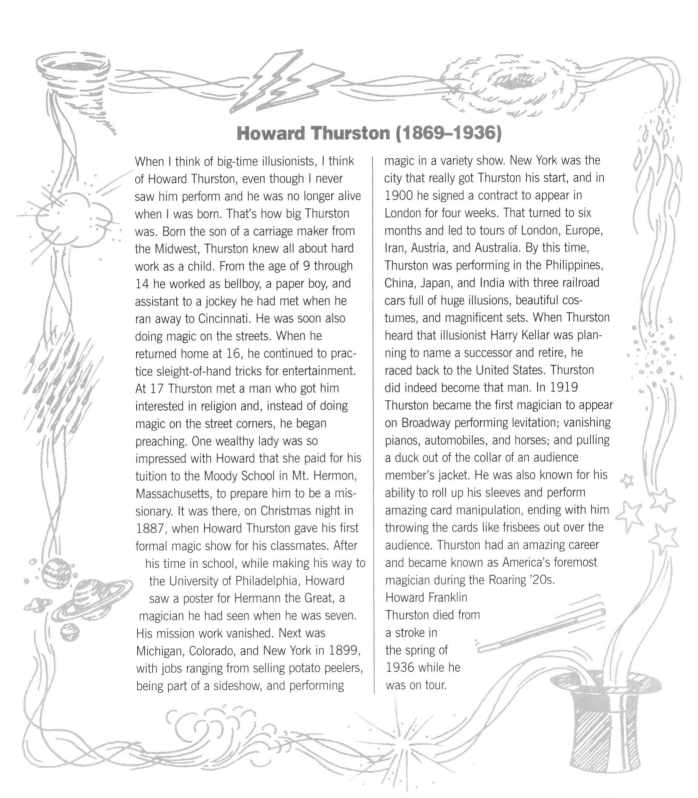

Howard Thurston (1869–1936)

When I think of big-time illusionists, I think of Howard Thurston, even though I never saw him perform and he was no longer alive when I was born. That's how big Thurston was. Born the son of a carriage maker from the Midwest, Thurston knew all about hard work as a child. From the age of 9 through 14 he worked as bellboy, a paper boy, and assistant to a jockey he had met when he ran away to Cincinnati. He was soon also doing magic on the streets. When he returned home at 16, he continued to practice sleight-of-hand tricks for entertainment. At 17 Thurston met a man who got him interested in religion and, instead of doing magic on the street corners, he began preaching. One wealthy lady was so impressed with Howard that she paid for his tuition to the Moody School in Mt. Hermon, Massachusetts, to prepare him to be a missionary. It was there, on Christmas night in 1887, when Howard Thurston gave his first formal magic show for his classmates. After his time in school, while making his way to the University of Philadelphia, Howard saw a poster for Hermann the Great, a magician he had seen when he was seven. His mission work vanished. Next was Michigan, Colorado, and New York in 1899, with jobs ranging from selling potato peelers, being part of a sideshow, and performing magic in a variety show. New York was the city that really got Thurston his start, and in 1900 he signed a contract to appear in London for four weeks. That turned to six months and led to tours of London, Europe, Iran, Austria, and Australia. By this time, Thurston was performing in the Philippines, China, Japan, and India with three railroad cars full of huge illusions, beautiful costumes, and magnificent sets. When Thurston heard that illusionist Harry Kellar was planning to name a successor and retire, he raced back to the United States. Thurston did indeed become that man. In 1919 Thurston became the first magician to appear on Broadway performing levitation; vanishing pianos, automobiles, and horses; and pulling a duck out of the collar of an audience member's jacket. He was also known for his ability to roll up his sleeves and perform amazing card manipulation, ending with him throwing the cards like frisbees out over the audience. Thurston had an amazing career and became known as America's foremost magician during the Roaring '20s. Howard Franklin Thurston died from a stroke in the spring of 1936 while he was on tour.

back down over the tube. It is a square tube. Now the magician shows the tube the same way. It is also empty. The tube is placed back and is seen to enter the box. Some magic words and a magical gesture are made, and the magician reaches into the box and produces . . . well . . . anything he wants—silks, flowers, a rabbit, a dove, or a six pack.

Preparation

Here's an illusion you can make. Just so we are straight, I'll discuss making a small square circle. That's probably the easiest to make and to get used to working with. You can, however, make this thing as big as you can imagine. You could pull a Buick out of it if you want.

1. You'll need two large cans that will nest inside of one another. Large coffee cans or oversized canned food cans will work fine. If you can find a can without the reinforcing ribs around it, use that; it will look nicer.

2. The larger can needs to have its top and bottom removed so it is just a tube. Decorate this outside of the can with bright colors. The slightly smaller "load" can should have its bottom left intact and it should be covered with velvet or velveteen. Note that this type of material has a definite nap and it should be running up. If you run your hand from the open top of the load can to the bottom, it should be rough not smooth. This is important in making sure that the black looks as dark as it can.

3. Now, you'll need to build a box. Because the box doesn't need to have any structural strength, you can make it out of plywood or even foam-core poster board. The box needs to be large enough to fit the larger, outer can and must have a design cut out of its front so the colored tube may be seen through it. Make sure the design is not too big so you can see the sides or the curved top of the black inner can when the colored tube is pulled off. Paint the outside of the box with contrasting colors and either paint the inside flat black or, better yet, cover it with velvet like the load can **(Figure 12.1).**

Figure 12.1

4. Finally, you need a little base for this prop. This allows the audience to see the underside of it as the load is being produced, so they don't think it's just coming out of your table. The stand needs to be a couple of inches wider than the box all the way around and should be held at least an inch off of the table by some type of legs. Keep the base simple.

Setup

Place the black load can on the base with the colored can around it. Make sure that any seams in the velvet or the cans are pointing upstage so they are not seen during the performance. Load all of the items you want to produce inside of the inner can. Place the box around the outside with the cutout opening toward the front.

Routine

Bring the entire setup out and place it on top of your table. Pick up the box and remove it from the stand. If you like, you can also pinch the load chamber and the outer tube together and just lift them as one, slightly off of the table to show you are using only two objects (not too far or people will see underneath).

Place the tube back down and concentrate on showing the box empty. A pretty way to spin the box is to pick it up by corners A and B and spin it toward you so that it revolves on the corner axis held between both palms. Hold the palms tight so the box can spin freely and quickly. Place the box down over the tube.

Now, lift the tube (but not the load chamber) and show it to be empty. A neat spin for the tube starts by holding it upright between the two hands with the fingers arched and the index fingers directly opposite each other. You are going to have the tips of those two fingers be the axis this time. Spin the tube toward you and let go of every finger except the index fingers and it will spin smoothly. It takes a little balance and practice, but once you get it, you'll have it forever. Place the tube back down in the box, surrounding the load compartment.

All you have to do now is reach in and produce the items from the box that the audience has just seen as completely empty. With black art magic, you'll really leave them in the dark.

Magic vs. Illusion

People often come up to me and say, "Hey . . . about that magic trick that you did . . . or am I supposed to call it an *illusion*?" Or they'll say, "I saw that magician on TV, or should I call him an *Illusionist*?" There's definitely an unclear vision in the public eye of the difference between *magic* and *illusion*. To help you in your quest for understanding, consider these definitions:

Illusion
1. Something that a person wrongly supposes to exist
2. A false belief about the nature of something

Illusionist
1. A magician
2. An artist who uses techniques (such as perspective drawing) to make a pictorial representation look realistic

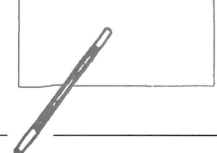

Smoke and Mirrors

"It's all done with smoke and mirrors." Boy, have I heard that a million and one times! However, most magic effects aren't done with smoke or mirrors. Yes, there are some illusions performed with the use of reflection or other optical effects and, yes, some of them do utilize mirrors, but they have to be used sparingly. As for smoke, I would say that smoke is used as a technical add-on or texture more than as an absolute element to many magic illusions. With the amazing design and technology that goes into the creation of modern illusion, smoke and mirrors are not exactly at the top. I do, however, think that we *should* go on letting people believe that it is all done with smoke and mirrors, so that when we create magic with all of the other great methods, they are still trying to figure out where the mirror was and what happened to the smoke!

I will show you one of the many applications of producing an illusion with a mirror. It will give you an insight into how mirrors can be used in magic, especially with illusions.

The Mirror Glass Illusion

Effect

A glass is shown to be empty and it is covered with a blue silk. When the silk is lifted, the glass is filled with a red silk.

Explanation

The glass is a gimmicked glass. It is created by placing a double-sided mirror down the center of the glass. You can use mirrored plexiglass, real glass that you have cut and ground or a contact backed mylar. A strip of pin striping is put around the lip to hide the edge of this mirror **(Figure 12.2).** Obviously, the glass cannot be shown from the side, but from the front, the illusion that the glass is empty is perfect. The front half of the glass reflects to look like the back half. The pattern in the glass hides any small discrepancies.

When the glass is first show, it is shown as empty. After it is covered with the blue silk, it is placed on the table and in doing so, the glass is turned so the red silk now faces the audience but

Figure 12.2

is hidden by the blue silk. When the silk is pulled off of the glass, the fingers can even reach down and pull a little of the red silk up so that when the blue silk is taken away, the read silk seems to fill and flow out of the glass.

This is one application of creating illusion with a mirror. Try looking at how the mirror reflects in other directions. You'll start to invent your own illusions.

Large Illusions
Voilà La Femme!

Here is a simplified version of an illusion originally created by the late Dr. Harlan Tarbell called "Three Kings and a Queen." I can say that this illusion really does pack *flat* but I can't say it packs *small*. It does however play big, especially if you soup it up with some costumes, music, lighting, and special effects. I use a high-tech, hinged variation of this effect in my illusion shows. Use your own creativity and you'll see how it can work for you too.

Effect

Three huge playing cards are brought center stage one at a time. After arranging them into a three-cornered, triangular screen, they are opened up to reveal a girl assistant dressed as a queen.

Preparation

You will need to make up these large cards. They should be six inches taller than your assistant and be made so that the height-to-width ratio is the same as a regular playing card. You can make these out of plywood or a plastic, corrugated reinforced signboard. With the signboard, the cards will be lightweight and the graphics can be scanned, cut on a computer plotter out of vinyl, and applied at a digital sign shop. The backs need to be finished as well. I suggest a red back pattern with a white border. The queen's costume should fit tightly enough so that it won't accidentally be seen as she is maneuvering throughout this illusion. She can hold a crown in one hand, but to keep the height of the cards down, I suggest she keep it off until she appears.

Figure 12.3

Figure 12.4

Figure 12.5

Setup

Together in a stack, the three cards are held upright on each side by an assistant. The faces of the cards face the audience and the queen is hiding, upstage of the stack, also facing the audience. The magician is on center stage and the illusion is ready to begin.

Routine

1. The magician signals for the cards to be brought onstage and the two assistants slide the stack of cards on, stage right. The cards shouldn't be too far downstage because of the audience's sight line. The stack of cards are slid as opposed to being lifted, so the feet of the hidden queen can't be seen. The assistant's position the cards far enough away from the stage-right curtains so the audience can't think that your assistant secretly slips in at some point. Too late for that anyway **(Figure 12.3).**

2. Next, the stage-left assistant walks to the front of the stack and slides one card stage left and away from the rest of the cards with both hands. The queen secretly moves with the card. The assistant places (and holds) the card upstage of the magician on center stage **(Figure 12.4).**

3. Next, the magician walks to the front of the stack and slides the next card off in the exact same manner (so everything looks the same). This card is positioned with its side touching the stage-left side of the load card, angled diagonally with the face of the card toward the audience **(Figure 12.5).**

4. The final assistant now slides his card stage left and downstage a little (toward the audience) enough to allow the queen to sneak in between his card and the downstage side of the back card when it passes the back card. The assistant follows along with the card as he continues "inside" the triangle **(Figure 12.6).** He is still just sliding

the card parallel to the back card and he stops about two inches from the inside of the magician's card. The queen is trapped between his card and the back card.

5. Now, the assistant pivots his card clockwise, sliding the edge of his card along the back of the magician's card. Any cracks in between the cards would reveal the queen. The assistant completes the triangle with the girl now in the middle **(Figure 12.7).**

Figure 12.6

6. At the correct moment that assistant and the magician open their cards away from the center, revealing the queen as she steps forward **(Figure 12.8).** The magician joins her while the two assistants manage the cards, restacking them and sliding them offstage.

I really love this illusion. It is beautifully simple. The simpler, the better, if you can get away with it. Again, the props shouldn't get the applause.

Dr. Tarbell originally suggested three kings be used, with an additional note that aces might be cheaper. If you have the cards digitally printed, it won't matter if they have one or one thousand colors, the price will be the same. If you have them covered with cut vinyl, Dr. Tarbell is right, the aces will be cheaper since they are only one color on white. I think the idea of using aces is good because it opens up patter opportunities related to the "Three-Card Monte" or "Cherchez La Femme" (or find the lady, as it was sometimes called). When the queen appears in multicolor, she will provide perfect contrast to the static image of the aces and . . . Voilà La Femme!

Figure 12.7

Illusion Designs

If you are interested in performing stage illusions, it's a good idea to keep your eyes open. Find out what makes certain designs better than others. Think about what makes some illusions get a kind round of applause versus those that make people literally gasp or scream with excitement. You'll find that line to be

Figure 12.8

a very slim one. I have seen wonderful illusions get poor reactions so many times that I feel sorry that the magician has invested that much time and money into the giant beasts. I myself have performed many illusions that were very well received but just didn't "kill," as they say. I found out why. An illusion needs to be constructed and choreographed in a manner that creates natural tension, wonder, and speculation but also has naturally built-in moments for the audience to reflect and react. (That means amazement followed by applause in magician lingo.) Give them time to savor it. Take them on your journey, and allow them to thank you if they're pleased. Going quickly doesn't necessarily mean it's the right pace for the audience. As a magician, your main goal should be to give the audience the best timing and the best opportunity to connect with your magical moments.

Lighting

Lighting is a big part of making illusions not only look good but play well. We'll discuss lighting in more detail in Chapter 20 when we discuss how to mount your magic show. Even if you already use technical support professionals, you'll want to know what you need in this area. That means understanding what lighting can do and what makes it happen. Don't ever let a person light a magic show who doesn't understand what you are trying to achieve, even if they are great at lighting. Lighting magic is a different ball game and it's something for which you need expertise. If you are considering performing illusions, get ready. Outside of all the usual considerations behind magic, you will also need to understand another aspect of your show and *that* is working with a team of experts.

Assistants

Illusionists need assistants. They are essential to the act. As the magic gets bigger, so does the commitment, and assistants are as important to the success of any great illusionist as the illusionist himself. Again, Chapter 20 will give you a brief overview of the respect and understanding that working with an assistant requires. It's something to look forward to.

Horace Goldin (1874–1939)

Horace Goldin might have been the first of the rapid-fire magicians. Today, illusionists move at lightning speed with huge illusions but it wasn't always that way. Goldin first decided to put an entire evening of magic into a few minutes because he had to. The press was eating him alive because when he performed his tricks he was almost impossible to understand. Goldin was the person who was very well known for cutting a woman in half, even though it was created earlier by P.T. Selbit. Later, Goldin improved on that concept when he created the buzz saw illusion. He was also known for vanishing a piano and a tiger. Of course, as we know, artists copy each other, so it was not long until those effects were mainstays for other illusionists too.

CHAPTER 13

Mental Magic—
Look into
My Eyes!

Mentalism and Mind Reading

Mentalism or mind-reading magic is one of my favorite types of magic. Why? Because it is different and audiences eat it up. When most people think of magic, they usually think of a tuxedo, a top hat, a wand or cane, and of course, a rabbit. There's nothing wrong with that image but it is pretty tired. One of the most precious of all gifts we as human beings possess is our different personalities. It is a shame when magicians don't take advantage of that in their magic. In magic with the mind, personality and presentation are paramount. The fancy boxes aren't featured, the fire and lighting isn't featured, it's just the mentalist and his connection to the audience's most personal of all possessions—their thoughts. Mentalism can be done without any props at all, for just a single spectator or in front of an audience of thousands. Either way, performed with conviction and attention to presentation, it's strong. It can be performed as an interactive piece of television with an audience at home waiting to assist. It can even be performed on the radio. If you have a commanding personality, speak well, and enjoy intellectual types of entertainment more than slapstick with rabbits, you will love performing magic with the mind.

"It's Okay to Pick Your Seat"

Here's a little beauty that is a slight variation on an effect I learned from mentalist, Gene Marvin of Las Vegas. I have used similar methods for close-up mentalism effects, but true to Marvin's tradition, his handling of this takes the idea up onstage and makes it bigger and better than ever. This plays big and, of course, packs small. I've made a few little changes and updates and I think this is a quick and easy addition to your mentalism repertoire (or a great place to start it).

Effect

At the beginning of your mentalism presentation, you bring a spectator onstage and offer them a seat in any one of three cushioned chairs that are numbered 1, 2, and 3. You explain that you will be reading her mind and her thoughts while she is onstage.

Jim Steinmeyer

Jim Steinmeyer is an incredible mind in the new world of magic today. Not only can he perform magic but he can also invent it. Steinmeyer has invented what are, in my opinion, some of the best illusions ever seen. Some of Jim's illusions include "Origami," where an assistant is placed into a box and the box is folded until there is no possible way she could be inside. The box is unfolded again and out pops the assistant, wearing a different costume. He also invented the illusion called "Interlude," where the magician steps into a box that has an opening in the front of it so the audience can see his legs and chest. His arms, shoulder, and head are outside of the top of the box and his arms are outstretched, clenching two grips for support. The magician's assistant walks behind the magician and through a

(continued on next page)

After she is seated, you prove your first miracle of mentalism when you reveal a prediction. The prediction tells which chair you knew she would choose.

Preparation

You'll need three chairs, three pieces of poster board (4 by 6 feet), two 3-by-5-inch index cards, and a marker.

Setup

This effect is a variation on a theme that is used in quite a few magic effects wherein no matter what the spectator chooses, you have predicted that choice. There is a prediction reading for instance, "You will choose chair number 1." The performance secret lies in placing these predictions on their respective chairs.

On one 3-by-5-inch index card write, "You will choose chair #1."

Tape this to the back of chair #1 but this time on the back of it (facing upstage or away from the audience). If this chair was turned around it would reveal the message. Make sure the card is taped firmly so it cannot move if the chair is tilted or flipped. Now, perform the following:

1. On the three pieces of poster board put bold numerals: "1, 2, 3."

2. On the back of the "2" card write "You will choose chair #2." Remember to print the message on the back of chair #2 upside down (opposite the numeral) so if it is flipped upwards, it will read correctly.

   With clear, good-quality tape, attach these three pieces to the front side (toward the audience) of the chair backs with two pieces hanging from the top of the each back. This will allow you to lift and flap each card upward by its bottom edge.

3. On the other 3-by-5-inch index card write "You will choose chair #3."

   Attach this to the bottom of chair #3. Make sure the card is taped firmly so it won't accidentally fall off or flip down.

Again, remember to orient the card correctly so that when the chair is tilted backward on its rear legs, it will read correctly.

Now you have three chairs, each with its own prediction and each in a different place.

Routine

While your spectator comes up onstage, you begin to tell her that you will be reading her mind, presenting mental suggestions, and channeling thoughts both to and from her during the performance. Ask her to take a seat and continue to explain your entertainment plans (whatever they are), finally stating that you want her to begin with her own thoughts and choices and to be completely relaxed. Even offer her a chance to change her mind on what chair she sits in, explaining that she will not be forced into any answer, decision, or action while she assists you. Once she is satisfied on her location reveal that the magic has already begun by revealing that on the one chair she selected (and no other), you have correctly predicted her decision. Here are the revelations based on her choice.

If she chooses chair #1, have her stand for a moment while you turn the chair around to show your prediction. Show the other two chairs to show that there was only one prediction and one chair that you knew she would select.

If she chooses chair #2, have her stand and lift the "#2" flap for the revelation. Show the other flaps to show that there was only one prediction and one chair that you knew she would select.

If she chooses chair #3, have her stand so you can tip her chair back to show the revelation of the bottom of the chair.

This effect is not really an effect I would suggest doing on its own because it uses a lot of large props (three chairs). Also, why would you need three chairs when you only have one person onstage? It makes the chairs look suspicious if they aren't used for anything else. Figure on using the other chairs later in your presentation for more people, to hold some props, or even to sit on yourself at some point. Gene Marvin believes that for mentalism the props should be common place. You are not a magician, you are a mind reader, and in Chapter 20, we speak of the beauty of using what's there and packing small. Think about it, you carry a few cards and some tape, and you have a pretty big looking effect. You might also want to try using prediction and number cards that are larger than the size outlined in this effect so more people actually have a chance to see what's written on them. This means you will have to carry all of the necessary items with you and assemble them on-site. Of course, every chair will be different so make up a stock set that will fit any chair and, if you have time when you get to your venue, make up a larger set. Just have the back up too so you don't let this kind of preparation cramp make you unready for the rest of the show. It's the sum of the parts that matters, not one particular part.

The Great Book Test

I love this effect! It has everything it needs and nothing else. No fillers, no goofy props, nothing but pure confusion. That makes perfect mental magic.

Effect

You request a spectator to pick two books out of his own collection, right off his own bookshelf. One book is given to you and explained to be the "selector" for his book, which he keeps. You begin rifling through the pages of your book, asking the spectator to say "Stop" at any time. The spectator is asked to open his book to the same page number and concentrate on the first few sentences or first few words on the page. You are then able to describe the sentences or tell him the words.

Preparation

Gene Marvin first taught me that what you need for this experiment is two books and a lot of nerve. Make sure you have access to at least two books and I'll tell you what I think about the nerves. Mentalists take risks, that's for sure. It's that walk along a tightwire of what is known, what can possibly be known, and what can be obtained during a presentation that makes mentalism exciting for both the performer and the audience. It's a nervous and possibly dan-

Gene Marvin

"Mental magic is much easier to learn than sleight of hand. It requires very few props. In fact, even the props should look ordinary. No flashy dragons or red/black/gold paint designs. You are not using tricks. You are using envelopes, papers, pencils, etc. Oh, and by the way, *never* refer to what you are about to do as a trick. That's a no-no! It's an experiment, a demonstration, or a test. Give the impression that you are never sure you will be successful. When your prediction or revelation is correct, be as happy and surprised as they are. And it doesn't hurt you a bit to miss now and then. This makes it all the more believable."

Gene Marvin, mentalist, author, and actor

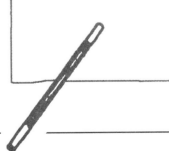

gerous proposition for both participants when private thoughts are brought out in public. That's part of the chemistry and, to me, it makes mentalism one of the most spontaneous and impromptu types of magic. The safe news is there are tools, controls, and methods that make great mentalists very sure that they will blow away any audience.

Setup

There is no set up for this effect outside of the preparation of a solid routine and smooth patter. Yeah, I guess that does sound a little bit like it takes nerve, now, doesn't it? Worry not, oh great one, you are in good hands.

Routine/Patter

Start the routine with some well-written patter outlining the impossibilities of true mind reading. Describe the focus, concentration, and chemistry that a situation must possess in order for mental transference to take place in a controlled environment with complete strangers. Then elaborate on your study of the unknown capacity of the human mind as you tell him that you'll need two books from his collection. Ask him to take them from a bookshelf or table and hand them to you. He has to do this one at a time. If he tries to pull out two, slow him down and ask him to be careful, start again, and pull just one book first. Tell him to allow his mind to flow comfortably so his energies are focused economically and not consumed on time or perfection.

Once he has done this, ask him to take his time and select a second book, a book that seems to speak to him louder than any other as he scans the remaining possible books. Try to stand in a position that allows you to be outside of his sight line when he turns to select the second book. When this happens, open your book somewhere near the center and memorize the page number and as many words or ideas as you can until you see him sliding the book out from the corner of your eye. Close the book casually and gently so he doesn't glimpse you trying to hide something, then have him hand you the second book. Keep in mind books are all numbered in different ways so get used to scanning the top,

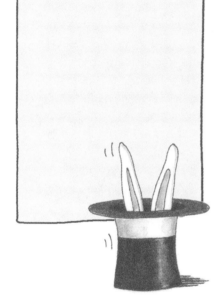

bottom, and corners for the page number as quickly as possible. Set both books down as you begin. Remember that in his mind the magic has not yet started until he has chosen both books. Of course, you are secretly armed and ahead of the game. Now you perform a subtle but effective force.

Ask the spectator to select one of the books but keep in mind, you need the spectator to get the book that you have already memorized. If he picks that book, tell him to pick it up. He will use that book and you don't even want to touch it. Tell him that you'll use the other book as a page selector and you pick up yours as well.

If he picks the other book (the one you know nothing about), you tell him that you will use that book as a page selector. Ask him to hand it to you and he can have the other book, which you will never touch.

The spectator never has a choice but he doesn't know it. He gets the memorized book. Now you have to get him to look at the page that you secretly know a few things about. Isn't this innocently beautiful? As an example, we'll say that I opened the book before to page 119.

Stand facing the spectator and ask him to select a page in your book at random by simply calling out "Stop" while you page through the book. When he says, "Stop," you stop. Look at the number in your book (which might be 90 or 348 or who knows) and quickly call out, "Page 119." Now, ask the spectator to turn to the same page in his book and ask him to look at the first words or sentences and concentrate on what he is reading. Suddenly stop him, ask him to keep his eyes on his book, and begin your explanation of what you are "picking up." Go slowly, draw it out, get some "cloudy images," such as "I see greasy, no, no wait . . . it's grassy, grassy plains." The more dramatic you can be, the better. Besides, you don't have a lot more to show off here than your amazing ability to read thoughts. There aren't a bunch of distracting props, dancing girls, or loud music. It's just you, two books, and a lot of nerve. That's all it takes, and believe me, when your spectator sees you pull this off, that will be more than enough. Book tests can be strong magic.

Max Maven

Max Maven has a definite look and a definite feel to his performances of mental magic. His image questions whether he really might be able to do some of the things he professes to do. With a commanding voice, deep set eyes, and a taste for the bizarre, Maven continues to astonish audiences both live and on television.

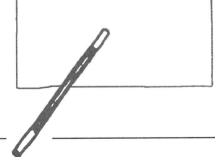

Billet to Me, I Tore It!—the "Center Tear"

One particular variation on a mentalism routine has always impressed me. It is the use of a billet. A billet is a small piece of paper, usually no larger than a playing card. On this paper the magician writes a message and tries to transfer that message to a spectator or visa versa. My favorite version of this is what is known as the "Center Tear," which I will explain. I have studied several variations by Joseph Dunninger, Theodore Annemann, Harlan Tarbell, Corinda, Foster, Morelle, Punx-Mier, Al Koran, Dai Vernon, Bert Reese, and Gene Marvin, and they are all very similar. When I started writing this book, I decided to consider what I liked and didn't like about all of the versions I was aware of (and I know there are tons I am not) and teach you a version that was straight-forward and uncomplicated but solid. Let me help you join the long line of magicians who think the "Center Tear" to be one of the best mentalism effects there is.

Effect

The magician has the spectator write a name or important word on a piece of paper and fold it in quarters so that the word cannot be seen. The paper is handed back to the magician who, in plain sight, rips the folded paper in half, then in half again, leaving only tiny pieces of paper. This stack of pieces are set on fire and placed in an ashtray, where they are watched until they are completely extinguished. The magician then reaches into the ashes with one hand and begins to pinch and feel the ashes with his fingers. He then begins to transfer ash onto the back of the other hand, forming parts of letters and symbols until he finally looks into the eyes of the spectator and says his word.

Preparation

The preparation of this effect is pretty easy but there are a few tips. You'll need some paper. I use one of those paper cubes or blocks of paper that are often given as promotional items at trade shows or print shops or that can be purchased at card shops with messages or pictures printed on the edges of the paper. This paper looks usual and normal, which is good. Make sure whatever you use, you do not use those pads with the temporary sticky backings or it will be disastrous. You'll also need something to write with. A dark pen or marker is good as long as it's not too thick so as to show or bleed through the paper. If you use a pencil, make sure it is soft enough to make a clearly visible marking. You'll need an ashtray nearby, matches, or a lighter and you should be set for amazement.

Setup

Your preparation already takes care of most of your setup. The only other thing you might want to do is put a lighter in your right pocket. It gives you a few options that you might want (or need) to take advantage of later on.

Routine

Begin by getting the pen and paper out, taking the pen and drawing a casual circle in the center of the paper to show the spectator where to write her word. I didn't mention this in the description of the effect at the beginning because it is a fact that is not considered of any importance to the spectator, but it helps cut down the odds of the outcome being a little, messy. You are just testing the pen and casually guiding the spectator to better understand what she is to do. She will be concentrating on getting it right, don't worry. You might ask her to print it in block letters. Make this request sound like an afterthought or make a joke about her handwriting, anything to help you get the result you need. Now, leave the pen and paper, turn your back or walk away (or both), and ask your spectator to write her word, name, or whatever your routine asks for. Ask your spectator to let you know when she is finished **(Figure 13.1)**.

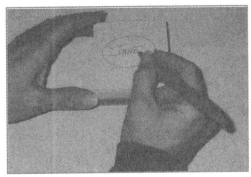

Figure 13.1

After your spectator finishes, ask her to remove the paper from the pad, fold it in half to hide her word, and fold it in half again so the paper is folded in quarters. Ask her to tell you once again when the folding is finished and ask her to hold the folded packet between two fingertips (she'll likely use the index and

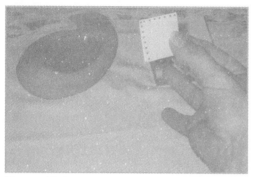

Figure 13.2

Figure 13.3

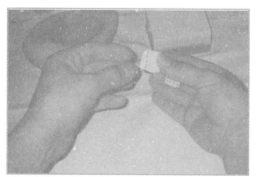

Figure 13.4

thumb). Some routines suggest prefolding the paper so your spectator will follow the creasing, but I think this only complicates and creates unnecessary questions. Hey, if it doesn't go right, crumple up the paper, have the spectator relax, and try again. No one knows what is going to happen yet, anyway. "Oh yeah, and by the way, fold the paper this way instead." Handling surprises is part of your job and you simply have to have an answer and a back-up plan for everything no matter how large or small.

Okay, so she has folded the paper and told you she is finished. You are on your way back to the table to take the paper from her with an open hand and silently prove your hand is empty. Try to see which way the paper is sitting in the spectator's hand. You want to eventually get it between your thumb and index finger so that the folded edges are to the left and up **(Figure 13.2)**. For learning and for clarity, the illustration shows dots along the left and upper folded edges of the paper.

Now, between the thumbs and index fingers of both hands, rip the paper in half. Try to appear to rip the paper casually but don't get crazy and make it too much of a mess **(Figure 13.3)**. Place the left-hand bunch on top of the right-hand bunch and give the whole deal a quarter turn. Rip it in half again and put the left-hand bunch on top of the right-hand bunch just like last time (only smaller) **(Figure 13.4)**.

Now you need to ask the spectator if she has a match or a lighter and, while she considers where they might be (a split second), you slip the top folded pack of pieces off into the right hand **(see Figure 13.4 again)**. A lot of people today don't smoke so if she doesn't have a need for fire she won't be distracted long. This is a good time to have a lighter in your pocket, don't you think? While you get your lighter you can drop the paper in your pocket to retrieve later, drop it on your leg (your leg acting as a little servante table), so you can unfold it and read it off of the leg later.

You have the lighter and the remaining papers are still in your left hand. Set the lighter down, move the ashtray toward the spectator, and torch the pieces. Be careful, especially when you are holding the paper. Drop it, whisk off both hands (because they are empty but you don't have to say it), and let it burn in the ashtray when it gets to be too much to hold. While the fire is burning, you have time to unfold, glimpse, and remember what is on the paper **(Figure 13.5).** I still think this part is cool. It's like a secret mini note. Take things slowly. Make sure the paper burns completely, it's important for the feel of the effect. You need the physical evidence to be gone before it seems so impressive to divine the information with your telepathic power. Ashes also create a dark mood or dingy backdrop and seem like something you wouldn't touch to get information. Watching the paper turn to ashes (especially if it was brightly colored) somehow brings a mood of seriousness and opens up many great possibilities for patter.

Figure 13.5

Now, it's time to do some dumpster diving. You have to reach into the ashes. Take as much of the ashes as you can between the fingers and thumb of the right hand and place them in a heap on the back of the left hand. Begin to break the ashes up, trace imaginary letters, trace veins in the hand, anything that seems to fit. I figure the wilder, the better. Gradually the letters, the pulses of life, and the ashes to dust bring forth the word—the one word that only the spectator could have possibly known, especially since she helped to destroy the evidence.

End this experiment by helping her get her jaw off of the floor. This is a very nice piece of mentalism and it can produce a powerful reaction, from amazement to fright. Gradually transition from this effect to whatever happens next, but be gentle and careful so you don't destroy the moment. Let the entire experiment sink in and continue to weave its spell. Don't suddenly jump up and yell, "Okay that was pretty scary, huh? Who wants to see me make a weasel out of a balloon?" Let your mentalism magic work for you. Unlike other forms of magic, the work of a mentalist is often over before the audience suspects it has even begun, and the effect of mentalism is often building even after the mentalist knows the work is complete.

Telekinetic Magic

You may have seen a mentalist or psychic on a talk show or documentary about the forces of telekinetic powers. They are usually bending a key, wilting a spoon, making pages flutter in a telephone book, or confusing a compass. Telekinetic experiments seem to rearrange the atoms of very commonplace solid objects, and they don't let the brain cells do much better. Seeing solid objects move by themselves is just plain magical. How many times have you looked at a jet in the sky and thought, "I'm amazed that can happen?" even though you've read about it in *Popular Science* and you've learned all about jet engines, lift, carry on, and bad food. Have you ever watched a feather or a leaf caught in an updraft and watched it just to make sure that it didn't just keep floating? Just in case it could just stay there until someone else came along and ruined the magic? Telekinesis is the study, the science, and the answer to moving an object with the power of the mind. As a mentalist, you also know that it's a good idea to have some fibers, atoms, pistons, and pulleys lined up in the right direction to make everything "move" just a tad bit easier.

Confusing the Compass
Effect

The mentalist, that's you, "The Amazing Dramamine," begins his experiment by introducing a regular Boy Scout's compass. The compass can be freely examined by a committee of audience members, perhaps a genuine Boy Scout leader. The mentalist begins to grunt and chant and make Yoko Ono noises when suddenly the compass begins to move. No way? . . . Way! That little sucker spins and jumps around like a grasshopper on espresso. Under the amazing powers held by the mentalist, the compass spins and jumps at his command until he wills it to stop. At that point (or any point in between), the compass can be examined.

Preparation

You'll need a simple, inexpensive compass. You don't need a fancy one with a navigational base or protective case. You're going to mess this compass up by knocking it around pretty badly anyway, so you might as well save your bucks for magic books. The other thing you'll need is a few magnets. There are a number of types of magnets available today that are strong enough to do some real damage if you're not careful. They are very strong and they are very small. Suppliers listed in the appendix will be able to set you up with some if you can't find them somewhere else. Don't get them near your watch, your television, computer equipment, or pacemaker unless you have a really whacked sense of humor and so does the person with the pacemaker. Seriously, these things are strong! My brother Chris put two of my magnets on his nose just goofing around and well, let's just say he yelled a lot, got this Pinocchio point, and he still can't smell very well. That's handy for him though, he has farm animals.

Setup

Wear a magnet on each wrist and around your neck on a leash or nonmetallic cord. Of course, the one around your neck has to be under your shirt or blouse and you have to be sure not to get the magnet too close to the compass so that your clothes jump out and grab the compass. The wrist magnets can be stitched into bracelets that you can easily sew onto elastic, fabric, with loop fasteners or sweat bands under your cuffs. Remember, no wristwatch! (unless you decide to hollow out an old watch and use it for the magnet!)

Routine

The routine for this effect is entirely open. Make this dramatic and take your time. Talk about honeybees communicating with each other through geomagnetic impulses, animal magnetism and Michael Faraday's discoveries about electric charge and magnetism in the 1830s. You can mention magnetohydrodynamics and plasma gas

---

George Kresge Jr., "Kreskin"

The Amazing Kreskin doesn't consider himself a psychic. In fact, he has often made fun of them on his many television and radio appearances while demonstrating his tricks that show mind power. He claims not to perform miracles but rather mysteries, and not hypnotism but attention manipulation.

Kreskin often ends his performances attempting to find his check, which has been previously hidden by his client. If he can't find it he doesn't get paid. He also offers $20,000 to any one who can prove he uses assistants or accomplices for this stunt. Once, at a show at the Waldorf Astoria in New York City, the check was finally found inside the stuffing of a turkey. It is true. Kreskin is amazing!

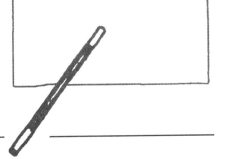

and magnetic data storage, anything. Then, begin to show how the force of human energies when focused together can counteract these natural laws.

With the compass on a table, approach it at chest level (or lean forward) until the compass moves. By waving the hands outside of the compass or grasping onto the wrists of others seated at the table and bringing their energy (and your wrist magnets) closer, the compass begins to move. You appear to take the energy from the spectators and allow their hands to drop and continue to control the compass yourself. Don't get your hands too close to the compass so that the motions look like your yanking the thing with some sort of invisible string. Caress the compass without touching it and you'll really sell the whole thing. Some magnets are even strong enough to move the compass through a wooden table, you'll be amazed. Just don't accidentally suck a couple of forks over to the compass on your way so you look like what you're doing really is too good to be true.

Hypnotic Magic

Real hypnotism is not something to mess with. The experiments I will explain here are what I would call, "light hypnotism." They are hypnotism by many definitions but they are not heavy, complicated, or dangerous and nobody goes into a sleep or an altered state even though the audience might think so.

The Doorway Flapper
Effect

The subject stands in a doorway so she can't move around too much. She is not a secret helper, confederate, stooge, shill, or a "plant." She is a mammal. Sorry, I just love that one.

The hypnotist has her anchor herself by locking her neck stiff and raising her shoulders, spreading her feet apart so that they touch each side of the threshold, and pushing against the sides of the door casing with the back of the hands. The subject's eyes close, and she imagines herself held tightly in a box. The hypnotist snaps his fingers, her eyes open, and she steps out of the doorway. Suddenly, both of her arms begin to rise up away from her body as if she is planning to fly. The subject is shocked because she obviously has no control of her own arms. She has been hypnotized.

Preparation

You don't really need any preparation for this experiment. It all happens as a natural body release action from the tension caused in the body, especially in the arms. When the arms are released from the confinements or pushing against the doorframe they, want to raise up. Stopping this action by the subject is unnatural and difficult unless she really tries. The trick is to only mention the stopping and suggesting the upward movement. Repetitious suggestion is an important tool in any hypnotism.

Setup

Always choose a subject who is interested and believes in the presence of hypnotism. Although this particular experiment will work anyway, it will work better if the subject is cooperative and enthusiastic. You also need an average-width doorframe (no more than 30 inches across), but a narrower one works even better. Make sure the doorway is in an area where all can see, so it doesn't tip the fact that the doorway has something to do with it.

Routine

Have the subject stand in the doorframe as explained in the description of the effect. Have her close her eyes and begin to have her relax her eyes as if closing them for sleep. If you like, you can ask her to close her eyes in a stage whisper as you walk in front of her and wave your hand over her face, softly touching her eyelids. The audience won't know you are telling her to just close her eyes and it looks as if something very strange is starting to happen. Ask her not to talk. The silence is also effective. Ask her to continue to push against the doorframe with the back of the hands, touching her at the wrists to enforce exactly where you mean. Ask her to picture herself sleeping and trapped inside of a

Lance Burton

One time at a magic event, a woman came up to me and asked if I'd heard of a guy she had gone to school with in Kentucky. She said this guy was always playing around with magic and that his name is Lance Burton. I laughed and said, "Yes, as a matter of fact, I do. Did you know that he's just landed a $100 million contract over the next 10 years with the new Monte Carlo Hotel in Las Vegas?" She laughed and replied, "Yeah, right, but have you ever run into him?" What I had told this woman was no lie. Lance Burton represents the classic story of "small town boy makes it good," real good! In 1977 Lance placed first in a competition at the Abbott's Get Together, a magic convention hosted by Abbott's Magic Company in the small town

(continued on next page)

box the size of the doorframe as if the doorframe had two doors on either side of it, one behind her and one in front of her. Now, suggest that she imagine the box getting smaller and tighter around her so that she feels the top come down and push onto her head (push down on her head with your hand). Have her imagine the back and front moving in and the sides pushing up against her wrists so that she is completely confined. Continue this talk at a warm, low, and confident pace. Always have your patter completely rehearsed so there are no "ums or ahs." After about one minute of asking her to push against the side of the box, say, "In a moment I am going to count to three and you will awaken. You will be released from this box and from your sleep, you will step forward, and you will spread your wings and fly." Count to three and ask her to open her eyes and simply step forward. As she does, her "wings" will slowly begin to raise as you quickly point out that no matter how she tries to remain in her position her dreams cause her to fly. Depending on how long you continue to describe the raising of her arms and how she physically reacts to your suggestions, the arms will continue to raise. The subject will probably begin to laugh. It's a weird sensation, and the fact that she suddenly speaks creates another layer of contrast that makes the performance look all the more like she has been hypnotized under your command to really "fly the coop."

Finger Tip Touch

Another experiment that is similar to "The Doorway Flapper" is the "Finger Tip Touch." It happens automatically, unexpectedly, and can be done in much more close-up and intimate conditions. It can also be done to an entire group of people at the same time. It will also help you determine who will be good to use in your final experiment.

Effect

The subject is asked to hold his hands together in a ball with his fingers interlaced. When the hypnotist gives the signal, the subject raises his index fingers toward the sky, stares at the space between the fingers, then into the eyes of the hypnotist and back and forth and suddenly the fingers begin to move toward each other even though the subject is not trying to move them at all. Closer and closer they become until they finally touch.

Preparation

You don't need anything for this except at least one subject. A group of subjects are even better and, if so, have them seated in a semicircle so you can be the center of concentration. Around a table works fine.

Setup

This experiment is entirely impromptu except for a brief explanation of what you are going to demonstrate, "hypnotism," a chance for some focus to set in. As I said, if you have already performed "The Doorway Flapper," you will know at least one person who might be considered a good subject. You need to get good at determining "who's naughty and who's nice" when it comes to getting helpers for your performance.

Routine

Begin by having the subjects close both hands in a ball with the fingertips interlaced. Talk about the relationship of the fingers and ask them to relax their bodies in their chairs and only think of the ball they are forming with their hands. Have them squeeze the fingers together and begin describing how they feel unnatural heat begin to build inside of the hands and seep through the cracks of their fingers. The backs of their hands will begin to become cooler and moist like an ocean breeze. Their fingers will begin to tighten where they come together and jewelry will begin to become tight and hot. If you have access to them, you can place your hand over top of each set of hands and give a light squeeze to reinforce that the hands should be held tightly. If you are doing this for a table of people in a restaurant, you won't have to worry about the waiter coming over and interrupting, it will look like you are holding some sort of prayer vigil and they will be spying on you through the

Lance Burton

(continued from previous page)

of Colon, Michigan. In 1980 he received the first Gold Medal awarded by the International Brotherhood of Magicians. That win led to appearances on The Tonight Show after which Johnny Carson requested he come back for another show. In 1982 Lance became the first American to bring home the gold at the FISM Grand Prix in Lausanne, Switzerland. Today he appears in his own theater, the 1,200-seat Lance Burton Theater at the Monte Carlo. Now, that's about as good as it gets!

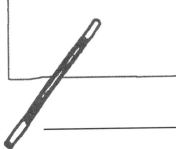

salad bar. Now, demonstrate how in a moment you will say, "begin" and ask everyone to keep the rest of their hands together but point their index fingers toward the sky. keeping them straight and pointing up. Immediately begin to describe that although the fingers are held straight up, when you say the word, "Closer," they will begin to move together. Ask the subjects to listen to your voice and think of that small space between their two fingers as the fingers move closer and closer together. Tell them to feel free to gaze through the fingers at you, back to the fingers, and feel little by little the fingers coming closer and closer together as they begin to weaken and touch. The fingers will touch and the reaction will be great. This is a cute experiment, and you can time your patter and explanation to match the subjects' actions. Ask everyone to quickly look at how fast "Gail's" or "Dale's" are moving if they are faster than average. Having them look up takes away any concentration of trying to stop this natural movement and, in most cases, their fingers will touch. Again, you look like a real hypnotist and the waiter also will probably treat you a little better!

CHAPTER 14

Escape Magic—
All Tied Up

E scape Magic has often swirled around in my head as a kind of oxymoron. It is not exactly what comes to mind if you do what I call "The Kid Test." If you ask a child to tell you something they think is Magic, they will say something that mentions disappearing, appearing, flying, floating, changing size, or changing color. Then they will usually mention smoke and surviving some kind of dangerous torture. Maybe that's it; escapes seem a little dangerous. Regardless, escapes have become associated with magic, especially when we think of Harry Houdini. Because so many of his escapes were surrounded in secrecy, and also because he was a skilled magician, he is most often thought of as a magician rather than an escape artist.

Close-Up Escapes
My Dad's Beads

Hey, I don't want you to think that my dad was a cross-dresser or something. It's just that he showed me this trick first and then he gave it to me. I still use dad's props today. It's commonly knows as "Grandmother's Necklace," but I had to give dear old dad a little credit. Granny, on the other hand, had nothing to do with it. The version dad gave me was produced in Canada by W. A. Elliott in 1965 and was called the "East Indian Bead Mystery." It's not really known as an escape as such but if you create some cool patter you can see why I put it in this part of the book.

Effect

Three beads are threaded onto two cords and set on a table. A spectator picks up the beads with the cords hanging out of each side of her fist. The magician ties one of the cords around the top of her hand and grabs both ends of both strings. Suddenly, he pulls the strings tight and the string melts through the beads and the hands. The spectator is still holding the three beads. Everything can be immediately examined.

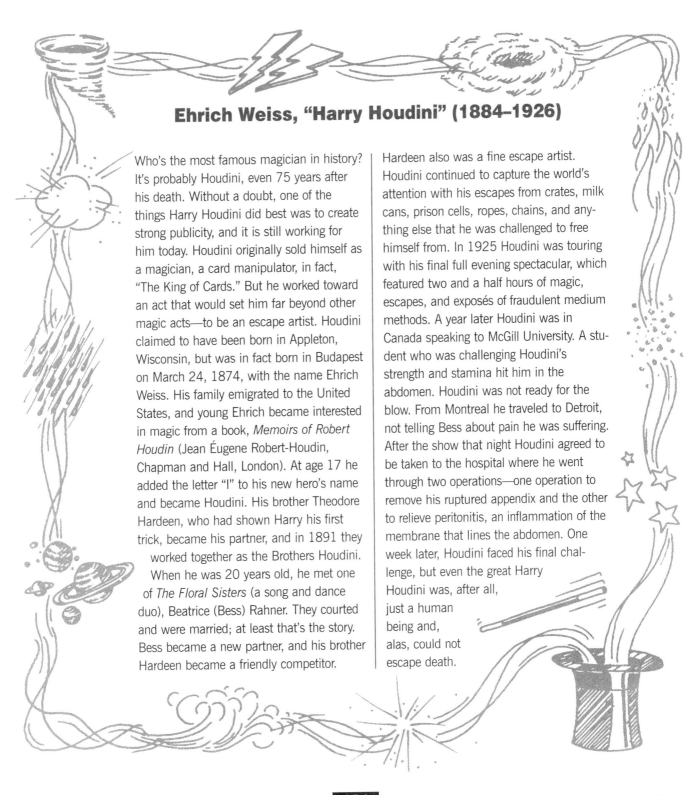

Ehrich Weiss, "Harry Houdini" (1884–1926)

Who's the most famous magician in history? It's probably Houdini, even 75 years after his death. Without a doubt, one of the things Harry Houdini did best was to create strong publicity, and it is still working for him today. Houdini originally sold himself as a magician, a card manipulator, in fact, "The King of Cards." But he worked toward an act that would set him far beyond other magic acts—to be an escape artist. Houdini claimed to have been born in Appleton, Wisconsin, but was in fact born in Budapest on March 24, 1874, with the name Ehrich Weiss. His family emigrated to the United States, and young Ehrich became interested in magic from a book, *Memoirs of Robert Houdin* (Jean Éugene Robert-Houdin, Chapman and Hall, London). At age 17 he added the letter "I" to his new hero's name and became Houdini. His brother Theodore Hardeen, who had shown Harry his first trick, became his partner, and in 1891 they worked together as the Brothers Houdini.

When he was 20 years old, he met one of *The Floral Sisters* (a song and dance duo), Beatrice (Bess) Rahner. They courted and were married; at least that's the story. Bess became a new partner, and his brother Hardeen became a friendly competitor.

Hardeen also was a fine escape artist. Houdini continued to capture the world's attention with his escapes from crates, milk cans, prison cells, ropes, chains, and anything else that he was challenged to free himself from. In 1925 Houdini was touring with his final full evening spectacular, which featured two and a half hours of magic, escapes, and exposés of fraudulent medium methods. A year later Houdini was in Canada speaking to McGill University. A student who was challenging Houdini's strength and stamina hit him in the abdomen. Houdini was not ready for the blow. From Montreal he traveled to Detroit, not telling Bess about pain he was suffering. After the show that night Houdini agreed to be taken to the hospital where he went through two operations—one operation to remove his ruptured appendix and the other to relieve peritonitis, an inflammation of the membrane that lines the abdomen. One week later, Houdini faced his final challenge, but even the great Harry Houdini was, after all, just a human being and, alas, could not escape death.

Preparation

You'll need three large beads and some cord from a craft store. Thread spools will work, too, if they are sanded smooth inside. You can decorate them, as you like. Shoelaces will work for the two cords. They should be about three feet long.

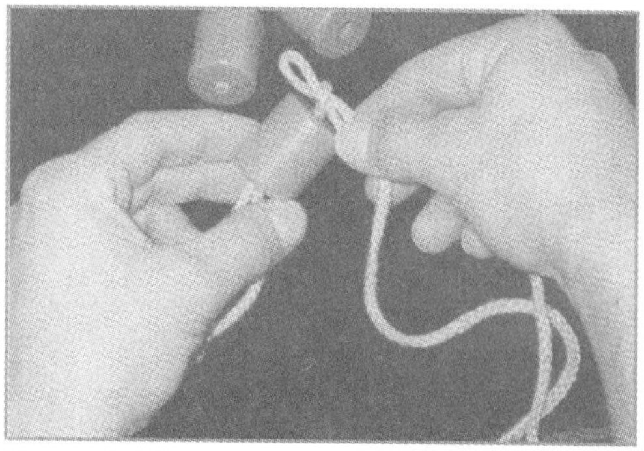

Setup

You have to set up at least one bead before you begin this. Take the cords and fold them in half. Push the looped ends of one cord through the bead and thread the other cord's loop up through it about ½ inch **(Figure 14.1)**. Now, pull the cord back into the bead and the other cord will be pulled in with it. You shouldn't be able to see any of the loops from the outside. You can thread another bead on either side of this one before you begin, but I like to thread them in front of the audience.

Figure 14.1

Routine

Bring the beads out and lay them on the table. Thread the other two on if you haven't already. One should go on each side. Now, have the spectator reach down and pick all three beads off of the table with the cords hanging down. Tell her to squeeze tight so the beads can't get away.

Tie any two ends (one from each end) over top of her hand. Take the ends of the cords (two in each hand) between your two hands. When it's time, pull outward on the strings. The loops inside of the center bead will release and the cords will appear to penetrate not only the beads but also the hand. Drop the cords onto the table and ask the spectator to turn her fist with the fingers up and open her hand. After this, the beads and the cords are completely examinable.

Variations

As an added touch, you can also put two finger rings onto the cords on either side of the three beads before the spectator first picks up the beads. When you pull the cords, the beads will be released but the rings will stay on the two strings. The spectator will shift her eyes back and forth between the beads in her hands and the rings still on the cords and wonder how she did it. This is a fantastic little illusion and it will even fool you when you first perform it.

As far as making the plot and patter for this effect into an escape, have the beads represent the three Houdinis—Harry, Hardeen, and Bess. Explain that although cords or ropes were tied securely around them, they were able to escape every time. The rings can represent handcuffs, the marriage of Harry and Bess, or the plot can be whatever you think up. Coming up with your own story is part of the fun and what makes your magic your very own.

Rope Escapes
Rope and "Straight" Jacket Escape

No, this is not a "Strait Jacket Escape" like the straight jackets that are used in psychiatric institutions. This escape uses two real ropes and a "straight jacket," an ordinary *blazer, double breasted jacket, or windbreaker.*

This escape works on the same principle as "My Dad's Beads." It will help you see how you can take an idea from even an effect from Close-Up Magic and make it large enough for Cabaret or Stage Magic. That's the way great magic minds think. That's how you begin to create new and original routines and tricks.

Effect

Two ropes are placed behind the magician's back. Two spectators are asked to hold each side, and on the count of three, they are to pull as hard as they can on the ends of the ropes. When they do, the ropes penetrate through the magicians body and he is free! Well, he is moderately priced.

Preparation

Two pieces of white magician's rope (I would suggest six to eight feet in length) and white thread.

Did You Know?

The World's Most Dangerous Trick

No, it isn't the "Chinese Water Torture Cell" or the "Buried Alive" illusion, or even the "Strait Jacket Escape." The effect known as the "Bullet Catch" has claimed the lives of at least 15 magicians. There are a number of ways to perform this trick, and those that perform it as a stunt invite disaster. The most famous bullet-catching death was that of Chung Ling Soo (William Robinson), who was shot on stage in 1918. Rumors persisted that his death was not an accident caused by equipment malfunction, but was a murder motivated by jealousy.

Setup

Lay the two pieces of rope together and tie them at their centers with the white thread. Don't tie so tightly that the thread cinches the rope. Just tie the knot firmly enough so the rope pieces are close together. The thread should be invisible against the ropes. **Figure 14.2** shows the ropes with black thread for clarity.

Routine

Have the ropes draped across the back of a chair or on a table and stretch them out so the audience can see they are just two long ropes stretched side by side. Of course, you don't let them separate and you don't mention that they are two "separate" ropes. The audience can see that.

Now, bring the ropes to your waist behind your back and as you do, get your thumb between the ropes on one side of the thread and your fingers between the ropes on the other side. By holding onto just one side of this separation (which is just *one* of the two side-by-side ropes), you can let the other side drop and the ropes will be linked by the thread **(Figure 14.3).** This link should be behind your waist.

Now bring the ends of the ropes around each side and to the front. Have two spectators tie a half knot in front of you with two of the four ends. Be sure to keep holding the ropes at each side of your waist so they don't accidentally pull and break the thread too soon.

When the half knot is successfully tied, have the spectators each take two ends of the rope and move as far to each side of you as possible and tell them to stop there. Ask them to allow a little slack so you can breathe, remove your own hands from the ropes, and explain what they should do next.

Tell them that you will count to three and when you do, you want them to quickly pull the ropes in their direction. Tell them to hold on tight so one doesn't pull the rope out of the other's hand. On three, they pull and you are magically free from the ropes.

Variations

For a change, you and an assistant can tie the ropes around someone else's body and use it strictly as a penetration effect.

You can also thread the two ropes through the sleeves of a jacket, hiding the thread/link at the collar until someone slips into the jacket **(Figure 14.4).** Button the front of the jacket and the ropes will penetrate not only the spectator but also their "straight" jacket. Again, you hang bracelets, coffee mugs, dried fig rings, or Polish sausage on the ropes outside of the sleeves. The audience is left with an astounding escape and you are left with a tasty snack.

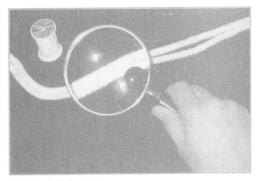
Figure 14.2

Lock and Chain Escapes
The Chain Escape

This is an escape you can make yourself if you have a pair of pliers and a couple pieces of hardware. It's simple to make up and once you do it, you have a pretty convincing piece of escapeology that can be performed either straight or with comedy.

Figure 14.3

Effect

The magician shows a chain, a padlock, and a set of keys. They are handed out for examination. After they are returned, the magician has a spectator assist him in tightly tying his wrists together with the chain and locking the ends with the padlock. The magician frees himself.

Preparation

Either make the escape yourself or purchase one from a dealer (or me!). To make it, you'll need:

A length of chain 24 inches long and two one-inch metal rings. Connect one ring to one end of the chain making it 25 inches long. Connect the second ring about four inches from the same end, that is, including the length of the first ring.

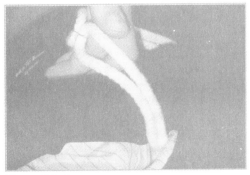
Figure 14.4

Figure 14.5

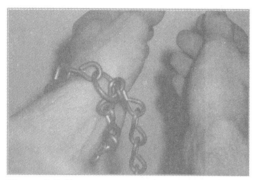

Figure 14.6

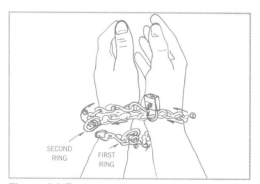

Figure 14.7

You'll also need a substantial looking padlock that will fit through the chain links. Don't buy a toy, it will make the escape look like child's play. Keys would be handy too. **(Figure 14.5).** Have a newspaper on hand if you decide to do the optional variation of the routine.

Setup

Have all of the props laid out on a table so the audience can see them. Have the table tilted or "raked" toward the audience. This gives the escape a bigger look.

Routine

Wrap the chain around one wrist and out through the end as in **Figure 14.6** with the chain coming up the wrist, over the end of the ring, and down the side of the wrist again. Hold the other wrist tightly against the chain that is hanging down and whip both hands around in a circle together, swinging the free end of the chain back over top. Have a spectator pull it through the inner ring (not the end ring) and lock it **(Figure 14.7).**

To release yourself, you only need to move the second wrist you tied over top of the other wrist, and the chain that hung down during the fastening will allow you plenty of room to remove that wrist. With the free hand, you can slide the chain through the end link in the other hand to allow it to also escape.

You can do this escape quickly by showing the hands locked, turning around and coming back to face the audience, and holding the whole apparatus still locked but dangling from the fingertips of one hand. It takes practice to get some speed with it, but it isn't difficult. You can cover the needed pause when your back is to the audience with some loud patter.

Variation

To add some comedy, another option of escaping is to have the spectator lock the wrists and place a folded newspaper over them in the shape of a roof. Once covered, remove one of your hands quickly and keep it under the paper. Be sure not to move the hands any more than necessary. As you are asking the spectator to "pull this corner over a little" or some similar instruction, bring the free hand out and adjust the paper for her. The hand goes back under the paper into the locked position. Ask the spectator to take the paper off and start again. When she does you are still locked. Often the spectator will not even notice that you are helping with a free hand but the audience will. It is very funny. Using your imagination, you can use this option in a number of different ways or a number of times until you finally do escape. Try to create a surprise ending.

Box and Trunk Escapes

Escape artists love to get locked up in boxes. This is when you will often find them making faces at policemen. Here's a large escape effect that will make you look like a real pro. It won't get you out of jail, though.

Houdini's Trunk

Effect

A person-sized wood or metal box and its top are inspected by a committee. Four bolts with small holes in the ends, four cotter keys, and four nuts are also handed out for examination. The committee keeps the nuts and the performer takes the bolts inside the box when he gets in.

A lipped lid is placed on the box and the performer pushes the bolts out through holes that align with the lid. The committee turns the nuts onto the bolts, pushes the cotter keys through the holes in the bolts, and spreads the cotter keys to lock everything tightly.

A curtain or suitable screen is placed around the box, a narrator steps forward to explain about the escape, and music is played behind him. At the crescendo of the music, the screen is opened or falls and the triumphant magician takes his bow.

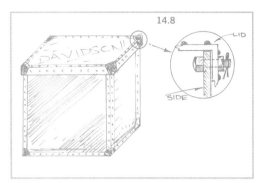

Figure 14.8

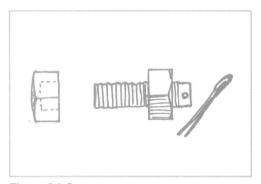

Figure 14.9

Preparation

You need some serious construction for this piece. This is definitely not close-up; this ain't no carry-on. Have a box built to the smallest possible dimension you can fit into made out of metal or wood. The fact that you can even get into it will look impressive and give the audience some idea of your contortion abilities. Audiences love to believe that all escape artists and all magic assistants are masters of contortion. There's absolutely no reason not to take some of that credit now. As far as the material you build the box out of, consider the weight of such a beast, and then remember that you have to get not only yourself but possibly a fresh hernia inside of that thing. Wood or lighter-weight aluminum are good alternatives since the box will sit on the floor and won't really be stressed or have to support any weight by itself. The lid should slip over the base like a shoebox and each of the four lid sides should be drilled in the center so a bolt can be inserted through it and into the box **(Figure 14.8)**.

You'll also need four regular bolts with holes in them to accept the cotter keys and four pieces of threaded rod with holes that will match the bolts when the magician switches them and pushes them out from inside of the box. Put another set of nuts on the other ends of these rod/bolts so they act like genuine bolts when the committee tightens them **(Figure 14.9)**. Since there are no wrenches supplied for them to use, the bolts will just be finger tightened, unless some freak shows up with one of those fold-out McGuyver knives.

You'll need four cotter keys that will fit the holes and a pair of pliers for the committee to bend them with. Finally, you need a screen, some music (I suggest the Rocky theme because it's about "boxing" . . . oh, sorry) and a narrator.

Setup

Have the four duplicate (all thread) rods hidden on you somewhere. You be the judge as to exactly how dedicated you want to be on this one. Have the box open with the top beside it and the hardware on a table.

Routine

Bring the committee onstage and have them inspect everything. Have one member hand you the four bolts and get into the box. Your narrator should instruct the audience as to how the top should be placed on. Once the top is on, get out your fake bolts and push them through the holes. While the committee is fastening everything, relax and think of how glamorous magic is.

When the music starts, you begin to escape by taking the inside nuts off of the bolts and pushing the bolts back out the holes. The music and narrator will hide the noise. Push up on the lid of the box, get out, and put the lid back on the box. Be careful of your fingers; nobody likes a whimpering escape artist. If you don't need to have the box inspected again, you can just push the bolts back into the box without the inside nuts on. You can also just leave the nuts inside of the box.

Now when your narrator has woven his velvet spell over the audience and the music is blaring ". . . Gonna' fly now!" drop the curtain. You're out and the audience will be applauding like crazy.

Underwater Escapes

Harry Houdini was known to the world as "Europe's Eclipsing Sensation," and "The World's Handcuff King and Prison Breaker." Probably his best-known escape, and the one most people believe killed him, was the sensation known as "Chinese Water Torture Cell." Just so you know, Harry Houdini did not die in this or any other escape.

Harry was 38 years old in 1922, the year he introduced this sensation. His ability to create publicity and mystique surrounding his very existence is nothing short of genius. Houdini's water escapes are shrouded in a veil that are even more mysterious today than they were way back then, there's no escaping that.

If you are thinking about performing escapes under water right now, stop it! Just get it out of your head Jacques. If you are reading this book, chances are you are trying to get to know where you fit in with magic and where magic fits in with you. You're just not ready. I'm not going to tell you that you can *never* do water escapes, but it's just not in the picture right now. Escape artists are a rare breed but they are not as crazy as you might think. Just like stunt people, they understand all of the risks involved and they try to remove them or at least reduce them to a sane level. Escapes take careful planning, exact routining, and physical ability. I have only given you the tip of the iceberg, but if you are interested, I tip my hat. You can be sure if you ever see me underwater, thrashing around trying to get out of some kind of tangle, I have either had too much Aqua Velva or I am just caught in the fringe on my baptismal robe.

CHAPTER 15

Magic for Children—Tricks That Kids Can Do

Paper
Flying Peter, Flying Paul

My mother, Mary Lou, showed me this trick when I was just a little tiny ankle biter. I thought it was amazing, had no idea of how she did it, and I was sure that she must be really, really smart.

Effect

Two pieces of paper are shown resting on the backs of both index fingers. As the magician recites a little rhyming story, the hands are raised one at a time off of the table and back again. The pieces of paper described in the poem as two birds "one named Peter and one named Paul," have disappeared. As the rhyme continues, the move is repeated and the birds are back.

Preparation

All you need for the little cutie is a couple of pieces of paper of a weight no heavier than regular writing paper. Lighter-weight paper is also fine. The pieces should be a little smaller than a dime so that they aren't a whole lot wider than your fingers.

Setup

Attach a piece of paper to the backs of each index finger just above the fingernail. To attach the paper use spit. That's right, I said spit and I don't want to hear any "ewww" or "gross" sounds. This is magic spit and another fine example of the glamorous life of magic. The proper thickness of paper and the right amount of your magic drivel will make sure the paper stays on but doesn't wet through. This is another reason not to use paper that is too thick. You would have to have a mouth full of grits to make it stick. For you people from the north, it would have to be maple syrup, but you catch my drift.

Routine with Patter

Start out with your index fingers pointing straight out, resting on the edge of a table, "birds" up. Try to let the fingers rest on the table with the rest of the hand bent down the side and as out of sight as possible. You begin to speak.

"Two little birds sitting on a wall,"

"One named Peter"

(Raise one hand a couple of inches then back down.)

"And one named Paul."

(Raise the other hand a couple of inches and back down.)

"Fly away, Peter."

(Raise the first hand all the way up past your ear until your elbow is pointing toward the spectator. Now, switch fingers, closing your index finger with the bird into the hand. Hey, maybe that's where they got that "bird in the hand" thing. Your thumb can help hold the finger. Immediately stick the middle finger out and bring the hand back down and rest the middle finger on the table. All the changing action happens when the hand is behind you.)

It appears as though the paper has gone from the finger. Most people think that the paper has fallen off when the hand was swung backward. It couldn't stay on upside down. That's because they are not aware of the secret ingredient—sticky spit. Now continue.

"Fly away, Paul."

(Do the same raising of the hand and switching of the fingers.)

"Come back, Peter."

(Switch the fingers back again.)

"Come back, Paul."

(Switch the other hand too.)

That's all there is to it. You can now take the papers off of the fingers and discard them. This is a quick trick, is good for improving coordination, and has patter that is easy to remember. It's good for anybody who is starting out. Whether you decide to perform it for a child or help a child learn it, it's a nice little piece of enchantment. If this doesn't sound very exciting to you when you read it, try it out on someone. It's simple but it can be a quick fooler and that's nothing to spit at.

Rosemagic

Rosemagic is the magical endeavor of two bright and talented young ladies, Katy (16) and Allie (13) Rose. As a duo, they perform magical birthday parties, stage shows, and balloon artistry.

In 1989 when the girls were but five and two, they attended their first magic convention and Katy begged her parents to purchase a scarf-to-rose trick. As children, the girls learned to promote their own business, negotiate their fees, and go into homes and perform. Their uniqueness at being young and female were recognized and they were asked to write their story in a book, *Girls and Young Women Entrepreneurs* (Free Spirit Publishing, 1997).

Rubber Bands

There are a ton of rubber band effects in magic today. Go to a magic convention and sooner or later you'll see someone with some rubber bands around a wrist ready to lead another unsuspecting spectator into the old latex labyrinth. Here is a rubber band effect that I like and that can be done with any thin band. This is a good impromptu piece of magic. You'll be surprised how many rubber bands are just laying around out there waiting for some magic to happen to them . . . perfect!

Effect

A rubber band is stretched until it is broken, "Snap." It is rolled into a ball and it is put into the spectator's hand. After a couple of magic passes, a wave, and a grunt or two, the magician asks the spectator to open the hand. The rubber band is restored.

Preparation

All you need is a rubber band. I'm not sure what size or number of rubber band is the best but I can tell you anything $1/8$ of an inch or less in width will work pretty well. If it's any thicker the illusion is not as good.

Setup

You need to get the rubber band in a starting position between the time that you pick up the rubber band in front of everyone and when you start to break it. The set up needs to be fast but with a little practice and a little misdirection it's not that tough.

Routine

Say something about the rubber band before you pick it up so everyone has a chance to see it is just one rubber band, your hands are empty, and the rubber band is whole. Pick up the rubber band and hold it with the thumb and index finger of each hand. Now it's time for the misdirection.

As soon as you touch the band and naturally begin to bring it toward you, look at the audience. Look right into someone's eyes in front of you, lean forward, and in a lively voice, say something. Don't worry about not being able to address everyone. If you address one person properly, everyone else will be magnetized with not only your words but also the reaction of the person you are talking to. Say something that will require some sort of response even if it's a laugh. This almost forces the rest of the audience to look away from your hands. They want to know the answer, they want to be in on it. They don't want to miss anything but they will. This is when you do the set up move. "You would like to help me create some real magic, wouldn't you?" you say.

Pull the rubber band slightly outward and pinch the two "ends" so you have two pieces of it lying together as one. Now twist the right hand fingers forward and the left-hand fingers backward just enough to twirl the two strands together. These two pieces will be shown as one later, so it's important that they don't get separated from one another. The twirling helps this.

The right hand keeps a firm pinch on it's end loop and the left hand moves the other end down and pushes it's loop between the third finger and pinkie finger of the right hand at the first joint. The pinkie closes and squeezes as tightly as possible. The left hand's second, third, and pinkie fingers immediately slide between the rubber band and right fingers, curl around it, and pull it away from the right-hand fingers **(Figure 15.1).** This is about where you would ideally have the spectator refocus after the misdirection back onto the rubber band. It all happens very quickly. To the spectator it just looks like the fingers are inside of a rubber band and it is being stretched between the two hands.

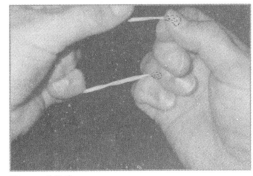

Figure 15.1

I try to keep things moving around during this part so that no one gets a chance to burn the band and discovers it is really two thicknesses. The farther apart you can pull the hands, the tighter the two thicknesses squeeze together and the thinner the band looks. Just keep squeezing one end/loop with your right thumb and the other with your pinkie.

After a few bouncy tugs stretching the band, bring the left thumb and index finger up against the right and pinch the band

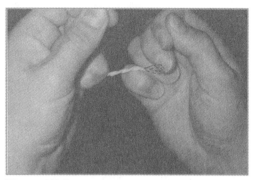

Figure 15.2

as close as possible with those left fingers. Keep pinching and pull the hands apart, tilting the thumbs toward the spectator so he is looking directly at about ½ inch of rubber band now stretched between the two hands. Really, it's more like you are pulling the left away from the right, but you'll get the feel for it.

Finally, when it's time to "break" the rubber band, keep pulling with the left hand and slightly release the right pinch. The band will slip out of the right hand pinch with a snap. The left hand naturally jumps to the left a little because of the release. The right-hand pinch should remain in position to give the illusion that the band is still running through the right hand up to the right thumb and finger. It's just broken off there, that's all **(Figure 15.2).** If the amount of rubber band stretched between the two hands just before the break was small enough, just a tip of band will be visible within the left hand pinch. It will appear to be the broken end. Now it's time to restore it.

Begin rolling the end in the left hand into a ball moving toward the right hand. When the left hand reaches the right hand, let go of the right hand grip and completely open it. Continue rolling the rubber band in the left hand while you ask the spectator to open one hand palm up. This once again takes the heat off of your hand. When the spectator's hand is ready, place the ball of rubber into his palm and with the other hand, close his fingers over the ball. Take the left hand out just before it gets trapped. The idea is to get the rubber band in his hand without it uncurling and ruining the finale. After you summon your magic powers, ask the spectator to slowly, ever so slowly, open his hand. Ask if he feels anything. Chances are he will because the rubber band is in the hand trying to unwind and untangle and it wriggles around quite a bit. When the hand is finally opened all the way, it is often necessary to use one index finger to straighten the rubber band out while it is still on his outstretched palm. Leave the rubber band in his hand. It won't be long before he will pick it up with his other hand and give it a stretch and a good looking over. You have made magic right in his own hands.

Crayons

Here's a piece of mentalism or mind reading that can be performed *for* or performed *by* anyone of any age. What's great about this is that the magician teaches the spectator how to be the magician. He instructs the spectator how to channel and transfer a thought, a vision, and finally a description of a real object by magic. Here's the most important part: it will fool them all! Again, it's simple but it's also easy. Simple to understand, easy to perform. Sounds like a winner to me.

Color Me Psychic

Effect

The magician asks the spectator to remain silent. The spectator opens a box of crayons and simply concentrates on one color of crayon. The magician faces away from the spectator with his hands behind his back and the spectator places a crayon into the magician's hand. When the magician turns around, he asks the spectator to touch his shoulder. At that instant the magician knows the color of the crayon that the spectator has chosen. This is an old trick with a few new twists that I think make it better than ever.

Preparation

There is very little preparation for this trick except to have a box of multicolored crayons and to practice the routine until you are confident about it. Because the secret and the size of the trick are very simple, the routine should be interesting and dramatic. It should seem like magic, not a puzzle. The secret lies in scraping a piece of the wax crayon off under the fingernail when it is behind your back so when you bring the hand back around, you can glimpse the color. This little "scraperoo" happens as the magician turns back around to face the spectator (marked by the * in the routine), and starts to go over what has happened so far. The rest is showmanship and performance, but there are some subtleties to make it even more mysterious.

(continued on next page)

Method

One tip is to make sure the crayons in your box are very different colors so you can tell them apart. You don't want to be saying, "Place your hand on my shoulder now as I tell you that the color of your crayon was pink, no salmon, I'll get it . . . peach?"

Most versions of this trick have the magician bring the hand with the "sample" to his head, get the glimpse and pretend to concentrate until the color is named. This will work, but the secret move, glimpse, and pose need to happen at the exact time. It would be better if you were looking at the spectator, not at your finger as you became crossed eyed and go into your Karnac/Swami pose. My idea is to make the spectator the star. Have the spectator "channel" his thoughts and finally transmit them to you at the moment you are touched. Putting your hand on his shoulder first gives you lots of time in a natural position to look at the color. It's also not goofy looking since you're just showing him what to do later. Having the spectator concentrate on closing the box, not touching your hand, is great misdirection for what you are doing. All eyes will be on his tasks. Asking him to remain silent seems unusual, interesting, and hypnotic. Having him speak only once (to reveal you have picked up his message) adds some tension and drama to what is usually just a casual and cute stunt. It makes it magic!

Setup

You'll need a box of crayons and an assistant from the audience. Place the box of crayons to the side so people don't think they are anything special. In other words, don't carry them on you; they'll call attention if they're tucked in a pocket somewhere.

Routine

Show the spectator where the box of crayons is sitting and ask him to pick up the box, open it, and just mentally select one of the colors. "Just think of the color. Do not touch it. Now, continue to think of the crayon and stare into my eyes. Please do not speak or make any sound."

After that is done, show your hands as empty, and put them behind your back. Turn around. You are now facing away from the spectator.

Instruct the spectator to take his mentally selected crayon from the box and place the crayon into your left hand. Tell him to be careful not to touch his hand to your hand but to simply place the crayon lightly in the hand. Again, remind the spectator not to speak and to close the crayon box so that if you see it again, you cannot possibly have any idea of what crayon he has chosen. If you are to gain any information it must come from him.

Now, turn around to face the spectator* and tell him to remain silent as you go over what has happened so far. Tell him to agree or disagree with what you say only with a nod of the head, if he agrees, or a shake of the head, if he disagrees.

"You were handed a regular box of crayons that you opened yourself. You then mentally selected one particular crayon. You did not touch the crayon but simply concentrated on it while looking into my eyes. Is that true?" The spectator nods.

"I then turned around, and you pulled your selected crayon out from all the others in the box and silently placed it into my left hand, is that true?" The spectator nods again.

"You did not touch my hand, is that true?" The spectator nods.

"In a second, I'm going to ask you to take your empty right hand just as I am and place it onto my shoulder. Please consider that you have not talked to me, touched me, made any decision in front of me, or communicated with me by any other means except by looking into my eyes. And now, it is time for you to channel your energy and information to me."

"Please place your hand on my shoulder now . . . as I tell you that the color of your crayon is green. Is that correct? Speak now." The spectator says, "Yes, it is! However did you know?"

If you want to add a little extra drama, time things so he puts his hand on you during the middle of your sentence and you act stunned. Build your voice up and let his touch spark you and interrupt your sentence.

James Randall Zwinge, "The Amazing Randi"

(continued from previous page)

combined with his intelligent and well read reactions of his audience, are very entertaining to watch. His numerous lectures, books, and television appearances have enlightened audiences all over the world. In 1996, the James Randi Education Foundation was established to further Randi's work. Randi's challenge to the world offers $1 million to any "psychic" who can prove their abilities without his explanation. No one has ever been able to collect the cash.

Paper Clips
The Linking Paper Clips

Here's a puzzling little trick with some usual objects that will make you smile the first time you try it. It's one of those magic tricks that you do and then you say, "Hey how does that work?"

Effect

The magician takes a dollar bill, folds it twice, and clips two paper clips a short distance from each other along one edge. When the bill is grabbed by each end and pulled, the clips jump off of the bill and magically link together in the air.

Preparation

The preparation for this trick happens as part of the routine. There is no advance prep work or secret set up. First of all you'll need a dollar bill (or any other bill) and two paper clips. The trick is in the folding of the bill and the placement of the paper clips. Here's how it goes.

Setup

This whole thing happens automatically once you have the bill folded correctly and the paper clips in the right places. Pulling the bill's ends causes the paper clips to be squeezed together in a way that cause them to quickly link and finally pop off of the top edge. It's really a neat little stunt. Everything is set up in full view so there are no special slights or anything to hide. Now, let's continue with the real set up, which is the routine.

Routine

Hold the bill horizontally between the two hands with the thumbs to the back (your side) and fingers on the front (their side). Looking down on the top edge you need to push the ends inward until the bill forms an "S." The right thumb goes inside of the top curve of the "S" and the left fingers in the bottom curve.

Once in position, move the right thumb to the back of the whole thing and take the left hand away. Hold the "S" in place while you pick up one paper clip with the left hand. Place the paper clips one at a time along the top side of the bill **(Figure 15.3).** Show the position of the clips to the audience and point out that the clips are separated away from each other. Now, simply hold tight on the left edge of the bill with the left hand and the right edge with the right. Pull the ends apart and the magic happens. I told you it was cool! You can practice and catch the clips in midair if you want to add more surprise.

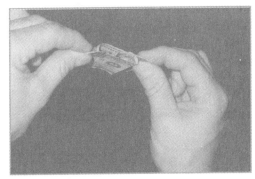

Figure 15.3

Before starting the fold, place a rubber band that is a little larger than the width of the bill around the center of the bill. Fold the bill as usual and add the paper clips just like before. This time when you pull the ends the paper clips won't jump off of the bill. They will link in a row with the rubber band and hang in a chain below it. This looks very tricky and seems as if it must be a very difficult piece of magic to master. We know different. This is a good follow up after performing your rubber band magic from the beginning of this chapter and you can even tie one routine into the next. Create your own patter so that one effect blends right into the next not only with the props but also with the story.

Figure 15.4

A Trick You Can Make
Popsicle Paddle

You can make a paddle for the paddle move by cutting a popsicle stick so it makes a handle, leaving the end of the stick as the paddle face **(Figure 15.4)**. By drawing a straight line on one side and a wavy line on the other, you can make a wavy line turn straight or a straight line "get dizzy"—just by shaking it and flipping it with the Paddle Move from Chapter 7.

CHAPTER 16

Magic for Grown-Ups— the Adult Table

Magic to Perform for Children
String-n-Straw
Effect

The magician threads a piece of string through a soda straw so it hangs out of both ends. He then bends the straw in half with the ends still showing and cuts the center of the bend off with a pair of scissors. He shows the two separate ends of each straw and restraightens the cut straw out. Pulling on the string from on end, he shows that the straw is still in two pieces but the string remains unharmed.

Preparation

You'll need a straw, a two-foot piece of string, a razor knife, and a soda straw. Cut about a two-inch slit through one side of the soda straw.

Setup

Place all of the props on the table and you are ready to begin.

Routine

Thread the string through the straw and fold it in half. As you are making sure that the two sides are even, hold the straws in one hand and pull on both ends, causing the string to be pulled down into the slits. The string now crosses from one straw to the other and you cover this with your thumb and fingers **(Figure 16.1).** Cut off the center loop of the straw and make sure everyone sees the center fall off and that the two ends are completely separate. Straighten the straw out so you're holding it like the handle of a suitcase, wave your hands as you say the magic words, "Badda Boom Badda Bing, fix this string." Pull one end of the string from the hand and the other end will follow it, completely restored. Drop the pieces of the straw to give the audience a chance to see the three pieces (including the loop) and you are left high and dry. Your audience will scratch their heads and think, "Now, I've seen a lot of tricky stuff but this, . . . this is the last straw."

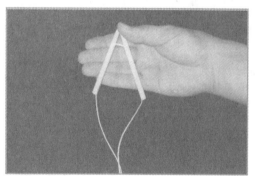

Figure 16.1

"Hey, That's Thumb Kinda' Trick Ya' Got Der"

Effect

At any given moment, the magician takes one hand and pulls on the thumb of the other hand, and it is seen to come off, slide back on, and work good as new. Kids love this trick but I'm warning you, they will want to see it over and over and over again. It's even one you can repeat within your routine.

Preparation

Just two hands. Even if you don't have both thumbs or index fingers, this can be done with a couple of the others.

Setup

This is totally impromptu and that's why it's great for children. They don't exactly wait until the time is just right to scream, "Hey . . . hey, can you show me a magic trick?" As a magician, it's you're job to not let them down.

Routine

1. Put one hand in front of you with the back of the hand toward the kids, and the thumb up, and fingers held straight, together and pointing off to the side. Now, you are going to make it look as if you are reaching over top of that hand with the opposite hand and squeezing the thumb at its first joint. You will be squeezing with the index finger and the thumb of that opposite hand. That's what you want it to look like anyway.

2. Here's what really happens. The other hand does come over the original hand but there's some trickiness with the thumbs. The hand that is originally held across the body holds its thumb firmly against the side of the hand and bends its thumb in at its first joint. Just the first joint, don't let the second section of the thumb (the one that hooks to the rest of the hand) move back. It needs to stay right on top of the side of the hand.

Attention!

If you are a child reading this, do not try these tricks. This section is "Magic for Grown-Ups." There are plenty of great tricks in the rest of the book, but these are off-limits. This can be very dangerous, and you should never play with razors or any other sharp objects.

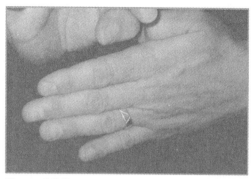

Figure 16.2

3. The approaching hand needs to pull the thumb into its own palm as tightly as it can. Just clench the thumb in hard and it should be okay.

4. Now you need to "line up" both thumbs so the two halves come together and form one. It's kind of like the front and the back of a horse costume **(Figure 16.2)**. You also have to hide the crack between the two thumbs.

5. Your original hand remains the same and your approaching hand lines its half up with it. Make sure the thumb doesn't look twisted from the front. By raising the approaching hand's finger up, you can twist your hand around until you finally get a match. When you do, just bring the index finger down and cover the crack. The other fingers all remain raised out of the way. Remember, all of these steps happen very quickly and smoothly and look like you're just grabbing your thumb in the middle with your hand. You'll get a feel for it just like you get a feel for where your car keys fit into your car's ignition (as opposed to how it feels when you have a rental car).

6. Now, slide the thumb tip to the side, along the side of the index finger, but stop it before it gets to the end. The illusion is really quite perfect, but you can't leave it there too long because it does have some angle problems. Slide the thumb back against its "stub" again and back and forth a couple of times.

7. At the end of this trick I usually quickly shift my hands as if to show another angle, and when I do, I take my thumbs out of "presto position" and regrasp the thumb with the other hand for real. This also happens extremely quickly. Holding it that way, you twist it at the joint to make sure that it's on tight and take the covering fingers and hand away. Wiggle your thumb to show that it still works and you're finished. There's nothing to hide, nothing to reset, and your audience is sure to give you the thumbs up, tah dah!

"Ah Ah Ah Chew!" Chewing String Together

My uncle Dick showed me this trick a long time ago. My brother Chris learned it too. Chris and I probably could have put the magic world on its ear with this one. We could have teamed up to be just like Siegfried and Roy, but we didn't because there was only one trick that we both agreed on and we were fresh out of tigers.

Effect

The ends of an ordinary piece of string are tied together to form a large loop. The loop is twisted in half, forming two small loops and a spectator is invited to cut through them. Two of the newly cut ends are plainly shown to be placed in the magician's mouth. The other cut ends are held apart and the magician begins to chew. After a short amount of time, the string is pulled from the mouth and miraculously, the string is seen to be completely restored. The magician has chewed the string together. The string may then be examined.

Preparation

The explanation of this small miracle lies in the looping of the string with the hands and the forming of a secret loop in the string. I prefer plain old, white cotton string, the kind the butcher used to use in the old days to hold the brown paper around a couple of pounds of brontosaurus burger. I use a piece about three feet long. I don't actually measure off three feet, I simply hold one end at the tip of my nose and stretch my arm out as far as I can and that's the length. I also have a pretty big nose so you might want to make it four feet.

You'll also need a pair of scissors. If you are a child, please use safety scissors or ask a grown-up to help you. I don't want anybody getting hurt. Remember, never run with string.

Setup

Once again, this is done right in front of everyone, so no set up is required. I never knew my Uncle Dick could be that sneaky!

Did You Know?

Argentina's Rene Levante is famous for his beautiful card magic, even though he has only one arm. Along those lines, Meir Yedid, who specializes in a weird kind of illusion magic that seems as if he can make his fingers vanish and reappear, actually lost a finger during a car accident. Meir made the best of the accident and works the fact that he lost one finger into his act.

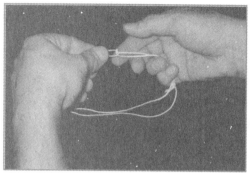

Figure 16.3

Routine

Start with a length of string. You can let the spectator examine it if she wants. Tie the ends together forming a loop. Now put your hands inside of the loop with your fingers pointing toward the audience like you were lying about "the one that got away." It's a good idea if you keep the knot on the left side—over the back of the left hand is good. Now, it's time to create the secret loop that no one will ever see. Keep your left hand still and rotate your right hand twice. The rotation of the right hand is as if you were motioning "Speed it up." You might also say that the right hand rotates clockwise. When it rotates and is back to its original position, that's one rotation. Do it again and your hand should be back in its original position for the second time. There will be a couple of twists in the middle. It looks like three twists but it's only two.

Move the right hand with its loop to the left and put the right fingers through the front of the left hand loop. The back of the right hand slides against the palm of the left hand. Carefully remove the left hand leaving both loops hanging on the right hand. Pinch the two strings together that rest on the right index finger and pull the two strings out to form a loop. Move the strings with your left hand until the secret loop is drawn exactly between your right thumb and first two fingers. **(Figure 16.3).** These fingers pinch and hide the secret loop. This will take a few practices to get the feel of it, but once you do you'll improve fast.

Keep a firm grip with the right thumb and first two fingers and move your left hand up to grasp the strings opposite your right hand, leaving about an inch between the two hands. This is where you will have the spectator cut the strings. Make sure the spectator is very careful when she cuts the string. Never ever try to substitute a knife for the scissors. It's way too dangerous, and sooner or later, a spectator will slip and you'll end up with a career as a one-fingered pickpocket who can only steal doughnuts.

Once the strings are cut, let go of the left-hand strings and let them fall. The right-hand thumb and index finger hide the secret loop. The second, third, and pinkie fingers of the right hand should be extended out of the way as if you were holding the handle of a tea cup. If you keep them closed, it will look like you are trying to hide something (only you know that you really are).

Check out "the secret loop." It consists of the one long string looped around a tiny piece of string. The tiny piece makes what appears to be the two cut ends. The other ends are still hanging down. Now, you just have to get rid of the little piece and it will appear as though the string is together. That's the next step.

Draw attention to the two separate ends and put them into your mouth. Make sure the secret loop makes it in there too. What you're trying to do is get the little string off of the big string and hide it between your cheek and gum.

You can either hold each of the other ends in your hands or let the spectator hold them. Here's a word of caution. If you let spectators hold the strings, "spot them" with your own hands between their hands at the ends of the string and your mouth. If the string gets pulled, it will come out of the mouth with the little piece attached, either that or a partial plate. Be careful if you're holding them yourself too. It's easy to want to pull the big string to help get the little string away. If it pops out of your mouth too quickly, the spectator doesn't get a chance to see what happened even if the little string is already off. Remember that chewing string together takes time. Tongue weaving is not easy. Don't worry about your facial gestures, they will take care of themselves. If you don't believe me, just practice in the front of the mirror and then write me and tell me how much you laughed.

Once you have the little string off and hidden in the mouth, draw attention to the mouth with the hands and slowly reveal the string. Before ending let me warn you, you can choke on string. Be careful and make sure there isn't too much string between the two hands when the spectator is asked to cut it. This means the little string of the secret loop won't be very large. When you have a chance, take the little string out of your mouth and discard it. Don't let anyone see you do this, it's ugly.

Here's another idea. I have performed this effect using very thin licorice string. The good part about this is you don't have to cut it, you can break it. It doesn't seem weird to put it in your mouth and you can swallow the gimmick. There! We have solved all of the problems and I won't have to send you a get well card. Besides, we've got more magic to do.

Neil Foster
(1921–1988)

Neil Foster didn't always want to be a magician. He was set up to become an artist but somehow decided to enroll as a student of the Chavez College of Manual Dexterity. Not only did he become a student, he later became an instructor. Neil traveled internationally as well as throughout the United States sharing his magic with people, ranging from nightclubs to schools. He was often assisted by his wife Jeanne. I can remember seeing Neil Foster when I was a child, attending the "Abbotts Get Togethers" in Colon, Michigan. He was vice president of Abbott's Magic. Neil would always perform at the evening shows, and everyone waited in hopes that he would perform his beautiful "Zombie Ball" routine. A silver sphere floated over and around a silk handkerchief held between Foster's out-

(continued on next page)

Magic for Other Adults
Poker Hands—I'm Royally Confused!

Because adults love the theme of poker, here's one for them. Keep in mind, most kids don't care about playing cards the way adults do. They either don't know the names, the suits, or really care why the doggy paw is called the spade and the clover is called the club. Kids need the trick to pass "the kid test," remember?

Effect

The magician takes a deck of cards and asks five people to think of a number between 10 and 20 but not to tell it to him until he asks them. Then he gives the deck to the first spectator and asks her to tell him her number and count that same number of cards off onto the table one at a time into a small pile. Next, he asks her to add the two digits of her original number and deal *that* number of cards from her small pile into a new pile. She keeps the last card (her number), regroups the deck, and passes them to the next spectator.

Each spectator has a chance to do this and when they are all done, you explain about how people love to the gamble (love to win money, really) but that they are always up against the odds. Tell them that the odds of them choosing any specific number or getting any given card in this demonstration would make a computer smoke. The odds of them coming up with cards that would work well together would be even greater. Ask the first person to turn over her card, followed by the second, and so on until the fifth person. In order, their cards are the ace, king, queen, jack, and 10 of spades. They have created a royal flush.

Preparation

All you need is a regular deck of cards and a little set up time.

Setup

This is a variation on the countdown force you learned in Chapter 3. It just uses more cards. As an added bonus, when the cards are brought out of the deck with this mathematical method, they also come out in the order they were stacked. That's how you are able to get the royal flush. Place the cards in a packet and in order. Put nine more cards on top of them and set them all on top of the rest of the deck. So that you know which way the cards will come out, remember that the first card in the five-card stack will be the first card to come out after all the selecting and counting is done.

Routine

This effect is self-working but you need to keep your eyes on the helpers. One wrong count or misunderstanding could really screw things up.

One thing you do need to know is what to do with the remainder of the cards after the one card has been counted down to and laid on the table. The following is what you need to do between the steps.

1. You give the deck to the first spectator and ask her to tell you a number between 10 and 20. She needs to count off that same number of cards face down onto the table, one at a time into a small pile.

2. Next, you ask her to add the two digits of her original number and deal *that* number of cards from her small pile into a new pile. The last card dealt is her card (and she takes it). The rest of that little pile are placed on top of the *deck* (not the smaller tabled pile) and the smaller tabled pile is placed on top of them. Basically, the cards that are finally counted to find her card are placed on the deck, and the remainder of the cards that are still tabled from the first count are placed on last.

3. She keeps the last card (her number), regroups the deck, and passes them to the next spectator. The cards are handled the exact same way each time.

This is a cool effect. It involves a number of people who are able to interact for some magic that will leave them "royally" confused.

Neil Foster (1921–1988)

(continued from previous page)

stretched hands as if it were a zombie ghost traveling on fog. Under the control of Neil, the trick seemed closer to a miracle than magic and would always get thunderous applause, even though almost every person in the audience was a magician and knew how the trick worked. I guess it's just like knowing what colors are in the palette of paint. It's knowing how and when to use each and how to layer every stroke that makes the painting a masterpiece. Such was the magic of Neil Foster. In 1979, Neil retired in Colon, Michigan, where he spent the next nine years, the remainder of his life, teaching the Chavez Course, the course that accidentally created his career and the careers of many others who were fortunate enough to study with him.

A Razor Head

Effect

This is an effect that was inspired by Warren Simms. It's a simple version of the "Razor Blade Swallow" that doesn't cost a lot and doesn't look too gimmicked. Follow the instructions so you don't cut off your tongue and get angry at me for it. I guess you couldn't yell or anything, but I just don't need you getting angry anyway.

The magician shows a rack of 10 razor blades and a cup (preferably a tumbler). He removes one of the blades and proves it is sharp by slicing through a sheet of paper. He drops this blade into the cup and proceeds to empty the rest of the stand into the cup. The magician shows a spool of thread, pulls off a piece about an arm's length, balls it up, and places it onto the end of the tongue. He swallows and shows the tongue to be clean. Next, he pours the blades from the cup into his hand and places them half way in his mouth. With a snapping back of his head, they are gone. The magician begins to hold his sides, his stomach, and his throat as if he is going through serious pain and strenuous regurgitation. His lips begin to pucker and he points at his mouth, takes his empty hand up to it, and pulls out a short piece of white thread. Continuing to pull, a razor blade is pulled out and it hangs from the thread, then another, and another until all 10 are stretched out between the mouth and the outstretched hand.

Preparation

You'll need:

- 20 razor blades (ten left normal and 10 filed or ground down until they are dull. I also recommend putting some sort of identifying mark on the blades so you never confuse what's sharp with what's dull.)
- The plastic box from the razor blades
- An opaque cup
- A strong magnet
- Cardboard
- Thread

- A dowel rod
- Nails
- A block of wood

Then:

1. Make a stand for the blades by cutting a length of dowel and drilling the wood block to accept it. Use small nails as hangers for the blades (five on each side).

2. Make a gimmicked cup by gluing a very strong magnet into it and covering the magnet with a disk of cardboard so the magnet is hidden **(Figure 16.4)**.

3. Make a secret box out of the original razor box and attach it to the inside of the cup. The box must hold the blades upright and be open only at the top end so that if the cup is turned upside down, the blades will fall out.

4. String the dull blades along an arm's length of thread, tying them into position so they will remain properly spaced. Allow extra thread at the end and tie it around the blades when they are stacked in the cup's holder.

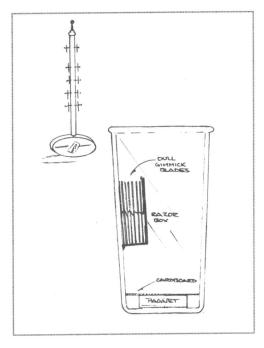

Figure 16.4

Setup

Place the real blades on the stand and the gimmicked blades in their holder. Have the thread on the same table.

Routine

Taking the first blade from the stand, demonstrate the sharpness by slicing a sheet of paper. To do this, hold the paper by one edge and start cutting into the paper in a diagonal cut. Now, fill the cup with the remaining blades, which you can shake to make sure they all stick to the magnet. The loaded blades will shake to help with the sound.

Show the spool of thread, tear off a piece, roll it into a ball, and place it onto your tongue. You can either pretend to swallow it by placing it between the teeth and gums, or you

Richiardi Jr. (1923–1985)

When I was 16 years old, I performed aboard a ship that docked in Nassau, Bahamas, at least three times each week. In Nassau's Paradise Island there was a huge hotel that hosted a show called *Dazzling Deception* starring Richiardi. I saw that show literally hundreds of times because I was so mesmerized by him. He was a real magician to me. He couldn't have been anything else. He didn't look like anyone I knew. He didn't talk or move like anyone I knew. He handled magic like it belonged to him. I wasn't the only one who felt this way about Richiardi. He appeared more than any other magician on the *Ed Sullivan Show*. People loved him. Born in Peru, Richiardi moved like a graceful tornado: fast and smooth. He was best known

(continued on next page)

might want to really swallow it. Just don't choke, it's bad enough you're messing around with razors.

Now, pour the gimmicked blades out of the cup and into your hand. Place the stack into your mouth so they can be seen. (The cup can be put mouth down on top of the stand. This casually reinforces the fact that the cup is empty.) Clench down and show a big smile so that everyone can see the stack. Now, shake your head backward like some people do when they are swallowing a pill. Go into your "regurgitation boy" routine and, finally, come up with the end of the thread from the mouth.

Pull the first few blades out of the mouth very slowly then speed up as the reaction begins to build. Count the blades to yourself as they leave the mouth so you don't just let them drop and hang. When you are finished, let the blades hang and seem as if you are trying to get out of their way as they swing. Very cautiously drape them into the cup to clean up.

Business Magic
Meeting Ice Breakers

Magic is a great way to break the ice for a business meeting. As in all forms of public speaking, a joke can loosen tension and create a more receptive audience. Meetings are inherently stuffy and a little magic can kick the stuffing out of it.

Business Card Magic

Think of using your business cards instead of regular cards for a trick. In both Chapter 3 and Chapter 10 you will find ideas for using your business cards in a magical way. Any way you can put a face with your card is important for name recognition, and adding some magic really makes it happen.

Creating Your Own Effect

As I have said, new magic grows from taking all of the "basic tool kits," all of the methods, and rethinking, reshaping, or rebuilding them. The more you learn about magic, the more you can flex it. Just for fun, take one of the favorite tricks you have learned so far and try to turn it into something else that parallels with your line of work. Customizing your magic or creating new magic can be fun too. I think the master of this type of magic was the late Karrell Fox. Karrell was knowledgeable about so many types of magic that he could constantly create magic to parallel situations and create brand new effects while keeping the apparatus and the method to a bare minimum or expense. Creating magic with what you have is a wonderful feeling. It takes a while to be able to do it consistently, but it will happen if you stick with it.

Richiardi Jr. (1923–1985)

(continued from previous page)

for his dancelike moves and his suspension of a girl from a broomstick, the "Lighting Vanish," and his extremely gory "Buzz Saw." When Richiardi cut a girl in half there was no mistaking when it happened. Blood gushed from the body onto the white linens of the master and his assistants. Whether it was the rhythmic snapping of fingers over top of a levitating assistant or the ghastly screams from the saw, Richiardi filled showrooms with the sounds of ultrarealism, and the mood of real magic. Even backstage in his dressing room, Richiardi was different from anyone I had ever met. He was both onstage and off, an artist.

CHAPTER 17

Street Magic—
Street Smarts

There aren't enough pages in this entire book to give you an accurate forecast for a future in street Magic. Let me tell you that it's a lot more complex than you could ever imagine. It's not just showing up on a street corner and trying some stuff out. It's more of a daily creation of your own theater out of concrete and sky. It's careful consideration of your show, your art, and the people who walk into it. You not only have to pass the test of stamina and confidence, you have to meet the legal and physical responsibilities of building your passion into a very public business.

There are some standard Street Magic classics that are synonymous with street performing, and that's what you'll learn about in this chapter. If you have a real interest in Street Magic, you'll find the answers somewhere between City Hall and the great books that have been written on the subject. The rest is up to you because Street Magic really comes down to you and *them* . . . the audience of the world.

Some Cool Street-Style Tricks

Three-Card Monte Over Easy

Effect

Three cards are shown, two black 6s and a red queen. The queen is in a fan between the two black 6s. The magician explains that the spectator must watch the lady and remember where she is. He turns the cards over and asks the spectator to put a coin on the back of the queen. She does this and the magician takes away the other two cards and her coin. The third card is lifted by the spectator and it is seen to be a joker.

Preparation

Make up a gimmicked card by cutting a slice off of a queen of hearts and hinging it to the back of one 6 as shown **(Figure 17.1)**. The queen cannot be seen outside of the 6 if it is turned over. You need another black 6 and a joker too.

Figure 17.1

Setup

Place the joker inside of the queen/6 set up as shown in the illustration. Now, continue the "fan" by placing the final 6 on top.

Routine

Show the three-card fan, explain the rules, and turn the cards over. Separate the cards (this pulls the queen fake away from the joker with one 6 and the other 6 pulls away by itself). Place the regular 6 under the gimmick cards to keep anybody from seeing the flap, and put the cards into the pocket. Take the coin too. Now, all that is left to be done is for the spectator to look at her queen. What a joke!

Variation

If you want, you can make it "easy" for the spectator by even putting a paper clip on the corner of the queen so when it is turned over it stays with the card. How could this be more fair?

Three-Card Monte/Find the Lady

The "Three-Card Monte," "Find the Lady," "Cherchez La Femme," or "The Monte" are all names given to a game of chance (so the audience thinks) using only three cards. Although this was originally devised as a betting game, magicians perform this as an entertainment piece and more of a lecture or exposure than a losing proposition. Although no real secrets are ever revealed, the audience is much more open and enthusiastic to learning how it's done and trying it out. The audience loves the chance to win a glimpse behind the scenes of this age-old hustle, much more than they feel like they might be victimized and lose by not paying attention to how it works.

Effect

The faces of three cards are shown, usually two black cards of the same value and suit (such as two aces of clubs) and a red queen (such as the queen of hearts). The cards are turned face down, moved around, and the spectator is asked to find the lady.

Harry Anderson

Most people know Harry Anderson as a television star of *Night Court* and *Dave's World* but he started on the streets. He's been arrested, had his jaw broken, and been banned from playing cards in Nevada for playing "games of chance" where other people didn't seem to like their own odds. Sure, he was out there doing the comedy clubs, casinos, and showcases like every other budding comic when he was starting. We got to know Harry and his con man, wise guy, scam artist character from *Saturday Night Live, Cheers,* and later when he played Judge Harold T. Stone on NBC's *Night Court.* That show lasted for nine seasons. Of course, we also have seen Harry on a

(continued on next page)

At first the spectator appears to be "hot"—he apparently is very good at following the game. The magician decides that it's a good time to put some money on the game, and the spectator lays some money down. This time, the spectator loses for the first time. The magician "Throws the Monte" again and the spectator wins. The spectator feels confident he knows what he did wrong, and the real game begins. Now, no matter how he tries, he cannot seem to win. In most routines, the magician gives the spectator a final chance by marking one of the cards. This can be done "accidentally" or as an opportunity for the spectator to make some of his money back. The spectator still loses. In this chapter, there is only space to explain the overthrow handling and execution. If you want to specialize in this trick, you'll need to really study the material from a supplier (see Appendix).

Preparation

The Cards Themselves

First of all, you need two black cards and a red queen. I personally prefer two lower value cards like the 6 of clubs. The 6 seems pretty unglamorous, a little chubby, and definitely doesn't have going for it what, say, a 7 or an ace of spades might have. This in comparison makes the queen seem powerful and valuable. All of the cards should be solid backed (patterned but without white borders) and they need to be "bridged" before you begin.

Bridging the Cards

To *bridge* the cards, place all three cards together and hold them from above by the ends with the thumb and the middle finger of one hand. The backs of the cards should be toward the palm. The opposite hand reaches underneath and bends the cards with the thumb and fingers halfway at the center of the sides. The bend is centered along the length of the cards. You'll want the cards to arch no more than ¼ inch off of the table when they are set down. You can readjust the cards throughout the routine to make sure they stay in the correct condition. This can be done in plain sight because the audience is supposed to think that this only helps to pick them up from the table. It does, but it also helps with what is called the "overthrow" or "hype move."

Setup

The three cards are set on the table with the queen in the center. We will call your right (stage right) simply, "right" for clarity. I assume you are facing the audience unless you are very very shy in which case "Three-Card Monte" is not for you.

Routine

The Basic Move or Overthrow

This move really happens the second time you throw the cards or any other time you want the queen to go someplace other than where the audience believes it goes. I want to explain the overthrow first so you can do the actions in the same way whether it is a real throw or an overthrow.

The first step is to pick up the cards in position for the overthrow. The move begins with one card being held on top of another and it appears as though the bottom card is thrown onto the table. What really happens is that the top card gets thrown.

Pick up the right card between the thumb and the second finger. The card should be held in position by the portion of the pad of the second finger that is closest to the joint. The tip of the finger will hang off of the card a little. The other fingers are there too but the second finger does all of the holding. Show the face of the black card and turn it face down again, moving it over top of the middle queen. Pick up the queen underneath the 6, holding the queen with what's left of the thumb and second finger. Keep the left sides together and keep a small break on the right side. The right index finger is on the outer left corner, the second finger is holding the center of the cards, and the rest of the fingers are covering the break. Again, you turn the cards over to show the queen on the bottom

Now you pick up the left 6 with the left hand in the exact same way, showing the face and turning the hand back down. To throw the queen (really the 6), the right hand raises the cards again and

Harry Anderson

(continued from previous page)

number of talk shows. Many times he will perform magic on one of these shows even though he might be there to talk about a television project. In 1989 he was even voted Magician of the Year by The Magic Castle. Whether you see Harry onstage or on the screen, beware, he's a scammer. As Harry put it himself in his book *Harry Anderson's Games You Can't Lose, a Guide for Suckers* (Simon & Schuster, 1989). "It's not whether you win or lose. . . . it's whether *I* win or lose."

Figure 17.2

on an arc back to the left, the following takes place. The little finger anchors the inner/upper corner of the queen, and the index finger stretches to the left, pivoting the 6 on the thumb **(Figure 17.2).** The other fingers have to move out of the way to allow this pivot to happen. At the end of the arc, when it's time to let the card fall to the table, the index finger lifts off of the corner letting it drop onto the table. The right hand moves back a little along the same arc, with a whiplash kind of action, tossing the card down. The card should hit the table as flat as possible, so you need to watch and repeat the same arc to perfect this.

The left 6 gets tossed the same way, landing on the right hand side of the queen (really a 6), and the right hand tosses the 6 (really the queen) to the left-hand side of all the other cards. This crisscross action of the hands is the usual pattern and rhythm of the "Monte."

The Real Throw

When throwing the cards "for real," treat the cards the same way. Handle them, grip them, and seemingly throw them in the same manner. Of course, instead of throwing the top 6 down as with the overthrow, you need to really throw the queen. This makes everything look the same when you start to control the queen.

After throwing the cards for real you might also want to change the positions of the outside cards by crisscrossing your arms and exchanging them. Whatever you do, the spectator will always try to keep his eye on "the money card."

Practice using each hand. You need to be ambidextrous with this handling. Make sure the rhythm, the hand positions, and the arcs are the same in each direction and in each variation of the throw, and you'll be on your way to "Three-Card Monte" mania.

The Three Shell Game

The "Three Shell Game" is one of my favorite Street Magic tricks. I love to perform it, and it's a little like dancing to me. The "Three Shell Game" is an extremely interactive and fun puzzle that everyone recognizes and wants to try, especially when they know you are a magician and they aren't going to lose any money on the deal.

Effect

The magician shows three walnut shells and a pea. The pea is placed underneath the center shell and the shells are mixed, but the middle shell is not even touched. When the magician asks which shell the pea is under, the spectator points to the middle shell. The magician shows the underside of the middle shell and she is correct.

The magician now explains that it gets even tougher when he begins to actually move the shell that the pea is under. He moves all of the shells and the spectator guesses incorrectly. The magician gives the spectator another chance and she still guesses incorrectly. He shows that it was under the final shell. There are a number of ways to end this routine, but I will suggest one that makes the spectator the hero when she finds the pea without even thinking about it.

Preparation

The Shells

You'll need three shells, one pea, a close-up pad, and a clear tumbler. Shells can either be purchased or you can make your own by using half walnut shells from the grocery store, coating their insides with wood filler, and sanding them smooth after it dries. The purchased shells are available in hard and soft plastic and there are even some beautiful metal shells out there. Some of these shells have a very gentle arc cut out of their backs to make getting the pea out a little easier.

The Pea

The pea is made of dense foam rubber cut into a sphere about the size of a genuine large pea. If you want to make it look more realistic or at least green, you can dip it in latex paint or a product called Plasti-Dip found at your hardware store. This product is made for coating the handles of tools. I make my peas out of a rubber makeup wedge. Start with a cube of foam, trim off the corners, and

---

Penn and Teller

Penn and Teller are known as "The Bad Boys of Magic." Their magic is sometimes questionable, often challenged, certainly shocking and all their own. Beginning in small clubs, theaters, and Renaissance fairs, they put together a stage show that played Off-Broadway and got some real attention. That attention turned to offers such as *Late Night with David Letterman, Saturday Night Live,* and *Miami Vice.* Then they were on Broadway and were favorite guests on almost every imaginable talk show.

Penn and Teller have authored two best-selling books, *Cruel Tricks for Dear Friends,* and *How to Play With Your Food.* They also have a new book entitled, *How to Play in Traffic.*

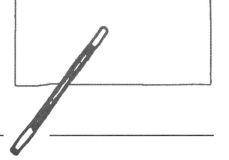

keep trimming corners to make it rounder. The pea I use is large (over ½ inch in diameter), because I think it makes things look all the more impossible. Try making your first pea ⅜ of an inch or smaller in diameter.

The Grip

You will have to learn to grip the shell correctly before anything else. The hand comes over top of the face-down shell with the index finger about halfway along the inner edge. The thumb is on the opposite edge at about 7:30. These two fingers pinch together to hold the shell and the remainder of the fingers curl in toward the palm **(Figure 17.3).** This is the way all shells should be gripped every time you touch them. The left hand uses the exact same, but only opposite, grip.

Moving the Shell and the Pea

You'll find that if you take your pea, place it under a shell, and move the shell forward with a little downward pressure, the pea will escape from the back of the shell. This happens automatically and is the root of "The Three Shell Game." It's also a secret and something that the audience does not know about it. This is one reason to never let a spectator try it out. They will see that the pea doesn't want to stay in the shell and will conclude that you are doing . . . well, *what* you really are doing. This means if you want to move a shell and keep the pea in it, you have to move it, retain the pea (as in "The Steal") and put it back in the shell again (as in "The Load").

Display Move

Every time you show a shell, no matter which hand you use or if it has a pea in it or not, you have to show it the same way. Holding the shell in the grip, you rotate your wrist inward and pivot the second, third, and pinkie fingers to the right so their backs finally rest flat against the table. The inside of the shell is shown and the action is exactly reversed to place the shell back down.

The Steal

To steal the pea from the shell, you simply move the shell forward with a slight pressure and the pea comes out the back. The pea is trapped and pinched between the thumb and the second finger tip **(Figure 17.4 underneath).** The shell can continue to moved forward or back as long as the pea is not pushed down into the table.

With the pea still in "The Steal" position, the tension of the thumb and index finger can be relaxed and the hand can be lifted off of the shell and move to another shell to load it. The pea remains firmly pinched between the thumb and the second finger tip. The hand can then be moved to any shell you wish to load the pea in.

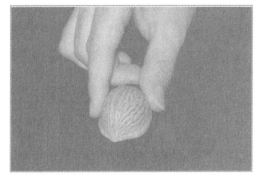

Figure 17.3

The Load

By gripping the shell as usual with the pea still pinched in "The Steal" position, move the shell backward and push the pea down against the table a little. You shouldn't have to move the shell far for the pea to load inside successfully and invisibly.

The Holdout

The "holdout" allows you to turn over a shell that really does have the pea in it but show it as empty. The move looks just like the display move but it hides a very ingenious secret. Holding the shell in the grip, you turn your wrist inward but let the fingers slide along the table. This moves the shell sideways and, of course, the pea wants to leave. It leaves but immediately rolls under the backs of the sliding fingers (usually along the line between the second and third fingers **(Figure 17.5).** The inside of the shell is shown to be empty and the action is exactly reversed to bring the pea back into the shell and place the shell back down.

Figure 17.4

The Tumbler Choice

I always leave the pea in the middle shell before I begin my last sequence. I have the spectator pick the shell the next time by placing a clear tumbler over it. I use the tumbler for the finale because it makes it seem like I'm giving the audience a fair chance. They make the choice, I don't touch it and they can see what's happening through the tumbler at all times. I say that I'm not going to touch the shells. No matter which shell the pea is in, I have the spectator place the glass over one. If it *is* in that shell, I have him tap the tumbler, lift it up and then lift up the shell. A miracle!

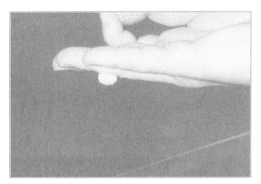

Figure 17.5

If he doesn't pick that shell (which, by the way, is usually the center one) I have to force the shell on him using the Magician's Choice.

If he puts the glass on an *empty* shell I slide that shell off by moving the tumbler (and the shell beneath it) off of the close-up pad and away. Then I ask him to place the tumbler over another shell. If I know it's *not* in that shell either, I take that one away too. Then I have him tap and look at the remaining shell. Miracle a second way!

If on the second tumbler placement, he puts the glass over the shell that *does* have the pea, I simply remove the other shell and place it with the first shell which is to the side. When he taps and looks, hey, lookey there!

This of course is a force or "The Magician's Choice" as it is called. Really, no one but the magician has a choice, I guess that's how they got the name.

Setup

Place your close-up pad on the table with the three shells in a row and the pea in front (downstage) of them. The tumbler is off to your right.

Routine

Begin by showing all three shells to be empty using the display move. Place the pea under the middle shell and move the other shells around it.

Ask the spectator to point to the shell or tell you which shell the pea is under. Don't ever let them touch the shells except for the very last reveal with the tumbler. You don't want anyone ever getting it right, and you want to set a precedence of how you show under the shells. She picks the center shell (hopefully) and you continue.

You explain that it gets a little tougher when you actually start to move the shell with the pea in it. Start with the center shell and steal the pea. Either load it back under that shell, the next shell you move, or move it under the last shell. This is part of the beauty of "The Three Shell Game"; you can change things any time you want to. Let's suppose you leave it under the first shell. She gets it again. This is the last time she will be successful.

Move the shells again and this time she misses. Leaving the shells where they are, give her a second chance. If she guesses, okay, if she doesn't, that let's you show the last shell to really contain the pea. Any time you want you can have her pick a shell and she will get it wrong. Use "the holdout" move if she guesses correctly. If she guesses correctly the first time (this will be by sheer luck or confusion), use "the holdout" and then show the others to be empty as well. Move on to "the tumbler choice" to bring it back, where she last guesses.

Practice this and get it smooth and fast. It can be a very fun game for the audience to play. It makes you look like a real expert, and eventually you can perform it even on a slick surface without a close-up pad. I will admit that the spectators will often pick up the pad to see where the trap doors are (or whatever they are snooping for). It just gets them more confused. Definitely start out with the pad. It has taken me quite a while (I mean years) to be able to confidently perform the "Three Shell Game" on just about any surface.

Fire Eating

I'm not going to go too far with fire eating because honestly, I don't want you to try it without the help of a professional. I also don't really view it as magic. It's cool (I mean hot), and it's a crowd pleaser, but it's not magic. It *is,* however, something that magicians perform, especially on the streets. There are laws for performing dangerous tricks on the street, and every city has different laws and regulations. Find out if you have to have a permit not only to perform but if there is any additional red tape you have to go through for the dangerous stuff. If you are thinking of doing this inside a building, *absolutely* clear it with the venue, which includes consulting a fire marshal and making sure fire sprinkler heads will not come on once you really start to burn. Pardon the pun (again), but that's a sure-fire way to dampen the spirits of any crowd, even if they are a great crowd. I have seen it happen. I want you to be able to understand the basics and the necessities of fire eating so

Attention!

I am not responsible if you hurt yourself trying to play *Conan the Fire Boy.* I'm serious, this is dangerous stuff so don't goof around with it unless you are prepared. You might burn your tongue off or something and have to put together a weird act where you just put saltines on your tongue and scream a lot.

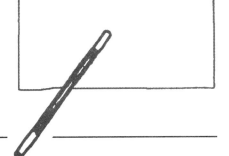

you can see if it's something you really want to pursue and add to your magic repertoire.

The Secret, or Not

There really is not a secret to fire eating. It is a practiced technique and a regimen of individual handlings and safety precautions. You also need some specialized tools, and some nerve.

The Tools

The Sticks

The sticks you need can be purchased professionally from a magic or juggling dealer in a variety of shapes and sizes to suit your taste. Or, you can make your own. If you prefer making your own, cut and straighten a heavy weight coat hanger and make loops in each end about the size of 50-cent pieces. One of these will be your handle so you can make that one a little larger and flatten it out a bit. The other end will be the action end. Cover the other end with some wicking from a juggling supplier or cover the wire with strands from a floor mop. Buy a new one for goodness sake, yuck! Tie these around the circle and knot them firmly. You can also wrap strong, linen thread or metal wire around this material to further anchor it, but be careful, metal wire gets hot too. Whatever you use, make sure it cannot drop off and into your mouth while it's on fire. Oh sure, it will look cool but it's nothing to play around with. When any type of wicking becomes too burned, replace it so it doesn't fall off and hurt you. The idea is to have the fire burn the fuel on the wick and not the wick itself. Incidentally, the most expensive mop heads are supposed to have the best material to use. The strands are thicker and longer.

The Fuel

Okay, let's get this out of the way: NO GASOLINE, NEVER! The best fuel is lighter fluid. There are several different brands and some of them taste a lot better than others. My personal favorite is Ronsonal in the yellow and blue bottle. Store your fluid in a cool, safe area. I double-bag mine in two Ziplock bags, so if one bag leaks, I'm still okay.

Alexander Herrmann (1844–1896)
and wife, Adelaide (1853–1932)

German born Alexander Herrmann and his brother Carl teamed up at the age of 10 and became very good at sleight of hand. They got so good that they appeared for the queen of Spain when Alexander was just 15 years old. Eventually, they separated and performed as their own acts. Their cousin Leon was also a magician. Alexander Herrmann was one of the first magicians that looked the way many of us picture a magician to look. He added a cape, silk top hat, and a goatee to the black-and-white evening dress that became synonymous with magicians. Herrmann was America's leading magician from 1870 until his death more than 25 years later. He performed such illusions as "After the Ball," where he vanished his wife, Adelaide. In "Cremation" he burned her in a box until she was nothing more than a charred skeleton (an illusion that is still featured in many illusion shows today). Another illusion featured a head that had been severed from its body, allowing Herrmann to have a conversation with it. When Alexander Herrmann died in 1896, Adelaide was left without a cent so she decided to ask cousin Leon to join her and keep the Herrmann show alive. They toured as *The New Herrmann, The Great Company* but because they fought so often, it didn't last long. Adelaide, born to Belgium parents in London in 1853, became possibly the world's greatest female magician. Starting out as a teen dancer, then of course as Herrmann's lead assistant, she learned what it took to present grand illusion with great style. Adelaide's act eventually played every great European theater and showroom, but she loved the American audiences most of all. She was known as "The Queen of Magic." Adelaide continued in magic and show business even touring the vaudeville circuits into her mid-seventies. On February 19, 1932, in a New York hotel suite, Adelaide Herrmann died at the age of 79.

David Blaine

David Blaine is relatively new on the public magic scene, but people are watching him. Blaine is different, dark, strange, slow, maybe even creepy. That's the way he plays it. He even claims to be the grandson of a witch and a tarot card reader. It does make the plot thicken. Blaine's stage is the street. His costume is simple (jeans, T-shirt, sunglasses), and his audience is ever changing. Whenever there is a magician on television I get phone calls from friends and family asking, "Hey did you see the guy that blah blah blah." When Blaine was first on television, my phone rang off the hook. People reacted wildly to his spontaneous and dark mysteries with ordinary objects and his own body. David Blaine started

(continued on next page)

Basic Fire Eating

Before you light your stick, or torch, as it is sometimes called, remember a couple of things. If you are going to do fire eating, you are going to get burned. Are you still reading? That will happen accidentally and is just part of the picture. You also can blind yourself or even kill yourself if you don't take this seriously. Okay, if you're still here, this may be what you're looking for. Good luck!

Before you start, you need to do many dry runs. Before there is any real fire, practice all of the moves below without anything lit. Make sure everything is well rehearsed and that you are familiar with every step of the way.

Also take into consideration anything that might not affect you where you are rehearsing but might affect you on the street. *Wind* is the major one. Sun in the eyes would be right up there too.

1. You can put the fuel on your sticks before your performance, or you can dip them during the performance. Just make sure there isn't too much fuel so that it drips off. By shaking the stick off, you can remove most of the dangerous excess. If you are going to dip onstage, make sure you use a container that won't be knocked over. It can be bottom-weighted or attached to your performance table, but a spill of fuel can cause a disaster. Also, make sure that the container can be sealed or covered so that a stray ember won't light up the city.

2. You have to study how a flame always rises straight up and where your hand can be on a stick so it doesn't get burned trying to place the end of the stick into your mouth.

3. You also have to make sure you have plenty of spit in your mouth and around your lips so you have a good coating of protection.

4. Whenever you near your mouth with the flame, and more importantly, when you are putting the flame into your mouth, you have to breath out. The breath should be slow and steady not fast and gusting. You could blow out the flame or blow the flame onto you somehow.

5. If you don't breathe out you will be in big trouble. You will breathe in the fumes and that is the combustible part of the gas. If you get those fumes down your esophagus or into your lungs, hello Mr. Barbecue! I'm trying to make this light (cause that's the kind of guy I am), but it's not funny. If you are going to have to breath during all of your stick handling, you have to take a *big breath* before you start, right? Practice all of the breathing, reaching for your props, and placing of the stick.

6. Lean your head back and open wide looking up all the time. Make sure the stick is out of the pass of the flame or it will burn your hand.

After you fully understand these steps and rehearse them to perfection, it's time to ignite the stick. This should be rehearsed too, and you should know exactly where all of your props are every time. You shouldn't have to look down or fumble around for anything, ever.

Light the stick, wet your lips, and let 'er rip. Move slowly and deliberately and you will be very happy that you rehearsed and know what you are doing. Of course, the flames are going away from you and not toward you, but it's still close enough.

Extinguishing the Flame

You can extinguish the flame in a fireproof bag or box but you can also do it in your mouth. On your last swallow of the stick, bring your lips around the end of the torch being careful not to bite down too hard and touch the hot shaft with a lip, tongue, or other sensitive area (yeah, like there is an area that wouldn't be sensitive in the mouth.) If you close carefully, you can keep the oxygen from the flame and put the flame out. End by exhaling a cloud of smoke and . . . I don't know, have a breath mint or something.

There are a lot of other spectacular stunts you can do with fire eating such as putting flames all over your body or spitting a giant ball of fire. If it's for you, only you can say.

David Blaine

(continued from previous page)

magic when he was only four years old. By age 17 he had learned the basics and was appearing at private celebrity parties for stars such as Robert De Niro. Today, with a couple of television specials under his belt, audiences know that this is the man that levitates himself without a stage, tears the head off a bird and brings it back to life, and finds the intimate thoughts of an onlooker written in coal on his own stomach. Blaine seems to create magic with raw materials and without premeditation. He is magic's urban shaman and someone about whom we will definitely call a friend the next time he emerges from his own shadows.

CHAPTER 18

Magic with Science— E = MagiC²

Chemicals
"Water" You "Wining" About?
Effect

Three tumblers are shown. One of the tumblers is full of water, while the other two are seen to be empty. The glass of water is poured into the second glass and instantly it changes to a bright red liquid. The water has seemingly changed to wine. Now, the wine is poured into the third glass and it changes back to water.

Preparation

You'll need three transparent tumblers, some red adhesive pin-striping from an automotive store, red food coloring, and some bleach.

Setup

1. Put one line of the pinstriped adhesive around the bottom of all three tumblers and another row around the top of each tumbler about ½ inch from the lip of the tumblers.

2. Fill one tumbler with water to just below the top pinstripe.

3. Put some food coloring into the next tumbler.

4. Put a cap full of bleach in the last tumbler.

Routine

Show the first tumbler full of water and pour it into the second tumbler (the one with the food coloring).

Now, take the red "wine" and pour it into the third tumbler (the one with the bleach) and it changes back to clear. Remember, it's not really water, don't drink it!

Sounds

Transcurrency

Here's a magic trick that relies on the misdirection of sound for its success.

Effect

A coin is shown and placed under a handkerchief. A spectator is allowed to pinch the coin through the handkerchief and hold it over the top of a glass of water. On the magician's command, the coin is dropped by the spectator and the coin is heard to fall into the glass of water. When the spectator lifts the handkerchief away from the glass, the coin has vanished.

Preparation

You'll need a large coin, a matching disk of glass from a flashlight lens, an ordinary handkerchief or napkin, and a glass of water.

Setup

The glass disk is finger palmed and the rest of the objects are lying on the table.

Routine

Ask the spectator to examine the props. After he is convinced the props are normal, pick up the coin and place it under the handkerchief. While under the handkerchief, switch the coin for the glass disk, making sure not to let the coin and the disk "talk." Bring the handkerchief up to the spectator and ask him to grab onto the coin through it. Arrange the outside of the handkerchief so that it surrounds the glass. If there is another spectator at the table, ask her to grab two of the corners of the handkerchief and either you or another spectator hold the other two corners. Give the command to drop the coin and it is heard to fall into the glass. Ask the spectator to pull the handkerchief off and the trick is done. As soon as he pulls the handkerchief away, pocket the real

Did You Know?

Jasper Maskelyne, grandson of John Nevil Maskelyne, was an invaluable resource to his native Britain during World War II. With his great knowledge of illusion, Maskelyne was able to devise ingenious and very large-scale illusion systems that made tanks virtually invisible from the air, hid whole buildings full of ammunition and supplies, and even made an entire city vanish and reappear several miles away. Sadly, when the war ended, he was unable to gain success as a magical stage performer. The military had forgotten his achievements, and he died a broken man.

Jean Eugène-Robert Houdin (1805–1871)

Robert Houdin was born in France and didn't become a professional magician until he was forty. That is surprising, considering that he is known as the "Father of Modern Conjuring." Even the great Harry Houdini idolized Houdin, borrowing his name and adding an "I." Houdin was a watchmaker, mechanic, inventor, and an early experimenter with electricity, which he used in some of his magic tricks. He had learned much of his magic by traveling with a magician named Torrini, learning magic from street swindlers. Houdin did not believe in a stage filled with huge boxes for magic but felt magic was an art form and stressed the need for using sleight-of-hand skills and thinking up new ideas. He

(continued on next page)

coin and get your hands on the glass. The best way to view it is at eye level from the side. You can even pour the water out of that glass into another and the disk will stick to the bottom.

Gravity and Resistance
I've Got a Pair of Chutes
Effect

The magician challenges a spectator to drop playing cards from chest level one at a time into a hat on the floor. No matter how they seem to try, they usually can't do it until you tell them the secret.

Preparation

You'll need a deck of cards and a hat or a box.

Setup

Place the hat on the floor and hold the cards in your own hand.

Routine

Give the cards to the spectator keeping one as a demonstration card. When you demonstrate what he needs to do, hold your card at chest level and point one of the cards with its edges down as an example.

Then let him try several times to drop the cards into the hat. He will probably become frustrated. The reason is that with either the top or the side edges pointed down, the card will always miss the hat. If the side edge of the card is held downward, the card will always spin horizontally on its way to the hat and miss. If the top or bottom edge of the card is held downward, the card will always spin vertically on its way to the hat and miss. When he is so frustrated that he gives up, ask if he'd like to know how he could hit his mark. Then suggest to him that your solution is the only way you know to make the card float straight into the hat.

Hold the card parallel to the floor in the Biddle grip and release the fingers at the same time. The card creates air resistance and it will float gracefully into the hat like a parachute. Not too many people will try to drop a card in this way. It seems like it would flutter downward like a feather. If the spectator guesses the method right away, tell him he is very clever and steal his wallet! Nobody likes a smart alec!

Optics/Reflection
Now Here's the "Kicker!"
Effect

A story is told to a spectator about an old man, Pop, who is buying new glasses from a young salesman, Bob. As if there with the old man, the spectator first reads a card with the words "CHOICE QUALITY," but when he's asked to read the same words in a mirror, the phrase is illegible. The magician rubs the paper as if to clean it and this time the word "CHOICE" can be read but the word "QUALITY" is still illegible. The story has the old man lose his temper. The magician then flips the paper over and shows the words "pop KICKED bob." Then, when it is viewed in the mirror, it seems the message has changed to "bob KICKED pop."

Preparation

Print the words on the card the way they are described above, paying attention to uppercase and lowercase letters. Print "CHOICE QUALITY" on one side and "pop KICKED bob" on the other. Print in clear block letters in the middle of the card. You will also need a mirror.

Setup

There is no set up other than the above preparation, but there *is* a little secret. You will ask for one participant at the beginning.

Jean Eugène-Robert Houdin (1805–1871)

(*continued from previous page*)

also was costumed in very formal attire, which was very modern back then. Because of his ingenious creativity with mechanics, Houdin built automatons, the equivalent of mechanical robots. These entertaining machines were featured in his and other magicians' shows, and his ideas soon began to creep into the designs of large-stage illusions. Houdin was also the first to perform a second-sight act which, by means of a secret code, he described objects hidden in the audience to his son, who was blindfolded on stage.

Routine

Create some patter along these lines:

"I took my grumpy grandfather to get some new reading glasses, even though he didn't think he needed them, and he *sure* didn't want to spend a lot of money. The salesman, a nice young man named Bob, showed Pop a pair that he said was for a good price, and pointed out a label on the lens that read 'CHOICE QUALITY.'"

Show the spectator the card that reads "CHOICE QUALITY" when you mention the label.

"When Pop put the glasses on and looked in the mirror, *this* is what he saw . . ."

Ask the spectator to look in the mirror and then hold up the "CHOICE QUALITY" side of the card to the mirror. The reflection shows that both words are obviously illegible. Take the card down and continue . . .

"When Pop saw the jumbled words, he complained that he couldn't read a darn word with those so-called quality glasses. Nice Bob suggested that they probably just need a good cleaning."

Now act as if you are cleaning the card as if it were the glasses and then . . . (and this is one of the secret parts) . . . show the same side of the card, but turn it upside down.

"Pop looked in the mirror again, and could make out the word "CHOICE" but the word "QUALITY" was still all mixed up. Pop got so mad, do you know what he did?!"

You then flip over the card to show to the spectator (straight on) the side that reads "pop KICKED bob."

"Yep, Pop kicked Bob. And I think Bob must have been pretty fed up with Pop by then because look what happened next!"

Then hold the "pop KICKED bob" side upside down to reflect in the mirror and tell the spectator to read what he sees. (It reads, "bob KICKED pop.")

"That's right, bob kicked pop! It seems the shoe was on the other foot once Pop made such a spectacle of himself."

This routine relies on the reflection of certain letters when viewed in a mirror upside down or backward.

Magnetism
The Semi-Vacuum
Effect

The magician balances a paper cup on an ordinary dinner knife which is held in one hand. He places the other hand over the top of the cup as he claims to be able to merely press gently down on the top of the cup to create a vacuum of sorts." So, after a gentle press on the cup, the magician then inverts the entire set (cup and knife) so his hand is under the mouth of the cup and the knife is on the top. "Look what a semi-vacuum will do!" Suddenly, he lets go of the supporting bottom hand and the cup miraculously clings in a vacuum-like state to the knife. The magician's hand comes back up to pull the cup away from the knife (breaking the vacuum) and offers both the cup and knife for examination by spectators.

Preparation

You'll need a normal paper cup, a dinner or butter knife, and a magnet that is just strong enough to hold the cup to the knife.

Setup

Place the magnet in the bottom of the cup and place the cup and the knife on the table (not to be examined prior to the trick).

Routine

Start by taking the knife handle in one hand (flat blade side up) and carefully balance the cup on the knife blade. The magnet will grab immediately **(Figure 18.1).** After your explanation of how much "vacuum like" power your magical hands possess, press dramatically on the top of the cup (don't crush the thing) and invert the knife, cup, and holding hand. Slowly draw the bottom supporting hand away to let the cup "hang" from the knife **(Figure 18.2).** After the amazement subsides, bring the hand back to the cup mouth and wrap your fingers around it to break the vacuum and pull it away. If the magnet is too strong,

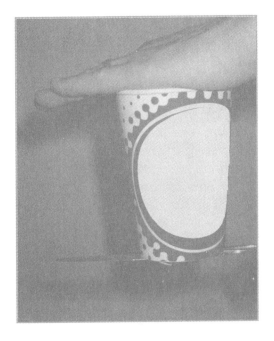

Figure 18.1

Figure 18.2

(continued on next page)

Jade

Jade was born on the island of Sumatra, Indonesia, and is of Chinese descent. In 1972, her family immigrated to America and made San Francisco their home. Although she graduated college with a degree in Communications, her love for the art of magic led her to pursue a career in the male-dominated world of professional magic. In 1990, she competed in the International Brotherhood of Magicians' World Magic Competition. Jade surprised everyone, including herself, when she won first place. In addition, a celebrity panel of judges awarded her the coveted Gold Medal of Magic. This award has only been presented six times in the 20-year history of the competition. To date, she is the only woman to receive this

your hands will jerk apart and broadcast "A MAGNET being used here" to all spectators. You also will possibly knock the guy beside you in the head with a piece of cutlery. Don't chance it. When the cup separates from the knife, the magnet will drop into your hand and you can either finger palm it or classic-palm it. Why? Because you can, and because you need to hide the source of your super powers. Now, after more displays of amazement, you can hand the knife and the cup out for examination. Hey, and if somebody guesses that you had a magnet or something, tell them they are *right* (wink, wink) and go on to your next trick.

Air Pressure
Magnetic Menthols
Effect

The magician borrows a menthol cigarette and states with confidence that "all menthol cigarettes are magnetic." To prove his point, he starts by displaying a piece of cardboard on which a magnet has been drawn. Laying the cigarette on its side, he puts the magnet near it and pulls it away from the cigarette. The cigarette magnetically follows.

Preparation

You need to make a "magnet card." To do this, take a piece of poster board the size of a credit card or playing card, and on it draw a "classical" magnet—you know, the red horseshoe shaped one with the white or silver tips. You'll be borrowing a menthol cigarette from someone in the audience.

Setup

Make sure you're sitting at a table surface that is smooth and relatively level. Any kind of texture or slant will prevent you from making this work well.

Routine

Ask to borrow a menthol cigarette. When you get the cigarette, begin to inform everyone that a lot of people are unaware of the ingredient that really makes a menthol cigarette, menthol. What is it? You're right, it's the iron filings. There is no mentholated medium, no mint, no green tea or medicated leaf, it's good old ferric flavoring. It scratches up your throat so badly, it just feels like you are tasting the warm tingling sensation of menthol, and you can prove it. Lay the cigarette down horizontally on the table in front of you, no more than 6 to 12 inches away. Bring out the magnet and give some ridiculous description of its thinness and special attributes. It is powerful and yet you can easily store it alongside a credit card in your wallet and it does nothing. In fact most of the time, it does nothing. But, put it close to a cigarette, and this is what happens. Hold the magnet card down on the table on the far side of the cigarette, with the magnet ends facing the cigarette. Lean your body forward as if to concentrate on the experiment and begin to lightly blow along the table just in front of the cigarette. The cigarette should slowly begin to roll away from you, toward the magnet card. Keep the magnet evenly ahead of the cigarette, creating the illusion that the magnet is really pulling it. Make sure you don't pucker up and do, "The Hippo Hurricane Holler." You just need a light, consistent breath. Separate the lips slightly and silently sigh out some wind. The cigarette will do the rest since all eyes will be on the mighty menthol at that moment. Of course, everything can be examined but remember to tell any spectator who has an expensive watch or a pacemaker not to get too close to the magnet. It's bad enough that you're letting someone smoke menthol cigarettes, you don't need to push your luck. You might want to have some back-up patter in case nobody has a menthol cigarette.

Jade

(continued from previous page)

honor. That award launched her into a world of adventure, travel, and a wide variety of venues all over the globe. Since then, Jade's repertoire has grown and her ability to speak fluent Cantonese, Mandarin, and English has been useful in her performances here and abroad. In 1999 she made a three-month tour of Canada, immediately followed by an engagement at Caesar's Magical Empire in Las Vegas and a six-month run starring in Hocus Pocus at Casino Magic in Biloxi, Mississippi.

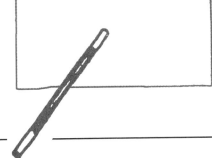

The Human Body

Men Are from Mars and Martians Can't Lift Chairs

Effect

A chair is placed with its back against a wall. A female spectator is asked to approach the chair, keeping both of her feet one shoe length from the front chair legs. She is to squat down with her back straight and touch the top of her head against the wall. She is asked to pull the chair up off of the floor by lifting the seat with her hands. Then she is simply asked to stand up. She does so.

The same thing is asked of a male spectator, and he can't do it. It seems that he has lost all of his power.

Preparation

You'll need some props for this: a chair, a wall, and two helpers (a man and woman or a boy and a girl). This trick works because men and women are different in their body alignment at the hips.

Setup

Place the chair as described and ask for the assistance of a female spectator first.

Routine

I'm sure you can make up some bogus patter about how Samson lost his strength when he got a haircut and couldn't even lift a light piece of carry-on luggage. He had to buy a special kind of luggage called Samsonite. It was very durable but much lighter. Most men are losing some hair, but what they don't know is that they are also losing some strength. Following the description from the Effect, go on to demonstrate this with this scientific experiment. Try this, it's a lot of fun and I'm hoping that one day it will get me out of taking out the garbage. Wait a minute, that wouldn't be magic, that would be a miracle!

PART III

Introducing "You"! Putting on the Show

CHAPTER 19

Planning Your Own Magic Show

etting started with putting together your own magic show is an exciting step but also a lot of work. You may want to forego the planning phase because you naturally want to just get on with the magic. Getting started means you are actually considering doing your stuff in front of people, people who aren't necessarily all friends, family, or fans . . . yikes! Don't worry; I'll walk you through some of the key ingredients and steps for becoming "the amazing you." To make things a little easier to follow, I'll just call your show, performance, demonstration, project or preproduction vision your "act." Follow the guidelines below, chart your progress, and the pieces will fall into place a lot easier than you may think.

The IDEA System

A few years ago I devised a program called "ImagicNATION" that uses a system for supercharging creative ideas. The whole concept is structured around the acronym IDEA. I usually teach this technique to corporations to help them put their own ideas to work. It will work for you and your new magic act too. Following is a condensed outline with the focus on creating your own act.

The four steps and your four tasks using the IDEA system are:

I Imagine and Identify = Dreaming up *every idea* you could imagine your act being like

D Dedicate and Decide = Finally deciding exactly what you will be doing

E Edit and Elect = Dividing the act up into pieces and plotting how you will build each part

A Activate and Ascend = Systematically putting all of the pieces into motion

Imagine and Identify (I)

The is the first step in putting together your own act. All you have to do is dream about all of the things you could do and could be. Write these thoughts down, even if you think they are no good; they might very well spark another great idea. To help your ideas start to flow, learn, read, listen to, and see as much magic as you can. This book provides a good overview of most of the areas of magic, but I suggest you also get out there to see what other established magicians are doing. Put a note pad and a pen wherever you linger and lounge and start collecting these thoughts. Draw pictures, collect clippings, make notes, read magic catalogs, and get to know what magic is available. Remember how each magic effect strikes you the first time you see it. Eventually, things will start to overlap and will fuel new thoughts. The Appendix gives you a great resource list for your research. Write everything down on this "dream list." There are no wrong answers at this point, just get all the possibilities out.

These ideas don't have to relate at all, just write them down and get them out of your system so the rest of your thoughts can flow.

What Do I Want My Show to Be Like?

Your show can be anything that you want it to be. Don't worry about how big or how small it might be. Don't necessarily think about what magic shows look like but rather think about what they *could* look like. Imagine different types of communication and stimulation. Think about tiny magic performed for a huge crowd. Be curious and think about what may make your act unique.

Where Will I Perform My Act?

Once you have what satisfies you as a good list of what your act will consist of, you should start to imagine where you would eventually like to perform it. Try to imagine your act fitting into a space. Because you are not stuck to any decision and you can change your mind or back up later on, don't worry if this is not too particular; again, be broad and create a comfort area wish list. Acts evolve. Theatre plays do the same thing. As a new play is being rehearsed, it is constantly being rewritten and rediscovered. It's part of the evolution. It's essential to dream, but you also need to be realistic. You need to build confidence so you will want to go on with this project. If you live in an area where there are nine people, six cows, an emu, and a Lion's Club, don't start out trying to put together a performance art piece suited for Radio City Music Hall. If you want to perform on cruise ships don't do something

My "Dream List"

- Purples and ambers used in backdrops and lighting
- Chiffon and stainless steel
- Virtual reality suit with head gear and gloves
- Head floats away from body and back
- Show my natural strength and physique
- Dreamlike but serious
- Card throwing
- Jimmy Hendrix music, choir music, industrial sound effects
- Multimedia and antiques

that insists on balance and steadiness, or sobriety for that matter. You get the idea: match your place with your act.

What Do I Want to Accomplish with It?

Do you want to bring something out of your use of magic? Have you ever thought of trying to use magic for a specific purpose? You should. It can be a very strong tool for communicating, and it will make you feel really great about what you do if you can feel an inner sense of accomplishment after you are finished. Remember, you want to put together something that you will enjoy doing over and over and over. That's how you get good at magic— repetition. Do you want to simply entertain and have your audience walk away or do you want to completely bamboozle 'em? Maybe your thoughts include inspiration, motivation, or education. Magician Doug Anderson uses magic as a tool to share Christianity with his audiences. It's something you want to think about so you can focus your mighty arrow toward the correct target.

Decide and Dedicate (D)

Now that you have collected all of the possible scenarios for your magic act, you need to make some definite decisions on which direction to go in and dedicate yourself to it. You need what you have to work with and what will happen during your act. Will you present a concert of magic where the audience sits and takes it all in? Will you produce a playlet with a theme and a plot, a one-person show, an interactive collection of effects, or a spoof. What is it that grabs you? You need to review your lists, get focused, and dedicate yourself to creating the act that fits with your goals from step one. The following sections will give you additional ideas.

Developing Your Character

Character development is a toughie. It takes a lot of thought, honesty, and imagination. You probably know yourself better than anyone else except your mother and perhaps a specialized medical practitioner or two, so you can pretty much trust your initial thoughts on how far "you, the person" are from "you, the magician." Actor and magician Max Howard lectures on theater technique for

John Gaughan

John Gaughan is another one of those very creative talents in magic that the magic community greatly respects but that the public may not know as well. You might say that John Gaughan is the magician behind many great magicians. John designs and builds illusions for all the best magicians. Throughout the years his work has been showcased through the stage properties and illusions he has created for magicians such as Mark Wilson, Doug Henning, and David Copperfield. John is also known in magic for his rebuilding and resurrection of self-working mechanical pieces (known as "automata") such as "Antonio Diavola," a mechanical trapeze artist that has been featured on television. John Gaughan is a magician, yes, but also a wizard of all things mechanical and magical.

magicians, or as he puts it, "Things You Need to Know After You Know the Secret and Before You Go Onstage." Max does not recommend creating a character, because it takes a long time, requires lots of inner understanding, and has nothing to do with making money. You need to be inspired right from the beginning. If you want to, you can work on a character while you are developing your own strength. Max recommends creating strong personalities or personas. Developing a personality means you would host your act as yourself on your very best day. You would be positive and interesting to see and listen to, but you would be yourself. Developing a persona means you would be a real person; however, you would be very unique, unlike anyone the audience had ever seen. Maybe you would be very funny, serious, dignified, or even foolish, but you would be exciting to watch.

Physical Appearance

What do you look like in your show? In this chapter, we will take you into detail as far as costuming, makeup, and physical appearance, but it's time to decide *what* you will look like before you learn *how* you can enhance or exploit it. This is also a time to realize what you really look like to other people and use that to your advantage. Maybe you are very short and very skinny. Maybe you have super straight posture. Maybe you have big blue eyes. Maybe you have a big hump and bulging Marty Feldman eyes! Oh, my god, you're a monster! Whatever you can see, your audience can too. You either have to bring it out or minimize it.

Personality

If you just develop and establish your own personality for your act, you will have to do it well. If your don't have a super strong personality, you will have to find out what your most redeeming traits are and let them shine in the very best light. If you are creating a persona, enhance some of your traits. Make them larger than life but not unbelievable. You want to be viewed as extreme, eccentric, and intense, but not unbelievable. The audience should not feel as though they have to take any part of who you are with a grain of salt.

Abilities

Consider what abilities you have at your disposal, what you have to choose from. These might be God-given abilities, trained abilities, or abilities you are still working on. First of all, how good are you with your magic right now? Maybe you have some theatrical strengths, such as the ability to dance, sing, or speak with conviction and confidence. Maybe you are naturally funny or rich. If you are too rich, feel free to call me and we'll work on it. Adversely, you could really be terrible at dancing and possess a voice with the range of a Daisy rifle. If so, don't figure on the song and dance number. See how many items from your dream list you can consider and commit to.

Textures

Consider textures, contrasts, and consistencies for your show. I think contrast is one of the strongest theatrical tools, whether it be for scenery, imagery, or character. You might be so articulate that you pop when you speak or you might be so inarticulate that your sound almost stumbles over your own tongue. Whatever you have, make it seem like you have a magnifying glass over it. Each one of these textures settles down to become a layer just like rock becomes sand. Think of what you have to work with and be noticeably different from anyone the audience has ever seen before. When I meet people on a plane, they almost always say, "I have never met a magician before." They seem to be surprised that we fly on airplanes just like normal people. Interesting textures let people enjoy watching you.

Learn to Look for Characters

Study people, actors, and magicians that intrigue you and decide what it is about them that attracts you. Is it James Bond, Marilyn Monroe, David Copperfield, or Spider Man? What characteristics grab your attention? Study theatrical characters, television stars, cartoons, even people out on the street. Figure out what makes you look and write it down.

What Kind of Magic Is Best for You?

You probably already have a favorite type of magic, and chances are, it's the magic you are the best at too. That will also be the magic that the audience will appreciate most. It's easy to want to do everything in magic. It's all pretty cool and each area has its own strengths and weaknesses. Right now, you need confidence and credibility.

Think about what effects and what ideas in your collection fit best with who you are or what your personality is. Do what feels right for you. Don't worry about what you've seen or what every one else is doing. It would be pretty darned boring if every magician looked, moved, and performed in the same manner. It still happens, but if you listen up, it won't happen to you. It's fine to study other acts and get ideas from that, but go one step further.

Okay, let's assume you're best at doing rope tricks, that comedy comes naturally to you, and that you can sing and play guitar and do some good impersonations. There might also be more comedy clubs and bars in your area than there are service clubs or theaters. You also wrote down on your wish list, "Superhero with cape."

So, you start thinking about doing "open mic" nights at your comedy club. Maybe you want your show to be slapstick and funny but also to contain some good magic. You could be costumed in a cowboy hat, a cape, and a T-shirt with CW ("Captain West") stamped on your chest. You play and sing your theme song, but the rope guitar strap gets caught on the microphone stand. You rip it off and do a cut and restored rope trick with it. Instead of using a pair of shears to cut the rope, you use your Bowie knife.

I realize this is far fetched, but it will give you an idea of how your different ideas can be temporarily put together so you can prepare to make a final decision. You still have some details to consider, though.

What Are Your Best Tricks?

Make a list of the tricks you want to perform, can perform, and dream about performing and put them down on paper. Don't copy other acts or you'll be viewed in the same light as someone who sings other people's songs; it sounds nice enough but you'd rather

Max Howard

Max Howard is the star and cocreator of the international award-winning, nationally syndicated television series for young audiences, *Max B. Nimble.* Winner of nine Emmy Awards, the program also received the Chicago Film Festival's Silver Shield Award and the Action for Children's Television (ACT) Award of Excellence for Children's Programming. With his partner, Diane Bray, Max is also the star and cocreator of the unique autobiographical drama, *The War Wizard,* which celebrates the astonishing career and adventurous life of the legendary American magician, Civil War soldier, and inventor, Professor Gus Rich. *The War Wizard* has been presented at the Magic Castle in Hollywood, at New York's Lincoln Center, at the world renowned Spoleto Festival in Charleston, South Carolina.

hear the real thing. Do yourself a favor. Work on something that will pay off emotionally and artistically and that means dreaming up your own act. This doesn't mean that you can't ever use a commercially created piece of magic in your show. You need some sure bets, especially when you are starting out. Just don't take someone else's act or personality and try to jump in the middle of it; it won't fit. Put your own fingerprints all over everything you choose.

Creating Your Patter

Good patter is extremely important for any great speaking magic act. The patter is the backbone, the camouflage, the icing, and the thermostat for your show.

Researching Your Voice

Your persona has a voice and it's important to listen to and for it. Recognize your optimum communication mode and monitor it for perfection. Your voice needs to be consistent, clear, and contagious. I have seen a lot of really great magicians put a big question mark in the minds of an audience when they begin to speak. Bad speech can be very distracting. The audience stops to question the magician and is given a chance to leave the focal point, the magic. The question mark should be in your amazing magic, not in your communication with the audience. Audiences appreciate being given clear signals. They want to have all the details without having to figure out which voice is really yours. They really want to like you and everything about you. It's also a wonderful contrast to the mystery. How could something so comfortable and fitting accompany anything but comfortable and fitting actions? It can be such a great tool, when taken seriously. Listen to voices of magicians Max Maven or Colin Powell. If you have the chance, listen to a tape of the late Harry Blackstone and you'll hear some real craft. Having a good stage voice doesn't mean that you have to sound like a trained announcer, but whatever you decide is for you, so stick with it and work on it. If your voice signals change, the audience will be expecting to find the reason for it within your work. Becoming part of a speaking association such as Toast Masters International or a local chapter of the National Speaker's Association can also really help. These people are professionals. Theatrical training is, of course, another excellent way to study voice.

Who's Doing the Talking?

Many times, a voice is developed around a character, and it is important that the voice stay consistent. I imagine you have at one time or another watched a movie where an actor jumps in and out of a dialect. It immediately rips you away from the illusion of the character and makes you feel sort of deceived. Your audience should feel tricked and fooled—that's why they are watching magic in the first place—but being deceived is something quite different. If you're not real, then neither is your magic. The whole thing becomes cheapened.

Speaking off the Cuff

Improvisation and faux improvisation (lines that sound spontaneous but are carefully contrived and expertly delivered) make audiences say, "Wow." They really love it, if it's done well. It's not something to fool with unless you practice and perfect it, but it can be very strong. Audiences love to be the first to hear something good, funny or insightful. It's an added bonus when they feel lucky to have been there when it happened. That's the way every audience should feel after they watch you: happy, lucky, and impressed. Why not work on it as another layer of a great magical performance? They are worth it. On the other hand, improvisation can bury you fast, so try it out only once in a while. Don't try to take a spin on a drag bike if you are used to driving a moped. You'll fall off and get hurt. Forget about the flesh wounds, people generally don't really throw things anymore (okay, in some of the places I have worked they did, but I was having a bad night). Improvisational crashes will also crush your confidence and credibility when you hit the wall. Don't be afraid of it, just be smart about it. Speaking off the cuff should be thought of more as shooting from the hip. Be ready but be armed. It can be dangerously exciting and wonderfully impressive.

Tobias "Theo" Bamberg, "Okito" (1875–1963)

Theo Bamberg was the fifth generation of a dynasty of magicians from Holland. By the time he was 11, he was performing magic for King William III. As a teenager, he became partially deaf and decided he would crate a new stage persona, fearing that the problem might become worse and that he wouldn't be able to communicate as he had before. It was then that the Japanese character "Okito" was born. His act consisted of an Asian pantomime and he was adorned with colorful robes, make up, a wig, and often a hat. Okito played throughout England and France and in 1907, while performing in Paris' Folies Bergeres, he signed an 18-month agree-

(continued on next page)

Silent Magic and Magic with Music

When I speak of silent magic, I mean both silent and musically accompanied magic. Silent magic has some real advantages, but don't think that it's easier because you leave something out or don't have to worry about patter; it's just different. Discovering the power of magic without patter has been no secret to many of the great masters of magic. The marriage of magic and music, when it's good, is great. It's magic in itself, but that's no accident. It's planned that way. Listen to music, especially instrumental music, and feel what it does to you. Watch how a soundtrack affects a movie and you will begin to notice something that you may not have before. It was there all along, but you probably didn't notice before you starting listening for it. If that happens, then the musical director did a great job. Imagine the movie *Jaws* without the "dum dum dum dum." Music speaks. On the other hand, imagine having a speaking act and suddenly finding yourself playing for an audience that doesn't speak the language. It's hard, very hard. If that could possibly happen to you, it's always good to consider having an alternate plan. On one occasion, I decided to use a translator to solve the problem and let's just say, it was apparently lost in the translation. Visual, internationally understood acts are solid and stable, so unless you speak as well as music does, consider adding some tunes. I have always tried to use a musical piece of magic to open my shows. It's a great start and gives the audience that moment to size you up as they always do in the first few moments of your presentation. Good music makes you look even better.

Edit and Elect (E)

Once you have decided on what you will do, you need to decide how you will do it and how it will flow. You are about to lay out a flowchart or a roadmap of where you are going. Once you have the map, you can follow along until you finally get there. If you get lost, you just need to check the map to get back on track.

Routining Your Magic Show

Visualization is a little unusual but it's neat to imagine your act in your mind's eye in perfect form before you try to hammer it out and, more importantly, before anyone else sees it. Close your eyes and try to see yourself actually performing different selected pieces of magic and imagine hearing yourself delivering your patter. If you have a tendency to let your eyes roll back in your head or your mouth drop open when you go into serious visualization or meditation, I suggest getting a Medic Alert bracelet and engrave it to read, "It's okay, I'm a magician and I'm working on my act."

What Will Happen During the Show?

Will you work on a stage or a bar? Will you have one assistant or 52? Will part of your act include birthday parties and the art of twisting children into the shape of poodles or will you mesmerize adult audiences with your mind-reading ability and a trick with a foam rubber wiener? Will you play a character like "Zippy the magical monkey boy," or will you just be yourself? Will you be an act or will you be acting all the time? It's up to you, but here are a couple of tips to consider. There are signals, natural paths, and logical choices for you to follow, that's one; and there is a difference between playing a part and being yourself, that was two.

What Order Should I Put Things In?

I don't know what you are planning to do but my formula for any presentation has always been:

- Open strong with music, high energy, and a pleasing picture (look professional)
- Let the audience get to know you and your personality (have fun)
- Involve the audience in a solid piece of magic
- Have some more fun and say good-bye
- Blow them away with your best trick and some more music and energy
- Return to accept their applause

Tobias "Theo" Bamberg, "Okito" (1875–1963)

(continued from previous page)

ment with the American Orpheum circuit. Although he never extended the contract, he stayed in the United States, where he founded the Bamberg Magic and Novelty Company in New York. His products were beautifully made and the quality was superior to any other equipment available at the time. Bamberg is probably best known for his floating ball illusion, a trick that is still being performed by many magicians to this day. Okito's son, David Tobias Bamberg, also became a well-known illusionist under the stage name of "Fu Manchu."

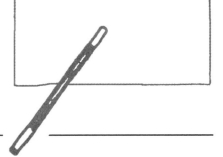

How Should My Audience React?

Keep track of how individual effects affect every audience. Don't just notice it, keep track of it. Audience reaction is a good barometer to what's going right and what's going wrong. When you know how your audience should react, you know when you need to give more or hold back.

Activate and Ascend (A)

This is the final step. It's taking all of your decisions, using them, and producing your act. You should truly consider all of the decisions you have made and see if they are possible. One way to do this is to consider Eugene Burger's 10 tips outlined below. They are good to know before you perform magic and while you are learning it. You might want to copy this section out of the book to use for reference and to help you make further decisions for your act.

Eugene Burger's 10 Important Points to Consider

We're going to talk about magic, not simply about how magic tricks work but rather about a question that is, I think, much more important: "What is the process by which we learn to perform magic effects?" A process hopefully that ends with a magical performance that is both deceptive and entertaining.

I suppose that there are almost as many views of this process of how to learn magic, as there are magicians. During the last eight years I have thought about it quite a bit. Much of my thinking was stimulated by working with magic students and trying to help them find efficient and effective ways to learn magic. Here are some words and some ideas to keep this discussion organized. Let's look at the first one.

#1, Easy or Simple

Here's a question. Is it easy or simple? Of course, we're told in magic lectures and many magic books that this is all easy. I don't believe it. I think learning to perform magic is really rather difficult. It is the case, however, that some magic is simple, not easy but simple: simple to understand and, even more important, simple for laymen to understand. I think that a good magic effect is one that when it's over, a layman can describe it to another layman. If they can't do that, perhaps the effect was far too complicated.

#2, Selecting Effects

What I'm looking for in a magic effect is, first of all, one that appears magical but, secondly, I want an effect that is within my own performing range, technically. Much of the very bad magic that we see is from performers who overreach, trying to do technical material that is far beyond what they actually have learned.

#3, Solitude

A strange word, "solitude," for this question of how to learn magic. I remember when I was a very small child, I would clear my mother and father's dresser of all the things on it and I would practice my cups and balls in front of the big mirror. I think that's often the way magic is learned. It is learned in solitude. It's learned in periods when we allow our imagination to simply inspire us. I think there are a couple of tools here. One of them is a notebook. When I get ideas, I write them down and later look through that notebook but, secondly, I think what we need is a mirror. I simply cannot understand how Close-Up Magic can be learned at all without a mirror.

Did You Know?

Every routine needs a definite beginning, middle, and end.

- The beginning begins your friendship and rapport with the audience.
- The middle offers a variety of magic that builds impact, each trick has its own complete unit from beginning to climax.
- The end says the act is over, puts the spotlight on you, and features your strongest trick.
- Depending on your time limit, keeping to this "rule of three" could mean only three tricks. That's all right, but make sure they fit into achieving a clear beginning, middle, and end.

#4, Practice

The fourth thing is practice. We've found an effect, hopefully from a book and not from a working performer's act, now we want to begin the process of learning it. The first step is practice. I think for practice to be effective it should be regular; that is to say, I think a person is far better off practicing 10 minutes a day than an hour once a week; a half hour a day would even be better. That leads us to the second thing about practice, and that is that practice should be structured. You should be clear what it is you want to practice before you do it. Practice is work! It's repetition. It's learning the moves. With complicated card tricks, one of the great ways to learn moves is to read the entire body of instructions onto an audio tape, because then you can close the book, turn the tape back on, and learn from the tape in an easier fashion. Practice is not always fun. It's work, learning the moves, learning the sequences. Above all, it's repetition with awareness, not rehearsal.

#5, Rehearsal

Rehearsal should also be regular and structured. In rehearsal what I'm trying to do, among other things, is find the frame that I'm going to put around this magical effect. Rehearsal means imagining that there is an audience with you and speaking out loud to these imaginary people. It's really quite schizophrenic. In rehearsal, you start at the beginning and you go to the end. If you mess up, well, you go to the end, because for rehearsal to be effective, it has to have that pressure of performing for imaginary people. A good piece of advice: Don't imagine that these imaginary people are always polite and kind. Sometimes you should imagine that they are frisky and that they're grabbing or asking embarrassing questions and you can then rehearse how you might deal with them. Surprisingly, one day you will have to respond to such things. Now, after we have practiced and rehearsed, we are then ready for the next step—the performance.

#6, Performance

I have a rule of thumb here that I want to mention. When I think that I am ready to perform a magic trick, I don't. I wait 30 more days. Give it 30 more days of practice and rehearsal, they really make a big difference. So, we've done all this and now we come to performance time, but performance is not the end. Performance is just a stage along the way, because this phase of performance is not going to be as good as the performances you make after completing step #10.

#7, Audio Taping

Since most Close-Up Magic is done with speaking, you should tape your performance and to listen to it sentence by sentence. Try to discover how many times you are putting yourself down, you are putting the effect down, you're just doing gibberish talk or idle chatter. This is what we call "patter" in magical lingo. I listen to my performance sentence by sentence, try to tighten it, to take away excess verbiage, to keep the directions tight and simple and not to be endlessly repeating myself. Once we've audiotaped our show and listened to it, then the next step is videotaping.

#8, Videotaping

When I videotape a performance I can watch it action by action. When you think about it, twentieth-century magicians have an opportunity that no magicians have ever had before; none of the great magicians of history, not Houdini, not any of them! The ability to get a video camera and to tape your performance and watch all of the little ticks and the little hideous things that you do is invaluable. It isn't easy to view these things, because it requires great honesty, to look at ourselves and to see what's there.

Eugene Burger

Eugene Burger is an important performer, teacher, mentor, and lecturer in today's world of magic. In 1999 he was named one of the 100 most influential magicians of the 20th century by the international magazine, *Magic*. Well-studied in the history, philosophy, and performance of magic, he understands, commands, and seamlessly fuses the mosaic of details that transform "tricks" into molten magic. Powerful playlets narrated with his voice of rocks and steam, are filled with mysteries as they quietly unfold, hypnotically surround, and ultimately capture any audience. Not only does Burger command this understanding of magic, but he also he shares it with other serious students of magic.

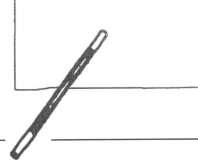

#9, Honesty

The great German Protestant theologian, Rudolph Bultmann, said, "Scholars must approach the bible with ruthless honesty." This phrase has remained in my mind since the '60s when I first read it. In magic, and in the arts even more so, we must approach our work with ruthless honesty, and the video camera and other devices that provide feedback allow us to do just that. Of course, sometimes we're not honest; that's the sad fact of it, but it's a goal to strive for.

#10, Other Eyes

Have another pair of eyes look at your work, perhaps a magician friend, perhaps a relative, perhaps a nonmagician friend, perhaps a professional director. What you hear from them is really up to you, but my point is that once we've worked on our act, once we've practiced it and rehearsed it and performed it, having another pair of eyes look at it can be an eye-opening experience. Look, what we're trying to learn is a performance art. Magic happens between people. It is a process to learn this. I think it is also a path. The important thing is going to the end of the path. And that's what we often don't see when we look at contemporary magic. Too often magicians have started to practice, they've started to rehearse, and then they put it aside to work on a new trick. Before they get that one finished, they find yet another one to work on. The end result is that we never go to the end of the path. That, I think, is where our attention needs to be—on going to the end of the path—where a magical performance that is deceptive and entertaining is awaiting us.

Seems like a lot of work, doesn't it? It is. As I said at Step 1, "This isn't easy but it can be simple" and therefore effective.

CHAPTER 20

Mounting Your Own Magic Show

Magic Equipment

Magic equipment is a subject that will make a lot of magicians cover their eyes and hang their heads. I think I can safely say, we all have way too much of it.

Deciding What's Right for You

You need knowledge first, and that doesn't come with props. Remember the entire secret never comes in the box. I like to think of a magic prop in the same way as I do a human being. The outer shell only makes up a small percentage of who that person is. The magic trick is only a small percentage of what the magic is.

If you are developing a comedy magic piece, you probably don't need a trick with the devil face, the fake blood, and the tombstones. If you have a formal, more serious piece in mind, walk by the drooping flower and the clown nose equipment. Understanding what kind of magic fits your performance style is the key. Of course, finding out who you are (at least on stage) is the key to finding out what your performance style is. We already know that from Chapter 19.

How Much to Spend

Boy, this is a good topic! Here's a good rule of thumb. Find out what's involved in a particular effect before you fork out the money for it. Advice from friends, reviews, and word of mouth are worth a lot in this area. Be careful purchasing something that sounds too good for too little—it usually is. Magic is often marketed with descriptions and claims that are only crystal clear once you really have a handle on what's out there. This weeding out process takes a long time because there is a lot out there. If you have a magician friend or mentor and wonder about an effect, ask him or her. It can save you a lot of money, heartache, and storage space. You don't need a bunch of junk, extra expense, or clutter. You need knowledge and an act.

Books, videotapes, and personal instruction are the wisest investments any magician can make, beginner or professional. There is nothing like personal instruction whether you get it one on one or at a lecture. It makes the process make perfect sense. It gives immediate satisfaction and it is both interactive and enjoyable. Books are great too. You can take them with you and you can get to them immediately. It's a good idea to highlight, note, and summarize your favorite parts of a book or magazine. Some magazines, such as *Genii,* offer summaries of what has been in the last year's editions. *MAGIC* magazine has an online search feature that is a pretty high-tech approach to making your magazines even more useable. Newer and newer study techniques are arising every day, but books will never be replaced. You get one "smart credit" already for investing your time and money in this book. You could have spent your money on a plastic mouse with a piece of wax described in a TV advertisement as "The Magician's Motor," as I did. It's sitting here on my shelf. Penn and Teller have a great story entitled "Invisible Thread" in their book, *Cruel Tricks for Dear Friends"* (Villard Books, 1989). It's a pretty realistic insight into the subject of buying something simply by its description and intrigue. Many times when you buy a magic effect without knowing much about it, what you get is an expensive lesson.

There are magic suppliers listed in the Appendix at the back of this book, and most of them have books and tapes. Get to know them; get on their mailing lists. Find out who is in your area and support them. Let them know what you are looking for and they will try their best. More often, one effect in a good magic book or tape can be worth far more than its cost. If you blindly purchase magic props, either from a store or by mail, you won't get the secret until you get out the wallet. Then it just may be too late.

How Big to Go

Magic comes in all shapes and sizes just like people and their tastes. Everybody is different and so is every type of magic.

Close-Up Magic

If you are a close-up worker, most of your props are already small, but presentations of Close-Up Magic differ quite a bit in size.

Dollars and Cents

You can spend a few dollars for a packet trick, a few more on a book, or thousands on an illusion. You can spend as much as you need to or as much as you want to.

Some close-up can be performed with something the size of a cigarette paper or a piece of thread and nothing else but the hands. There is not a need for a special work surface or area. It might be the bar top, the putting green, or the restaurant table. There may be no need for any technical support outside of the hands. That's the way some magicians work. I have been told by a number of professional magicians, "If it doesn't fit into my pockets or my jacket, I don't do it." Small props, big skill, and a casual manner seems to me to be the way a real magician would perform off of an actual theatrical stage setting. A real magician wouldn't need any special props, just those known and understood by everyone in everyday existence. David Blaine has become very popular recently. His television audiences seem to love magic performed with real people in real situations that somehow seem to yield unreal outcomes. To me it's a form of "magic jazz"—raw, perhaps unstructured, freeform and not packaged for looks, but it's high in personal impact. That's what we want as magicians—a personal impact on each person viewing our magic. David Blaine's success tells me that every magician doesn't need to have a fancy wand or a brand-new deck, a special close-up pad and a manicure, and every crowd doesn't need to see those things either. Magic is not one-size-fits-all. If it was, it would have been finished a long time ago. Every art form utilizes a large palette of possible colors, textures, and perspectives. Magic is no different.

Many times close-up magicians decide on carrying more than just what fits in the pockets. You can choose a variety of magic props that store well in a variety of places. I have seen special belts, belly bags, and fanny packs. I have seen aprons, pochettes, and even special vests adorned with magical motifs, ranging from playing cards to moons and stars. It's all a matter of preference, performing style, and individual needs.

Magicians often work on a close-up pad. This allows you to count on a specific working surface and texture and that's important if you are doing certain types of effects, such as in the shell game described in Chapter 17. I perform certain coin, card, and cups and balls effects that also count on the consistency of my work surface. The pad can act in other functions, like a back tray to hold objects ready for loading or to keep them ready to be ditched. Most magic stores will focus their close-up area around a close-up pad and I have seen these put to some terribly clever uses.

Magic cases, compact tables and specially-made close-up contrivances are another choice for some close-up performers. There are some real beauties out there but make sure you have something to put on them and "do" before investing or thinking about them too much. I use an adjustable case for my close-up work because it allows me to change the look of my presentation every time. I perform mostly for corporate events where the real reason for my being is to be part of an entire message or theme. I have developed a system that allows me to change the appearance of my case quickly, accurately, and very professionally for any need. It may be a conference theme, logo, or product, but I want to bring value through my magic to my client in any way I can. Trade shows, hospitality suites, special banquets often demand customization, and if I can make that a simple matter, it takes the strain and worry off of the client and allows me to fit into the big picture. I also have the ability to input my own media representation for jobs where gaining more business for me is the raison d'être.

There are situations that special lighting, music, and sound effects are also needed in the performance of Close-Up Magic. This means you'll need to learn about technical equipment so you can either purchase, rent, or recommend what will make your magic its very best.

Parlor Magic

Performing Parlor Magic automatically means the equipment is going to need to be a little larger than that cigarette paper and the piece of thread we just talked about. If you perform farther away, the magic needs to be able to be seen and understood. That still doesn't mean you can't control what you need and how to make it work for you instead of against you. There is a well-known description in magic for what many consider to be the end-all criteria for a great magic prop: the prop that "packs small and plays big" is a winner! There is no reason that an effect large enough to play for a moderate-size crowd needs to be a giant collection of equipment.

Did You Know?

Another Poetic Gift from Bob Farmer

"I never cheated an honest man, only rascals. They wanted something for nothing, I gave them nothing for something."
Yellow Kid Weil,
Con Man

"There's a sucker born every minute."
P.T. Barnum

"In the postwar years, there were two born every minute."
P.J. O'Rourke

Did You Know?

Some of the world's best stage acts travel in cases of a size that can be taken as regular luggage on commercial airlines anywhere in the world. Is this because these people can't have huge cases full of elaborate pieces of magic equipment? No, it's because their magic is in their talent and not in the cases.

How big do you go? For starters, don't let the size of your equipment overpower the magic. Be on the lookout for easy to pack props that fold or assemble with a minimum of effort. Patter is a great ally in Parlor Magic. You can create a mood, color a setting, fill a stage with just yourself and well-crafted patter.

If you're going to perform Parlor Magic, you need to be able to use every single element to make the situation the very best. Remember, you will be performing as if you are in someone's living room and living rooms aren't made for magic shows. It's a challenge that can really be a lot of fun and you can use it to your advantage. For instance, small tables can be draped to fill a stage with color and excitement. Silks are great for Parlor Magic since they pack up very small, and the color creates fantastic, flowing visuals even when you're not doing anything with them. Your favorite card tricks can be modified with a jumbo deck. Easels put things up into the air where you can see them, and they're also already available at a lot of small venues where Parlor Magic might be performed. Consider draping the tables, piano benches, or podiums with cloth. Use the hotel's glasses, goblets, knives, napkins, and liquid (water), just make sure they have everything you need before you show up. You don't want to try to find wooden matches, a lemon, and a legal-sized envelope on the spot. Don't count on anything and always have a backup plan.

Of course, there are some things that you just have to have to make your working area look professional. A sound system is something that will be a definite consideration. Chances are some of the rooms will be a little larger than your average parlor. If you are told there will only be about 50 people there, remember, there may also be their spouses, children, and perhaps a couple of their friends. All of them need to be able to see you *and* hear you. Also, if you are performing Parlor Magic, there is a good chance that you'll also eventually need to perform in a cabaret/stage setting soon. Some of these venues will have a public address system but some won't. Many of them will either be incomplete or insufficient for the room, and guess who's fault that will look like? You guessed it, yours. Keep all of your equipment manageable in weight and size and it will make your life a lot easier.

Cabaret/Stage Magic

If you are performing on stage, you will have to start "haulin' the stuff," that's for sure. It's just part of the deal. Your tables hold your equipment the way you need it to be, so you have to pack them. Then, there's the equipment itself, that's a given. If you are going to perform the *"Head Guillotine,"* chances are you'll need to take one with you. As you move from the simplicity of Close-up and Parlor Magic (and all that it *doesn't* include), you get closer to what makes magic big enough to see on a real stage—all those bigger props! It sure does seem to start to snowball, but if you carefully plan what your act is, what it needs, and how to transport it, you can keep things under control. I used to hear my childhood mentor, Max Scott, and his friend Al Monroe talk about trying to keep things small and pack as lightly as possible. Back then, I thought they might have just been getting a little tired of carrying a lot of equipment around. They weren't, they were getting smarter.

Some of the same rules apply to Cabaret/Stage Magic that apply to Parlor Magic in terms of equipment. Try to keep everything light-weight but look for sturdy and good-quality equipment. Try to create a strong impact, using lighting, sound, scenic treatments (such as backdrops), costume, props, and of course an act that fills up the stage. Again, I think silk magic is a friendly solution for stage and travel. Feather products also work beautifully. Think of using contrast in color, shape, and texture, such as white billiard balls, colored cards, or prismatic fans against a plain black backdrop. Almost all stages can supply you with a black backdrop. Think of using music as an element other than for plain accompaniment. There are many choices you can make once you decide to perform on stage. The distance from the audience, the size of the working area, and the inclusion of technical support are there for you; take advantage of them. It's very exciting to dream, plan, and mount your own show, but it doesn't have to break your back every time.

Carefully considering your magic both on stage and off stage makes the difference between enjoying working at your magic or working at enjoying it. Don't underestimate the power and presence of supporting your magic with magic equipment. You *do* need the right tools for the job. Just remember that you have to break the

equipment down and eventually get it home after the show, and you'll being doing it a lot!

Illusions

While attending my first magic convention, I saw a wonderful illusion act. Outside of the auditorium was a huge transport truck, an expensive car, and a very strange dog that I thought must have cost a lot of money. It looked like success on wheels. There were so many people on stage that the magician actually took time to introduce them. They had huge stage props, animals, a beautiful six-foot blonde assistant, costumes, and of course a star, the magician. They received a standing ovation. I was so young I didn't even know why people were standing up, maybe for a stretch. After the show we went back to where the dealers sold magic and the awards for the best of the convention were being given out. The magician from the illusion show was a winner, but he wasn't there. Where was he? He and his crew were still at the auditorium packing up the equipment. That should have told me something. Growing up in magic, I believed the natural progression in the art was from Close-Up Magic to Cabaret Magic to Stage Magic and, finally, to Illusions! I wanted to be an illusionist but there was that catch 22: I couldn't buy big props without big money and I couldn't make big money without doing big shows. I'll cut to the chase and tell you that I did end up doing illusions, though I never purchased the full set of props.

Care and Feeding

Taking care of your equipment is a must. Make sure everything is kept as clean and as new looking as possible. If you are trying to impress your audience with magic, your tools need to be kept in prime condition. Cleaning, painting, pressing, grooming, and replacing parts are all part of the game. Always put your props in a case with padding, even if it's just a suitcase with a towel. They *will* get beat up if you don't. If your props look bad, so do you.

Moving It Safely

Real equipment needs to be moved in real cases. As I said, if you are traveling by air and the equipment gets into someone else's hands to get there, you'll need flight cases or at least hard-sided luggage to make sure it gets there intact. I would also suggest that you insure your pieces. Most freight companies can help you there. Also, if time allows, try shipping your equipment by ground. This type of shipping offers tracking, insurance, and cheaper costs. If you are planning to ship by air, get to know each carrier's individual rules, regulations, and limitations. As a warning, freight doesn't go to every location every day. You need to find out when you're equipment needs to be at the airport to guarantee it by a given certain date. That often means you'll have to make two trips to the airport, one for the equipment and one for you. If you need to have equipment fly with you and get there with you it's best to put it on as regular baggage on a nonstop flight. That way it can't get taken off by mistake during a layover. I have had some very bad experiences, ranging from theft to extreme damage, so consider every possible way to get your equipment where it needs to be well in advance of when you need it.

Costuming Your Magic

Getting Ideas

The best way to get ideas for a costume is to keep your eyes open. Cut pieces out of magazines, see shows, draw sketches, read costume books, and ask people who know about costume design. There are people who specialize in designing and creating costumes for magic. Check out the list in the Appendix.

Costume for Effect

Sometimes, a costume just needs to be something that's good to look at. Make sure it is eye-catching without being gaudy. Make sure it is suitable for your performing venue. Don't wear a rhinestone tuxedo if you are doing close-up outside. If you are handy,

---

Harry Blackstone Sr. (1885–1965)

Harry Blackstone, Sr. inspired a lot of people to become magicians. Blackstone stood for grand illusion and was first class. When he was just 22, Harry Blackstone was moving beyond vaudeville with his own two-hour show.

Blackstone was a fresh contrast to the stiff Dante and Thurston shows. He was described as a flamboyant cowboy onstage, and audiences appreciated his huge illusions, his sense of humor, and his human traits. Performing his famous illusions such as "Vanishing Horse," "Vanishing Bird Cage," "Dancing Handkerchief," and "Buzz Saw," audiences got an eyeful when they saw Harry Blackstone and his *Show of 1,001 Wonders* come to town.

(continued on next page)

you can spruce up existing clothing or purchase a special magic tie, shirt, piece of jewelry, or vest from a supplier.

Costume as a Tool

If your costume needs to *do* something, such as hold a load in a special pocket or hide a gimmick or be an integral gimmick itself, make sure everything you do is first quality. If you can't afford to do that, don't do it at all. If your costume is a prop, care for it with the same attention you would any other prop in your act. Just because you wear it doesn't make it any different. The audience will be really looking at it a lot so make it nice.

Durability and Comfort

If you are performing magic for long periods of time or you have to travel with a costume in a tiny carry on, think of both comfort and durability in your choice of costume. Don't plan on wearing a light bulb suit with a chrome collar if you have to tuck it into a computer bag. If it does make it and still works when you get there, it will look like it *just* made it. Consider these kinds of things when you are deciding "what" you will do in your act. There are great fabrics available today that can be crumpled up and come out looking great. Travel with a steamer or some antistatic spray and never, *ever* wear your costume for anything other than rehearsal and performance. Wear washable garments under your costume to avoid overcleaning and distressing your costume. If you have to wear your costume for more than an hour at a time, think about comfort. There's no sense having your costume kill you. If you can stay comfortable and fresh, you will do a better job.

Makeup
What Do I Need?

If you perform Stage Magic, you need makeup. I don't care who you are. I don't care if you have a great tan or a wonderful complexion, you need it or you will look washed out on stage.

When Do I Need It?

If you use any kind of theatrical or high-intensity lighting, you need to be the correct color and you need to be able to be clearly seen. You can't be shiny and you can't look like a burned tomato. Any time the lighting is bright enough to affect your eyes on stage, you need it. Wearing makeup is part of a totally clean picture, and if you don't even out textures, create a matte finish, and highlight specific features, your shoddy work will be instantly visible.

What Am I Trying to Achieve?

Your eyes, your mouth, and the contours of your face need to appear clear and sharp. If you are a man, you are not trying to look pretty or in drag. Just clear up your features and accentuate the most important ones. If you are a woman, don't think that putting on evening makeup is going to get it. It's a completely different ball game and the dark shadows and exaggerated tricks that work for street makeup will make you look like you've been boxing with Zippy the clown.

What to Buy

You'll need a base color, cover stick, contour powder, brow pencil, mascara, and fixative powder. If you are prone to sweating, get permanent, waterproof products. Even water-based theatrical products are no good in this case.

Application

If you don't know about makeup, get a book on theatrical makeup application and learn what works and why. If you can, go to a theatrical store or get a consultation from a makeup artist who specializes in live shows, motion pictures, or television. I suggest doing half of your face yourself and letting the artist do the other side. Take a picture so you can remember what it looked like and see the difference. Also, write down any specific products and suppliers.

Harry Blackstone Jr. (1934–1997)

(continued from previous page)

while to decide he wanted magic as a career. He started with smaller tricks but eventually grew to love the grand illusions that his father had made famous. The Blackstone name continued to grow, and with new innovations and twists on illusions that were already famous with Blackstone fans, Harry, Jr. not only kept on vanishing bird-cages and buzzing women in half, but he also created new miracles such as "The Floating Lightbulb." To me, Harry Blackstone, Jr. was the last of a great era of magicians. Harry's last show was at the Carolina Coliseum in Columbia, South Carolina. The date was March 25, 1997.

(continued on next page)

Robert Harbin (1908–1978)

I'll bet you have seen some of Robert Harbin's magic in action and you might not even know it. Robert Harbin was the creator of the world-famous and, yes, perhaps overused, "Zig-Zag Lady Illusion." Created in the 1960s, just about everyone has seen it at one time or another. A girl is placed into an upright box and locked in place by three front doors—her face and left hand visible in the top box, her right and mid-section seen in the middle box, and a foot protruding and wiggling from the bottom box. Two large, flat, steel blades are slid from the front of the box through to the back, and the center section of the box (with fingers still wiggling) is slid to the extreme side of the other boxes. The young lady is, without a doubt, clearly divided into three separate

Technical Equipment

Microphones

Here's a good general statement. If you are in a large room you need to use a microphone, end of story. Don't think you can shout. Remember about keeping that voice of yours consistent? Won't happen. There are two major divisions in microphones, wireless and hardwire. One is a radio microphone that has no cord and sends a signal from the microphone to a receiving unit and amplifier. The hardwire microphone has a cord that runs from it to the amplifier. These microphones are either held or placed in a stand if it is necessary to use the hands. Within these two divisions of mics are two other major divisions: handheld and lavaliere. The handheld is just what it sounds like, and the lavaliere is worn on the tie, lapel, or sometimes on the head somewhere and allows the performer to use both hands without a microphone stand.

Sound Support Systems

A basic sound support system consists of a controller or mixing board, an amplifier, and the speaker enclosures. The mixing board allows several inputs from microphones, playback systems, or receivers, and controls those individual inputs by way of sliders and knobs. The amplifier boosts the signals coming form these inputs and sends the signal down a cord to the enclosures. The enclosures change the electrical signal to a mechanical signal and the sound is then heard.

Playback Systems

There are several types of playback systems for sound, but the most popular are cassette and compact disk. I recommend the use of compact disk over cassette because it is permanent and can't be affected by magnetic fields. New technology has made the creation of CDs possible so you can record just what you need for your act and carry it on one single CD. As far as a playback system, I usually let the sound man use his own, because he knows how it works. Learning a new machine in the dark can cause a technician to miss an important cue and make you look like a real loser. When anything happens during a magic show, it is the magician who takes the rap. As an added note, there is also a cool little system created by Kerry Pollack's Wireless Wizardry that allows you to record and wirelessly control a mini CD unit and control all of the cuts and volumes through a computer. It's portable and allows the performer to run his own cues and therefore might be a good option for you. It also has options for fades and control of other special effects. You just have to push the same button and the system remembers the rest.

Lighting
Basics

Very simply put, the idea of lighting is to control what and how you want the audience to see your show. First, you want to be seen. Next come props, assistants, and scenery. You can manipulate the attention of your audience, create discomfort, add class, or punch up a bright comedy act to maintain interest and attention. Here are some lighting guidelines I learned from experience and from lighting expert Tracy Lightel.

Areas and Uses
Front Light

Lighting from directly in front of an area is okay, but will flatten what is being lit. Instruments should be placed at an angle facing the stage, not directly in front. A 45-degree angle is preferred, using two instruments per area. This means that for one given area (stage right, center, etc.), two lights should be hung 45 degrees apart from each other with the center of the area in the center between the lights. Lekos, described later, are usually used for front light for their output and versatility. Divide the stage into areas with the center as one. Five is a good division for an average stage, although it depends on the size of the stage and how many areas and lighting instruments you need. Isolating areas gives you an easy way to use separate sections of the stage for setups, smaller illusions, and the like.

Robert Harbin (1908–1978)
(continued from previous page)

sections. The illusion is mind-boggling. Not only is this illusion very convincing, it is convincing close up, in full light, from any angle. That's the kind of design criteria many of Robert Harbin's illusions met. Not only was Robert Harbin a great inventor, he was also a performer. Unfortunately, just as he was reaching the highest point of his vaudeville career, such as his appearance at New York's Palace Theater in 1949, vaudeville was on its way out. Robert Harbin was instrumental in bridging the gap and fulfilling the need for illusions that could be equally effective in a theater or on television. In 1970 he published a book called *The Magic of Robert Harbin*, which describes many of his original thoughts and ingenious adaptations.

Martin Gardner

Within six months of writing up a trick for *The Sphinx*, his name appeared regularly on the cover as an ongoing contributor. He was only 15 years old. He wrote about magic, mathematics, puzzles, games, theology, philosophy, politics, science, psychic debunking, and shared some of the best darned practical jokes ever conceived. Martin Gardner is the author of more than 65 books.

Side Light

This lends definition to people and you may or may not want this angle if there are parts of illusions that would be visible or show shadows of people or objects not intended to be seen. It is what it sounds like—light from the side.

Top or Backlight:

This position is nice to subtly push people and objects back toward the audience. A more saturated color may be used to be pretty, but stark color or no color can also be utilized. Watch for blinding the audience by shining into the seats. This effect may be useful in certain instances in masking entrances and exits, but makes the audience uncomfortable if the use of it is prolonged.

Specials

These are used for one specific use in one area, hence the term "special." They can be tiny for a very small prop, or can be on one person or prop. They can be hung and shot from any of the angles previously described.

Washes

This adds a punch to existing lighting or lights a full area of stage. Several banks of instruments are connected in one group. Washes are generally set up from the front, can be warm or cool, and give versatility to other lighting by combining with them.

Equipment
Leko

The Leko, also known as the Ellipsoidal Reflector Spotlight, is the most useful of any lighting instrument. It comes in different sizes to create a pool of light in varying sizes. The pool of light from a Leko may have a sharp or soft edge by "running the barrel." The front of the light is moveable and creates more or less distance between the two lenses, creating the effect of the pool. Each Leko contains four shutters, which enable the light to be cut off of unwanted objects or cut down to frame a specific prop.

"Patterns," also called "gobos" or "templates." may be used in a Leko to break up and add texture to the stage. They may be focused sharply or softly by running the barrel of the instrument. A great variety of ready-made gobos are available, from leaves to clouds to varying shapes. Gobos can be projected across people, on a wall, cyclorama, you name it.

Par Cans

At one time this instrument was the staple of Rock and Roll lighting because of its swift setup and intensity while using heavily saturated color. It creates a strong, elongated beam of light from a sealed lamp (bulb). It is called a "par can" because the reflector, which is enclosed in the bulb, has a parabolic shape while the rest of the light is shaped like a large can. There isn't much else involved. The beam may be spun to any number of angles by spinning the bulb from the back. Par cans are generally used for back light, but can be used as front, side, and area light as well.

Follow Spots

These are good if there is an operator available. But, beware, a bad operator destroys a show. Choose wisely if you have the control to do so.

Color

Most lighting instruments contain slots where color may be added. Most color is a plastic medium called "gel" and comes in many brands and colors. Blending of color is useful for a more natural and dramatic use of lighting and also may mask aspects of the stage picture. An audience may be manipulated simply by a choice in color. Red is dramatic, blue is soothing or calm, purple may be mysterious or majestic. Warm colors often define a comedy or an upbeat performance.

Smoke and Fog

These effects are in the lighting category because they work in conjunction with lighting. They add a dramatic effect as well as

masking certain effects. Dry ice or CO_2-induced fog hugs the floor, smoke hangs in the air. Haze is another form of smoke which, if used sparingly, may not be visible to the audience yet allows the beams of light to be seen shooting across the stage, adding to the effect's dimension. Templates also show up nicely in fog and haze.

Your Soundtrack
Music, Sounds, or What?

The sound for your magic act doesn't necessarily need to be *just* music. Soundtracks are made up by of lot more than that and, really, what you are creating is a soundtrack for your magic act. Listen carefully to soundtracks and see how they combine orchestrated and specially arranged music, stock music, ambient sound, amplified actual sound, and sound effects to make the movie come to life. You can use this same powerful tool for your act, and you should. It's too good of a tool to waste!

Whose Taste Is Best?

Nobody's taste is best. The music you use and the way you put it together is up to you. The only advice I would give is to consider not making your soundtrack offensive in any way. It can't be too much of anything. Keep in mind that a soundtrack is to accompany the act, not *be* the act.

Finding Specific Music

Today there are a number of ways to find music. Hearing what's out there is obvious but you may not know that many music stores will let you sample the music before you purchase it. "Previewing" online is also a great way to find music and sample it. Blockbuster and Amazon.com are two companies that really do a nice job of this. You can search for a particular name or word using a search engine. Maybe you want a song about rabbits or magic. Some sites can tell you any recording that exists within that search and with choices of how you search for it (by date released, artists, or album name). They can also tell you if it's in stock, how to order it, or where their nearest store is (with a map of how to get there).

Creating Your Own

You can create your own soundtrack if you are talented in that area. Just don't fool yourself. If you aren't good at that sort of thing, if you don't have a good ear or often have visitors look at your music collection, point and say, "What's all of this junk for?" you might consider having it professionally done or use something that is already put together. You can also find collections of sound effects that are digitally created and available on compact disc.

Rules and Laws

There are laws against rerecording music. There are also laws against playing it in public. These are laws and not just friendly suggestions. BMI and ASCAP are the two regulatory organizations that can tell you what your rights are and what you have to pay for using an artist's music. Artists deserve to be paid for what they do and royalties handled by these organizations help control that. With the onset of better and faster methods of music duplication and pirating, this is more of an issue today than it has ever been. Some venues and events pay a blanket amount that may cover your performance so check into that too.

Rehearsing Your Magic Alone
Seeing Every Angle

When you are practicing magic you need to be able to see what every angle looks like to the audience. This usually means practicing in front of a mirror or mirrors; I suggest using three. Better than mirrors is a video camera to play back later. Of course, this doesn't give immediate feedback unless you attach your television to your camera and use it as a monitor. I think using a videotape is a good study tool when you are not physically rehearsing.

Tracy Lightel

Tracy Lightel is a lighting designer and stage manager. She's worked as an essential part of the production team of massive technical productions such as *EFX*, a Las Vegas musical extravaganza featuring many magic illusions, and the Canadian production of *Phantom of the Opera*, which also features many magic effects. These high-tech undertakings include computer-controlled scenery, lighting, magic, and special effects to synchronize these fantastic productions. Tracy currently tours with the Broadway musical, *Ragtime*.

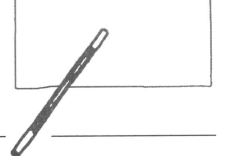

Recording Your Progress

Keep track of where you are in the process of creating your act. This lets you know at a glance what you have accomplished and what you have left to do. By comparing your videotapes, you can compare how you are doing, what's getting better, and what still needs work. Rehearsing the same mistake over and over can be a worse mistake and is often very difficult to repair once you have it ingrained in your "noggin" and incorporated with the other parts of your act that you might be doing correctly.

Be realistic with your magic. Look at your tapes and tell the truth. That doesn't mean you have to cut yourself down, but you really want your magic to be right and the only way to do that is with honest reflection, evaluation, and correction.

Rehearsing Your Magic with Others
Assistants

When you work with assistants, it's important to make sure your communication and direction is clearly shared with everyone involved in your act. Assistants look at a different part of the magic than magicians do and visa versa. I spoke with Gay Blackstone, wife of the late master magician, Harry Blackstone, Jr. I think Gay is the ultimate magician's assistant, because her duties with the Blackstone show included dancer/choreographer, money manager, creative talent, and assisting Blackstone onstage. Gay understands magic as well as any magician. She also offered some insight into working with an assistant. When I asked her who the best assistant is, she said, "Someone who has great awareness, because when you are an assistant, there are times you have to take stage and there are other times that you need to be on stage and be invisible, and many assistants miss that. In any project there is a perception of "a star" and that star can either be divided into parts or it can be one, but it's never multiple. You have to know when the magician is the star and you are the assistant and when you should take stage, but in other times when you need to be on stage and so invisible that people forget you were even there." There are a lot of considerations when you work with an assistant, that's for sure, but the best rule of thumb is to be considerate. Gay reminded me, "Magic has its own language, like dance or painting. Be aware that you are doing things that may be second nature to you but are not familiar to your assistants."

Considering Others

Technicians and Techno-Talk

The same consideration must be given to the technical expertise that supports your act. Technicians can make or break your show and you need to be able to communicate with them unless you have someone else taking care of that for you. My guess is that you don't. Even the world's greatest magicians handle a certain amount of this themselves. Learn to speak the language of the stage even if it's as simple as knowing upstage from downstage and house from stage. Learning to communicate with technicians and learning exactly what they do and how they do it is a smart idea. When technicians know you have taken time to learn about their craft, they are happy to help you with yours. It's also a good idea to know where you can start to look for answers yourself if (I should really say *when*) a technical problem rears its ugly head.

Musicians

For some reason musicians always get treated like dirt. It's completely wrong but that's the way it is. If you have the good fortune of working with musicians, they can really make your act great. If they are visible during the act, you can even integrate them into the act. Working with an orchestra is by far my favorite way to work, but it just doesn't seem to exist much any more. Working with live music means that you have to have arrangements (sometimes called charts) created for you. You can't just go to a studio and cut and paste some parts of music together. There are stock arrangements written for different orchestra voicing too. These can be an inexpensive alternative to having charts created from scratch.

A Helpful Hint

Bad habits are awfully hard to break and that's why you need to nip them in the bud as soon as you see them happening. Don't put things off for a better time to relearn your act the right way. By that time, it might be too late to interest you enough to put in the work that is necessary to fix them.

Gay Blackstone

Gay Blackstone was a television dancer when she met Harry Blackstone, Jr. after being hired by a magic producer to assist him in a show. She also assisted Orson Welles on the *Dean Martin Show* in 1971. Harry and Gay were married in 1974, and by 1976 Gay was coproducing the *Blackstone Bicentennial Tour* and the national tour in 1978. Gay was soon in charge of everything from rehearsals to finance and television projects. Today, Gay is the driving force behind Blackstone Presents, a California based corporation that produces magic experiences for television, corporate events, and live shows, and supports a 15,000-square-foot facility that supplies illusions and special effects for other magicians.

Since computers are used so prevalently by musicians today, arrangers can create music on their systems and print out perfectly readable charts complete with a director's score. They can also hear the music immediately so you don't have to wait to have it played before seeing if it is going to fit into your act. When it comes to performing onstage, there is nothing that is even close to working with live music.

Helpers

Sometimes you will get help from someone who is not your assistant. This might be a family member, friend, or someone from the client or venue. My advice here is to accept their help graciously but don't expect the person to fill the shoes of an assistant. As far as family members are concerned, sometimes this is great and sometimes it is not. Gay Blackstone pointed out, "As long as everyone gets along you've got great loyalty. The bad news is they're not always the best person to use. Sometimes it's not the person who wants to be doing it. Sometimes they are visually not the right image, but whenever you can do things together, it makes for a great relationship within the family."

Other Acts

Always treat other acts, whether they are magic acts or not, with the platinum rule I learned from a book of the same name. The golden rule says, "Do unto others as you would have done unto you." The platinum rule says, "Do unto others as they'd like done unto them." Take care of each other. It can help the journey be a great one!

CHAPTER 21

Marketing, Selling, and Performing Your Magic Show

Who Will Pay to See My Magic Right Now?
Private Parties

Private parties are occurring all the time. You could be part of them with Close-Up, Parlor, Stage, or Mentalism magic. Comedy is also great for parties. The budgets are usually low, but the jobs are enjoyable and hassle free.

Service Clubs

Find out how to contact the service clubs in your town through your chamber of commerce. These clubs use magicians for special events for club members and their families. They have established budgets so you need to find out what they can spend. Try to see who they had the year before and see if you can contact that person to gain some insight. Keep in mind that all of those people have employers who some day may need entertainment of some kind. It should be you.

Restaurants

More and more restaurants are starting to use magic as a side dish. They pay by the hour and allow you to collect tips.

Trade and Industrial Shows

Here's a great market but it's a tough job. Tradeshows are long and tiring and most magicians learn how to work efficiently and comfortably. The most valuable tip—wear the right shoes. Trade show floors are hard and unforgiving. Ecco and Mephisto are the two brands that seem to be most popular, and comfort can mean the difference between fatigue and exhaustion.

A Personal Story

Scott Tokar of Corporate FX offered this story about his first real voyage into tradeshows.

What does it take to become a trade show magician? How do you get started? Don't you make tons of money in the Industrial market? Isn't it the life, flying across the country, eating in fancy restaurants, staying in top notch hotels? "Slow down, hold it, wait a minute," says Scott. First things first. "There is an old Zen Buddhist saying that goes like this: Be careful what you wish for, because you just might get it."

Scott and I were standing in the main aisle of the National Restaurant Association trade show in Chicago. Ninety thousand people shuffled by us as we tried to speak. A typical trade show day for a magician isn't easy, Scott explains, and many young magicians look at this venue as a measuring stick or a sign that they have made it. Looking at trade shows as some kind of magical nirvana is not such a good idea. This type of performing requires a great commitment to the business, combined with flawless "commercial" routines or patter. You're never going to impress your passing audience with a complex, long, drawn-out card trick. It's sorta like working "street" magic in a suit; these folks are here to see the exhibitors, not your magic. You've got to instinctively know what kind of trick will work and what won't. Where are you currently sharpening your skills? Where do you perform regularly? If you are, say, appearing three nights a week at a local restaurant, you are on the right path to handling the rejection you'll encounter on the trade show floor. And, table-hopping will help you find the tricks that get the best reaction from your "commercial" audience. If you can't impress a drunk bar patron without making a nuisance of yourself, you'll never be able to deal with a typical, rude trade show attendee.

As we walked out of the exhibit hall, we stopped at the refreshment area to grab a quick bite. We had to eat fast because the next show clock was set for 2:00 P.M. Scott's typical set lasts 10 to 12 minutes and he repeats the show every half hour, which just goes to show you that this type of performing takes a lot of stamina. If you do the math, with the show opening at 9:00 A.M. and closing at 6:00 P.M., Scott will repeat the same show almost 16 times in a day. "This is a four-day show, so I guess I'll get real tired of my pitch after 50 or 60 run-throughs," adds Scott.

"Wow, when you dream about performing in a night club or on a cruise ship, you think two or three shows a night will tucker you out. How do you do it?" I asked. "Drink lots of water, that'll save your voice. And, most importantly, get comfortable shoes, not cheap ones.

Did You Know?

David Copperfield has repeatedly made the Fortune 500 list which lists the top ten highest-paid entertainers in the world. Lance Burton signed a 100-million-dollar contract at the Monte Carlo hotel. Believe it or not, there's still money left out there for the rest of us.

Percy Abbott (1886–1960)

I know Percy Abbott best as the founder of Abbott's Magic Company in Colon, Michigan. He was also the person who started the "Abbott's Get-Together," a three-day, 24-hour magic jam session. For any magic maniac, these are like camp and heaven all rolled up into one. Percy Abbott came to the United States from Australia and was not only a clever business man, he was a magician. Abbott's performances would include solid tricks such as the "Vanishing Cane," "production of a Flag," card manipulations, linking rings, rising cards, and a Chinese section, which he had costumed from a trip to China. Abbott also performed ventriloquism and chapeaugraphy, the creation of many different hats from a single donut of black felt. Percy was ingenious in get-

(continued on next page)

They'll become your best friend," Scott replied. "Remember, one of the first rules of any trade show is to *never* sit down in the booth. It looks unprofessional and your client expects the best from you."

"Oh, and speaking of unprofessional, make sure that your sound system doesn't totally blast out your neighbors. Eddie Tullock, the king of tradeshows never even used a sound system. Think about it, if you annoy a neighboring exhibitor, you'll never have the opportunity to sell your services to them. I don't care how many people you attract to the booth, or how big of a crowd you draw, if your sound system is too loud, you'll make yourself and the company you are working for an enemy of the other exhibitors on the tradeshow floor. To put it bluntly, you'll look unprofessional, and if it looks like you don't care, you'll be doing a disservice to the other magicians working tradeshows and you'll build a poor rapport with the attendees," Scott offered.

"Thanks. I guess that there is a lot to think about in the tradeshow market. It seems like hard work, and I bet you experience a bit of separation from your friends and family when you travel. But what about the money? Don't you make the big bucks in magic?" I asked. An uneasy feeling crept into the conversation. "Money . . . um, yeah, you can make a good living in tradeshows. I'm not sure if the living is any better than the average mid-to-upper level executive in the real-world of business. And, to become a success in the industry, it will probably take more time and energy than getting a masters degree. But, eventually, if you really keep working at it, there is a good living to be made. It is, however, a never-ending search for the next gig, this is not a one-time "destination" job. And it's unlikely that you will ever be discovered, per se. Just accept that you'll never become the next David Copperfield on the exhibit floor."

"Then, when you finally do arrive home from the road, it's non-stop marketing, PR, and phone calls. You'll always be busy writing the next script and packing for the next show. All in all, you need to *love* tradeshows, not magic, to be a success. Money isn't everything, but if you really are meant to be a tradeshow magician, you'll know within a year of performing the daily grind."

Lunchtime was over, and I thanked Scott for all of his input. And, to this day I'll never forget the advice he gave me during our lunch; "Be careful of what you wish for, because someday you just may get it."

Corporate Conferences and Conventions

Corporations have large events, including conferences and banquets. Stage Magic and Illusions, in particular, are a perfect match for these venues. Integrating your magic with these events creates an entertaining experience for them and a potentially lucrative situation for you.

Themed Parties

Parties that are themed around magic are very popular. The décor, the menu, and the entertainment can all support each other with a common theme.

Theme Parks

Theme parks use magicians but generally the shows are produced by the parks and the magician is an actor. I created my own theme park show in 1981 and 1982, but it entails a lot more than simply performing and is something to think about a long way down the road. You might be able to get a booking with a park to do your act as atmosphere entertainment. Theme parks are a good place for Close-Up Magic to Illusions. Many of them also have on-site magic shops that need to be staffed.

Cruise Ships

Ships still book magic acts, and each line has a different way they perceive and contract for magic. Check with an agent who deals with ships and find out what they are looking for. There's one in the Appendix at the back of this book. If you consider performing on ships, also consider time away from family and the motion of the ocean.

Hotels and Casinos

These are meccas for magicians. Hotels and casinos are one of the greatest opportunities for the professional stage magician or illusionist.

**Percy Abbott
(1886–1960)**

(continued from previous page)

ting magic to people who could pay for it. He created huge catalogues or "dream books" that were filled with magical apparatus and books that they would send to your door step postage paid. He also sold out when the magicians came to town. Eventually he expanded with satellite locations in Detroit, Chicago, New York, Indianapolis, and Hollywood. Percy Abbott knew how to sell magic and he could make magicians crazy for the Abbott's products. The company was purchased by Recil Bordner and later taken over by his son Greg Bordner who still gets the Abbott's magic to the masses.

How Do I Get These Jobs?
Agents

Agents are in the business of supplying entertainment to the venues previously discussed. They represent the magician and in turn receive a percentage of his income. The standard rate is generally 10 to 15 percent.

Bureaus

Bureaus are just like agents except they seem to cater more toward lecturers and speakers than they do toward entertainers. They are paid pretty much the same way as agents, but they usually charge 25 percent.

Associations

Belonging to professional associations that encourage networking is also a good way to get new business. I recommend joining Meeting Professionals International, National Speakers Association, and certain Convention and Visitors Bureaus.

What Will I Need to Market Myself?
Printed Media

You will need a range of printed materials, including:
- Business cards
- Stationery
- Envelopes
- A one-page description of what you do, in faxable form
- Brochure
- Video representation

Web Presence

Everybody has a different idea about the importance of having a Web site. In the first place, it depends on the image and information you'd like your prospects, fellow magicians, and even your family to have about you when they ask for it online. It also depends on your financial ability to pay for the site: monthly server fees, the cost to create and update the site, and other hidden costs. If you know you want a site but don't have it designed yet, you can reserve your domain name right away (e.g., *DavidsonMagic.com*) for around 70 dollars for two years and then when you have your page ready, you'll already have the domain. Before you make your decision, surf the net, look at other Web sites (see Appendix), and create your Web presence with the same approach as you create your act. One of the resources available to help you search for available Web site names, and to register your domain name, is *networksolutions.com*.

Word of Mouth

There is nothing like having an advocate to tell other people how good you are after they have witnessed your talent. You have got to get out there and be seen.

Fee Schedule/Price Guide

Have a one-page fee schedule in faxable form that you can send to clients who inquire about your different programs. You also have to commit to fee integrity, that is, everybody getting the same price. If you are counting on word-of-mouth recommendations doing some great things for you, changing your prices depending on how the wind blows is not a good idea. In fact, it's a terrible idea. Get a price and stick to it for everyone.

Contract

Have a contract ready to go when someone calls. When they are ready to decide, be prepared to provide your contract. One of the things that Beckwith shared with me is that, "Very few magicians approach magic as a business. They say, 'I like to do magic so I guess I can make some money at it.'" This is not always the case. Having a head for business will be an asset. At the very least, get organized and have all of the paperwork ready for your clients.

Karrell Fox (1928–1998)
(continued from previous page)

into driving him from their home in West Virginia to the Abbott's Get-Together in Colon, Michigan. He was there every year after that and he was a star. Karrell was a heavyweight in the areas of corporate magic and tradeshows and he shared this special knowledge in books such as *Clever Like a Fox* (1976), *Another Book by Karrell Fox* (1979), *For My Next Trick* (1986), and *My Latest Book* (1988), all published by the Supreme Magic Company. He was always learning and sharing with any one of the thousands who happened to meet him at a convention. Karrell Fox died on March 12, 1998, in a room at the Tropicana Hotel in Las Vegas. He was there to once again help magicians who were attending the Desert Magic Seminar.

What Will Others Need to Market Me?

Printed Media

I got some great tips from Tobias with regard to what you need to send to prospects for promotion. The most important thing is to know who you are sending the materials to. Tobias said, "Make sure that you get an idea of who you are and what market you want to go after—birthday parties or Vegas—and take it from there. The materials need to look like you could afford me and have a good time with me. You need to find out who's getting the material. Is it mommy? Is it the school principal? Is it the college booking committee? Who else is selling to these people? What are they used to seeing? Are they used to seeing a three-fold brochure? Are they used to seeing four-color?"

When I asked Tobias if he thought a magician should try to aim his media materials above the competition, he answered, "Yes, but not drastically. The point is that you don't want to scare them away by looking too expensive, or otherwise out of their league." Beckwith advises to make your media what the client is used to seeing in both format and quality.

"Make it like they are used to seeing but make it a little bit nicer than the other ones they are going to get, so they say, 'Out of these three pieces of paper, I want this one.' It needs to be the nicest thing that crosses their desk today, and you can know the quality of what's crossing those desks by seeing what the competition is putting out."

Video Media

If you have a videotape that you can send to a prospective client, you are way ahead of simply having printed materials. Try to get shots of the audience's reaction too. Remember, the client isn't just buying a magic show; they are buying happy guests.

Relationship and Track Records

There is nothing like a good relationship with a past client to propel your career. Take care of these relationships and they will probably surprise you. If you do a good job once, you will be hired again or be recommended to someone else.

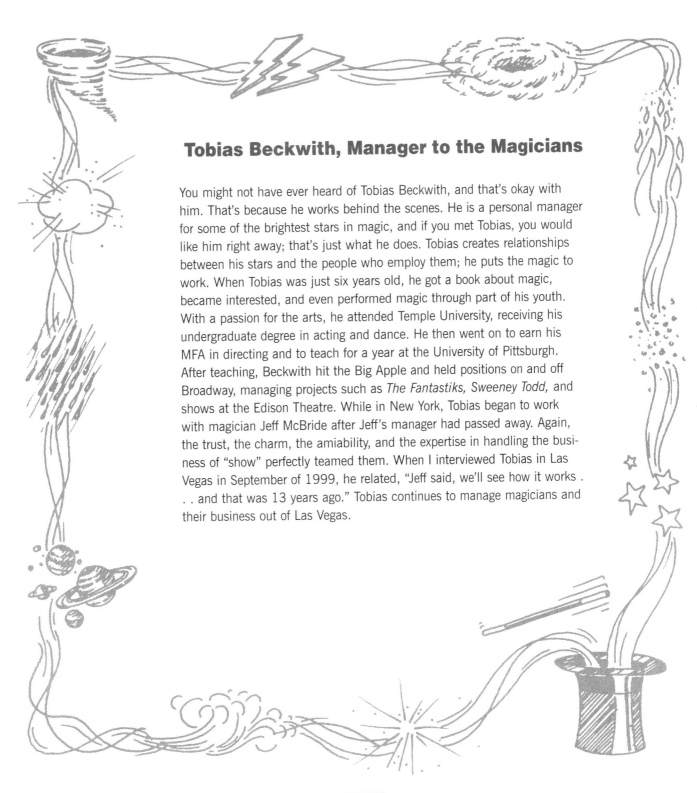

Tobias Beckwith, Manager to the Magicians

You might not have ever heard of Tobias Beckwith, and that's okay with him. That's because he works behind the scenes. He is a personal manager for some of the brightest stars in magic, and if you met Tobias, you would like him right away; that's just what he does. Tobias creates relationships between his stars and the people who employ them; he puts the magic to work. When Tobias was just six years old, he got a book about magic, became interested, and even performed magic through part of his youth. With a passion for the arts, he attended Temple University, receiving his undergraduate degree in acting and dance. He then went on to earn his MFA in directing and to teach for a year at the University of Pittsburgh. After teaching, Beckwith hit the Big Apple and held positions on and off Broadway, managing projects such as *The Fantastiks, Sweeney Todd,* and shows at the Edison Theatre. While in New York, Tobias began to work with magician Jeff McBride after Jeff's manager had passed away. Again, the trust, the charm, the amiability, and the expertise in handling the business of "show" perfectly teamed them. When I interviewed Tobias in Las Vegas in September of 1999, he related, "Jeff said, we'll see how it works . . . and that was 13 years ago." Tobias continues to manage magicians and their business out of Las Vegas.

APPENDIX

Continuing MAGICation

Periodicals/ Magazines

Genii, The Conjurors' Magazine
Richard Kauffman, Editor
4200 Wisconsin Ave. NW
[PMB 106-385]
Washington, DC 20016
(202) 363-4544
(202) 319-9723 (fax)

MAGIC, The Independent Magazine for Magicians
Stan Allen, Editor
6225 Harrison Dr., Suite 4
Las Vegas, NV 89120
(702) 798-0099
(702) 798-0220 (fax)
www.magicmagazine.com

The Christian Conjurer Magazine
Mike Stenberg, Editor
7739 Everest Court N
Maple Grove, MN 55311
(612) 745-7973
E-mail: mailcenter@fcm.org

MUM
David Goodsell, Editor
P.O. Box 338
26855 Saunders Meadow Road
Idyllwild, CA 92549
(909) 659-5990
(909) 659-5789 (fax)
E-mail: SuperG13@aol.com

Web Sites— My Favorites

The Magic of David Copperfield
www.dcopperfield.com

Siegfried and Roy: Masters of the Impossible
www.sarmoti.com

Doug Anderson
www.magicdoug.com

Jeff McBride
www.mcbridemagic.com

Lance Burton
www.lanceburton.com

Marco Tempest
www.marcotempest.com

Kevin James
www.kjmagic.com

Andre Cole
www.andrecole.com

Franz Harary
www.harary.com

The Amazing Johnathan's Cheap Thrills Page
www.amazingj.com

Penn and Teller
www.sincity.com

Web Sites—General

All Magic Guide
www.uelectric.com/allmagicguide.html

Magic Tricks
www.magictricks.com

Magic Channel
www.magicchannel.com

Magician's Alliance
www.magiciansalliance.com

The Linking Page (also known as The White Rabbit)
www.linkingpage.com

Proship Entertainment
www.proship.com

Trendy Magic
www.trendymagic.com

Magic Dealers

The All Magic Dealers Guide
www.uelectric.com/allmagicdealers/

Hank Lee's Magic Factory
allmagic.com/magicfactory/

Stevens Magic Emporium
allmagic.com/stevensmagic/

Magic Express
allmagic.com/magicexpress/

L & L Publishing
allmagic.com/llpub/

Owen Magic Supreme
www.owenmagic.com/index/cellz/htm

Magic Auction
www.magicauction.com

Magic Smith
www.magicsmith.com

Meir Ydid Magic
www.mymagic.com

Underground Custom Magic
www.ucmagic.com

Magic Organizations

International Brotherhood of Magicians
www.magician.org

The Society of American Magicians
www.uelectric.com/sam/events.html

The Fellowship of Christian Magicians
www.fcm.com

Magic Magazines

Magic, The Independent Magazine for Magicians
www.magicmagazine.com

***Genii,* The Conjurors' Magazine**
www.geniimagazine.com

The Christian Conjurer
www.fcm.org

Magic Resources and Suppliers

A-1 MultiMedia Magic Supplies
3337 Sunrise Blvd, #8
Rancho Cordova, CA 95742
(916) 852-7777
(800) 876-8437
(916) 852-7785 (fax)
www.1magicalmedia.com

Abbott's Magic Company
124 St. Joseph Street
Colon, MI 49040
(616) 432-3235
(800) 92-magic (orders)
(616) 432-3357 (fax)
E-mail: amagic@net-link.net
www.abbott-magic.com

Al's Magic Shop
1012 Vermont Avenue Northwest
Washington, D.C. 20005-4901
(202) 789-2800
E-mail: alcomagic@aolcom
www.alsmagic.com

Amazon.com
www.amazon.com

American Science and Surplus
3605 Howard Street
Skokie, IL 60076
(847) 982-0870
(800) 934-0722 (fax)
www.sciplus

Baran Entertainment
2021 East Gladstone
Building B
Glendora, CA 91740
(909) 394-5790
E-mail: Baranmagic@aol.com

Blackstone Magic, Inc
www.blackstonemagic.com

Brad Burt's Magic Shop
4204 Convoy Street
San Diego, CA 92111
(619) 571-4749
(800) 748-5759 (orders)
(619) 571-7943 (fax)
www.magicshop.com

Collectors' Workshop
38427 Snickersvilee Tpk.
Middleburg, VA 20117
(540) 687-6476
(800) mag-iccw
www.magiccw.com

Corporate-FX®
PO Box 1624
Tustin, CA 92781
800-MAGIC-13
www.CorporateFX.com

Creative Illusions
4405 E. Sahara Avenue #21
Las Vegas, NV 89104
(702) 641-6644
(702) 641-3887 (fax)

Dan Garrett Magic
4929 Salem Road
Lithonia, GA 30038
(770) 981-0310
(770) 981-0310 (fax)
E-mail: dangarrett@aol.com

Davenport's Magic Shop
7 Charing Cross/The
Strand/Underground
Concourse
London, England WC2 4HZ

Daytona Magic Shop
136 South Beach Street
Daytona Beach, FL 32114-4402
(904) 252-6767
(904) 252-9037 (fax)

Dean Dill Productions
2130 Fairpark Ave #110
Los Angeles, CA 90041
(323) 257-9062
(323) 257-7117 (fax)
(818) 242-0070 (work)
www.deandill.virtualave.net

Denny and Lee Magic Studio
325 South Marilyn Avenue
Baltimore, MC 21221
(410) 686-3914
(410) 686-6953 (fax)
E-mail: dennymagic@aol.com
www.dennymagic.com

Dick Barry's Magic Catalogue
176 Mira Del Oeste
San Clemente, CA 92673-3108
(949) 361-8620
(949) 361-3104 (fax)

Dock Haley Gospel Magic Co.
P.O. Box 915
Hermitage, TN 37076
(615) 885-4800
(615) 885-4874 (fax)
E-mail: DockHaley@gospelmagic.com
www.gospelmagic.com

Eagle Magic and Joke Store
708 Portland Avenue
Minneapolis, MN 55415
(612) 333-4702

**Frank Zak, co-author
with Keith Merrill of**
The Magic of Bartending
P.O. Box 43012
Las Vegas, NV 89116-1012
(702) 878-3283

Hank Lee's Magic Factory
127 South Street
Boston, MA 02111
(617) 482-8749
(800) 874-7400 (orders)
(781) 395-2034 (fax)
www.hanklee.com

House of Magic
2025 Chestnut Street
San Francisco, CA 94123
(415) 346-2218

**Flosso Hornmann Magic
Company**
45 West 34th Street, #607
New York, NY 10001
(212) 279-6079

**H. Marshall and Company
(flowers)**
1186 Shenk Road
Mogadore, OH 44260
(330) 628-9994

Kardwell International (cards)
P.O. Box 775-M
Orient, NY 11957
(516) 323-3880
(516) 323-3904 (fax)

Kennedy Enterprises
8 Winchester
Irvine, CA 92620
(949) 262-1164
(800) 247-7168 (orders)
(949) 262-1165 (fax)

Klamm Magic
1412 Appleton
Independence, MO 64052
(816) 461-4595
(800) 210-0800
(816) 252-1155 (fax)

Laflins Magic and Silks
203 E. Riverside Ave
Box 3003
Troy, MT 59935
(406) 295-7790
(406) 295-6076 (fax)

**L & L Publishing
(Books and Tapes)**
P.O. Box 100
Tahoma, CA 96142
(530) 525-5700
(800) 626-6572 (orders)
(530) 525-7008 (fax)

**Louis Tannen, Inc.
(commonly called Tannen's)**
24 West 25th Street, 2nd floor
New York, NY 10010
(212) 929-4500
(212) 929-4565 (fax)
(800) 72-magic (orders)
www.tannenmagic.com

**Lynetta Welch, "The Magician's
Seamstress"**
Designer/Consutant
P.O. Box 1402
Burbank, CA
(818) 623-6650

**MagiCraft Design and
Fabrication Group**
5722A Union Pacific Avenue
Commerce, CA 90022
(213) 724-2279
(213) 724-2693 (fax)

**Magic by Bruce Chadwick—
Illusion Fabrication**
P.O Box 6106
Ft. Worth, TX 76115
(817) 927-0581
(817) 927-1804 (fax)

Magic, Inc.
5082 North Lincoln Avenue
Chicago, IL 60625
(773) 334-2855 (tel/fax)

Magic Makers
4616 Rosebush Road
Mississauga, Ontario, Canada
L5M 5H2
(905) 567-4578
(905) 567-4826 (fax)
www.magicmakersillusions.com

Magic Ventures
3518 W. Post Road
Las Vegas, NV 89118
(702) 897-1224
(702) 897-0833 (fax)
www.magicventures.com

Malloy Modern Magic
220 East Ave K-4
Unit # 6
Lancaster, CA 93535
(661) 940-8871

Mecca Magic, Inc.
49 Dodd Street
Bloomfield, NJ 07003
(973) 429-7597
www.meccamagic.com

Meyer Ydid Magic
P.O. Box 2566
Fair Lawn, NJ 07410
(201) 703-1171
(201) 703-8872 (fax)

More Than Magic
Greg Davidson
110 Roswell Farms Circle
Roswell, GA 30075
(770) 587-0509
(770) 640-8411 (fax)
www.DavidsonMagic.com

Morrissey Magic (Canada's Largest Magic Dealer)
Herb Morrissey
2477 Dufferin Street
Toronto Ontario M6B 3P9
(416) 782-1393
(416) 782-4619
www.morrisseymagic.com

Oriental Trading Company (novelties)
P.O. Box 2308
Omaha, NE 68103
(800) 228-2269
www.oriental.com

Owen Magic Supreme
734 North McKeever Avenue
Azusa, CA 91702-2394
(626) 969-4519
(626) 969-4614 (fax)
www.owenmagic.com

Robert Nelson's Quality Used Magic
2601 White Fence Way
High Point, NC 27265
(336) 812-3061

Riley-Davidson
110 Roswell Farms Circle
Roswell, GA 30075
(770) 587-1292
www.RileyDavidson.com

Sorcery Manufacturing
2576 Mercatile Dr., Unite D
Rancho Cordova, CA 95742
(916) 852-4296
(800) 718-8188 (orders)
(916) 852-4298 (fax)
E-mail: sorcerymfg@aol.com

Stevens Magic Emporium
2520 E. Douglas
Wichita, KS 67214
(316) 683-9582
(316) 686-2442 (fax)

Sound Ideas
105 West Beaver Creek Rd.
Suite 4
Richmond Hill, Ontario
Canada L4B 1C6

The Magic Smith
64 Seafare
Laguna Niguel, CA 92677
(888) 222-2192 (orders)
(949) 249-8277 (fax, international)
www.magicsmith.com

T. Meyers Magic (balloons)
6513 Thomas Springs Road
Austin, TX 78736
(512) 288-7925
(512) 288-7694
(800) 648-6221
www.tmeyers.com

Tobias Beckwith, Inc.
(702) 697-7002 (phone/fax)
E-mail: tobias@yourmagic.com
www.yourmagic.com

Underground Custom Magic
P.O. Box 30186
Las Vegas, NV. 89173-0186
(702) 889-0002
Keith Merrill
www.ucmagic.com

Wellington Enterprises-Creators of the Finest Custom Illusions
55 Railroad Ave., Building 5
Garnerville, New York 10923-0315
(912) 429-3377

James Yoshida
99-579 Ulune St.
Aiea, Oahu, Honolulu, HI 96701
(808) 487-0590

Magic Fraternities, Clubs, and Organizations

The International Brotherhood of Magicians (IBM)
11137-C South Towne Square
St. Louis, MO 63123-7819
(314) 845-9200
(314) 845-9220 (fax)
www.magician.org
IBM is the world's largest magician's fraternal organization of magicians. It has more than 300 chapters (known as "rings") in 73 countries. They sponsor an annual convention that is usually held over the July 4 weekend in the United States. Members must be sponsored and be at least 18 years old; junior members can join at 12 years of age. They produce *The Linking Ring* magazine.

Meeting Professionals International
International Headquarters
4455 LBJ Freeway
Suite 1200
Dallas, TX 75244-5903
(972) 702-3000
(972) 702-3070 (fax)

The National Speakers Association
1500 South Priest Drive
Tempe, AZ 85281
(480) 968-2552 (phone)
(480) 968-0911 (fax)
www.nsaspeaker.org
Contact the national office to find the chapter nearest you. The National Speakers Association produces *Professional Speaker* magazine.

The Society of American Magicians (SAM)
P.O. Box 510260
St. Louis, MO 63151
(314) 846-5659
(888) 726-9644
www.uelectric.com/sam
SAM, founded in 1902, meets in approximately 250 chapters (known as "assemblies") throughout the world. Their official publication is *M-U-M*, which is an acronym for Magic-Unity-Might. Their annual convention is usually held in July in the United States. SAM has several categories of membership, determined by the magician's age and local assembly affiliation. Although the Society of American Magicians sounds like a national association, it is the oldest and most prestigious magic organization in the *world*. They also support the world's largest program for young people in magic, the Society for Young Magicians.

The Society of Young Magicians (SYM)
7101 Buick Drive
Indianapolis, IN 46214-3224
Contact: Char Gott
The Society of Young Magicians is a great way for young magicians (ages 7 to 17) to enter the world of magic. Some of their membership benefits include personal empowerment, self-confidence, better coordination, increased reading skills, and hands-on experience in public speaking and communication. Boys and girls alike are offered great life options through building confidence in their own abilities, a feeling of self worth, and a sense of belonging. Their publication is the *Magic SYMbol*.

The Academy of Magical Arts, The Magic Castle
7001 Franklin Ave.
Hollywood, CA 90028
(323) 851-3313
(323) 851-4899 (fax)
The Magic Castle is probably one of the best-known magician hang-outs and live showcase venues. With three different showrooms under one roof, visitors have a chance to see live magic from close-up to grand illusion. This private club was founded in 1963 and visitors are allowed to attend only if they are invited by a member. New members are approved only by sponsorship through a member in good standing.

The Magic Castle is the clubhouse for The Academy of Magical Arts, Inc., which is dedicated to the advancement of the art of magic. The active membership numbers over 5,000.

The Fellowship of Christian Magicians (FCM)
7739 Everest N
Maple Grove, MN 55311
(612) 745-7973
The FCM is made up of hundreds of people in all fields of gospel magic, ventriloquism, puppetry, clowning, ballooning, juggling, storytelling, and other related arts used for evangelistic purposes. One of the largest benefits of membership is their publication, *The Christian Conjurer Magazine*. Their conference is usually held in July for their entire international membership.

The Magic Circle
The Secretary Chris Pratt MIMC
13 Calder Avenue Brookmans Park
Hertfordshire AL9 7AH
England

The Chavez Studio of Magic
P.O Box 8054
La Verne, CA
(909) 593-5374
(909) 596-8596 (fax)
This is a highly successful school for magic founded in 1941. The studio offers both private instruction and home study under the direction of Dale Salwak.

The World Alliance of Magicians
P.O Box 33374
Granada Hills, CA 91394
www.MagiciansAlliance.com
This new organization, founded in 1998, is "dedicated to preserve the wonder and amazement of the magical arts for the general public, to protect the secrets of the magic profession from exposure, and to

reinforce the positive contributions of the magical arts to society."

Toastmasters International, Inc.
23182 Arroyo Vista
Rancho Santa Margarita, CA 92688
(800) 993-7732
Call for a list of the clubs in your area.

Magic Conventions

In addition to conventions held by the groups previously mentioned above, there are several regional associations of magicians and magic clubs that hold annual conventions. Because they don't have fixed head-quarter addresses for the most part, the best way to find out about them is to keep up with the magic magazines and one of the large magic Web sites. There are also several independent conventions held all across the United States:

Independent Magic Conventions

Florida Magicians Association (usually held Memorial Day weekend)

Michigan Magic Day

Magician's Alliance of Western New York

Midwest Magic Jubilee

New England Magicians Conference

Texas Association of Magicians (usually held Labor Day weekend)

Pacific Coast Association of Magicians

Southeastern Association of Magicians

South Carolina Association of Magicians

The Seminar of Platform and Parlor Magic

The Conference on Magic History

Professional Family Entertainer's Workshop (formerly Comedy College)

The International Festival of Children's Magicians

The Women-in-Magic Conference

Established Magic Conventions

Abbott's Magic Get-Together
This four-day family gathering is always held in Colon, Michigan, in early August.
Contact: Abott's Magic Company, (616) 432-3235

Tannen's Magic Jubilee
This four-day convention is held in early October at a resort in the Catskills mountains.
Contact: Louis Tannen Inc., (212) 929-4500

Hank Lee's Cape Cod Magic Conclave
This annual event takes place in April on Cape Cod, Massachusetts.
Contact: Hank Lee's Magic Factory, (617) 482-8749

Columbus Magi-Fest
Over 1,000 attendees have come for 30 years to this gathering held in February in Columbux, Ohio.
Contact: Jep Hosteltler, (614) 299-8995

Fechter's Finger Flicking Frolic (FFFF)
The informal weekend in held the last weekend of April, by invitation only.
Contact: Obie O'Brien, (315) 482-9068

World Magic Seminar
A combination of two previous and successful conferences, this seminar is held in Las Vegas in April. It's sponsored by Steven's Magic Emporium and Collectors Workshop.
Contact: World Magic Seminar, (800) 219-2200

Bob's Little Super Sunday
These are one-day events, usually held twice a year just outside of Philadelphia.
Contact: Bob Little of Guaranteed Magic, (215) 672-3344

Magic Collectors' Weekend
This conference is tailored for the collector of magical apparatus, memo-rabilia, etc.
Contact: Magic Collector Association, P.O. Box 511-M, Glenwood, IL 60425

International Battle of Magicians
The conference emphasis is on stage and close-up magic competitions.
Contact: Larry Durian, (330) 830-2206, or Tim Deremer, (330) 494-2823

Houdini Club Of Wisconsin
This Labor Day weekend event is attended by around 200 fraternal magicians.
Contact: Ed Litt, (773) 271-8489

Wizard's Weekend
This annual convention is held in the Midwest for all age ranges.
Contact: Gerald Smith, (612) 861-3240

Magic on Manhattan
This new one-day convention is held in New York City.
Contact: (800) 429-3433

The Professional Performer's Workshop
Theatrical and magic professionals meet on the west coast.
Contact: Bob Markwood, (213) 257-4433

Magic Camps/ Coaching

Jeff McBride's Master Class
(702) 868-8869
www.McBrideMagic.com
A three-day intensive class for advanced magicians usually held in Las Vegas

Tannen's Magic Camp
(212) 929-4500 (see listing for Louis Tannens under magic suppliers)
This is a week-long camp held in New York for over 100 students, ages 12–20.

Dave Goodsell's West Coast Wizards Magic Camp
P.O. Box 1360
Claremont, CA 91711
(800) 645-1423
Held annually in the summer in Idyllwild, California for students ages 9-17.

Where to See Live Magic

Here are just a few of the other places you can see live magic.

Caesar's Magical Empire
Caesar's Palace, Las Vegas
(800) 276-2442

Hilarities Comedy and Magic Dinner Theater Restaurant and Lounge
2035 East 4th Street
Cleveland, OH
(216) 781-7733

The Magic Castle
7001 Franklin Ave.
Hollywood, CA 90028
(323) 851-3313
(323) 851-4899 (fax)

Magical Nights Inc., Monday Night Magic
The Sullivan Street Playhouse
181 Sullivan Street
New York, NY
24 hr. Hotline: (212) 615-6432
www.magicalnights.com
(Shows every Monday night at 8:00 P.M.)

Magic: The Science of Illusion
A traveling exhibit developed by the California Science Center through February 28, 2001
(232) 724-3623
www.cascience.org

Warren & Annabelle's, A Magic Nightclub
900 Front Street
A202
Lahaina, HI 96761
(808) 667-6244
(Several two-hour experiences offered nightly, featuring the magic of Warren and the mysterious presence of legend Annabelle.)

Wizardz Magic Dinner Theater
1000 Universal Center Drive
CITYWALK #217
Universal City, CA 91608
(818) 506-0066, ext 121
(818) 506-1616 (fax)
(Wizardz has a 280-seat theater with nightly performances featuring a laser show and variety of noted magicians and illusionists.)

Index

THE EVERYTHING® GAMES BOOK

By Tracy Fitzsimmons & Pamela Liflander

The Everything® Games Book has everything you'll need for hours of family entertainment, featuring a wide selection of the most popular games. Not only will you find new and exciting games to play, but you'll also have a complete source of easy-to-follow rules and regulations for hundreds of activities right at your fingertips. Whether you're planning a party or just spending a rainy afternoon at home, *The Everything® Games Book* provides challenging fun and friendly competition for all ages and every level of play.

Trade paperback, $12.95
1-58062-643-8, 304 pages

OTHER *EVERYTHING®* BOOKS BY ADAMS MEDIA CORPORATION

Everything® **After College Book**
  $12.95, 1-55850-847-3

Everything® **American History Book**
  $12.95, 1-58062-531-2

Everything® **Angels Book**
  $12.95, 1-58062-398-0

Everything® **Anti-Aging Book**
  $12.95, 1-58062-565-7

Everything® **Astrology Book**
  $12.95, 1-58062-062-0

Everything® **Astronomy Book**
  $14.95, 1-58062-723-4

Everything® **Baby Names Book**
  $12.95, 1-55850-655-1

Everything® **Baby Shower Book**
  $12.95, 1-58062-305-0

Everything® **Baby's First Food Book**
  $12.95, 1-58062-512-6

Everything® **Baby's First Year Book**
  $12.95, 1-58062-581-9

Everything® **Barbecue Cookbook**
  $14.95, 1-58062-316-6

Everything® **Bartender's Book**
  $9.95, 1-55850-536-9

Everything® **Bedtime Story Book**
  $12.95, 1-58062-147-3

Everything® **Bible Stories Book**
  $14.95, 1-58062-547-9

Everything® **Bicycle Book**
  $12.00, 1-55850-706-X

Everything® **Breastfeeding Book**
  $12.95, 1-58062-582-7

Everything® **Budgeting Book**
  $14.95, 1-58062-786-2

Everything® **Build Your Own Home Page**
  $12.95, 1-58062-339-5

Everything® **Business Planning Book**
  $12.95, 1-58062-491-X

Everything® **Candlemaking Book**
  $12.95, 1-58062-623-8

Everything® **Car Care Book**
  $14.95, 1-58062-732-3

Everything® **Casino Gambling Book**
  $12.95, 1-55850-762-0

Everything® **Cat Book**
  $12.95, 1-55850-710-8

Everything® **Chocolate Cookbook**
  $12.95, 1-58062-405-7

Everything® **Christmas Book**
  $15.00, 1-55850-697-7

Everything® **Civil War Book**
  $12.95, 1-58062-366-2

Everything® **Classical Mythology Book**
  $12.95, 1-58062-653-X

Everything® **Coaching & Mentoring Book**
  $14.95, 1-58062-730-7

Everything® **Collectibles Book**
  $12.95, 1-58062-645-9

Everything® **College Survival Book**
  $12.95, 1-55850-720-5

Everything® **Computer Book**
  $12.95, 1-58062-401-4

Everything® **Cookbook**
  $14.95, 1-58062-400-6

Everything® **Cover Letter Book**
  $12.95, 1-58062-312-3

Everything® **Creative Writing Book**
  $12.95, 1-58062-647-5

Everything® **Crossword and Puzzle Book**
  $12.95, 1-55850-764-7

Everything® **Dating Book**
  $12.95, 1-58062-185-6

Everything® **Pregnancy Organizer**
$15.00, 1-58062-336-0

Everything® **Project Management Book**
$12.95, 1-58062-583-5

Everything® **Puppy Book**
$12.95, 1-58062-576-2

Everything® **Quick Meals Cookbook**
$14.95, 1-58062-488-X

Everything® **Resume Book**
$12.95, 1-58062-311-5

Everything® **Romance Book**
$12.95, 1-58062-566-5

Everything® **Running Book**
$12.95, 1-58062-618-1

Everything® **Sailing Book, 2nd Ed.**
$12.95, 1-58062-671-8

Everything® **Saints Book**
$12.95, 1-58062-534-7

Everything® **Scrapbooking Book**
$14.95, 1-58062-729-3

Everything® **Selling Book**
$12.95, 1-58062-319-0

Everything® **Shakespeare Book**
$12.95, 1-58062-591-6

Everything® **Slow Cooker Cookbook**
$14.95, 1-58062-667-X

Everything® **Soup Cookbook**
$14.95, 1-58062-556-8

Everything® **Spells and Charms Book**
$12.95, 1-58062-532-0

Everything® **Start Your Own Business Book**
$12.95, 1-58062-650-5

Everything® **Stress Management Book**
$14.95, 1-58062-578-9

Everything® **Study Book**
$12.95, 1-55850-615-2

Everything® **T'ai Chi and QiGong Book**
$12.95, 1-58062-646-7

Everything® **Tall Tales, Legends, and Outrageous Lies Book**
$12.95, 1-58062-514-2

Everything® **Tarot Book**
$12.95, 1-58062-191-0

Everything® **Thai Cookbook**
$14.95, 1-58062-733-1

Everything® **Time Management Book**
$12.95, 1-58062-492-8

Everything® **Toasts Book**
$12.95, 1-58062-189-9

Everything® **Toddler Book**
$12.95, 1-58062-592-4

Everything® **Total Fitness Book**
$12.95, 1-58062-318-2

Everything® **Trivia Book**
$12.95, 1-58062-143-0

Everything® **Tropical Fish Book**
$12.95, 1-58062-343-3

Everything® **Vegetarian Cookbook**
$12.95, 1-58062-640-8

Everything® **Vitamins, Minerals, and Nutritional Supplements Book**
$12.95, 1-58062-496-0

Everything® **Weather Book**
$14.95, 1-58062-668-8

Everything® **Wedding Book, 2nd Ed.**
$14.95, 1-58062-190-2

Everything® **Wedding Checklist**
$7.95, 1-58062-456-1

Everything® **Wedding Etiquette Book**
$7.95, 1-58062-454-5

Everything® **Wedding Organizer**
$15.00, 1-55850-828-7

Everything® **Wedding Shower Book**
$7.95, 1-58062-188-0

Everything® **Wedding Vows Book**
$7.95, 1-58062-455-3

Everything® **Weddings on a Budget Book**
$9.95, 1-58062-782-X

Everything® **Weight Training Book**
$12.95, 1-58062-593-2

Everything® **Wicca and Witchcraft Book**
$14.95, 1-58062-725-0

Everything® **Wine Book**
$12.95, 1-55850-808-2

Everything® **World War II Book**
$12.95, 1-58062-572-X

Everything® **World's Religions Book**
$12.95, 1-58062-648-3

Everything® **Yoga Book**
$12.95, 1-58062-594-0

*Prices subject to change without notice.

EVERYTHING  SERIES!

Everything® **Kids' Baseball Book, 2nd Ed.**
$6.95, 1-58062-688-2

Everything® **Kids' Cookbook**
$6.95, 1-58062-658-0

Everything® **Kids' Joke Book**
$6.95, 1-58062-686-6

Everything® **Kids' Mazes Book**
$6.95, 1-58062-558-4

Everything® **Kids' Money Book**
$6.95, 1-58062-685-8

Everything® **Kids' Monsters Book**
$6.95, 1-58062-657-2

Everything® **Kids' Nature Book**
$6.95, 1-58062-684-X

Everything® **Kids' Puzzle Book**
$6.95, 1-58062-687-4

Everything® **Kids' Science Experiments Book**
$6.95, 1-58062-557-6

Everything® **Kids' Soccer Book**
$6.95, 1-58062-642-4

Everything® **Travel Activity Book**
$6.95, 1-58062-641-6

Available wherever books are sold!
To order, call 800-872-5627, or visit us at everything.com

Everything® is a registered trademark of Adams Media Corporation.